*Our deep respect for the land and its harvest
is the legacy of generations of farmers who
put food on our tables, preserved our landscape,
and inspired us with a powerful work ethic.*
—JAMES H. DOUGLAS

HOME PLATE

THE TRAVELER'S FOOD GUIDE
to Cooperstown & Otsego County, NY

Brenda Berstler

Syl·lab·les Press

The author thanks Cornell Cooperative Extension, CADE, Otsego 2000,
The National Baseball Hall of Fame and Museum, Major League Baseball and The
National Soccer Hall of Fame and Museum
for permission to use graphics under their control of copyright.
Drawings are also from *Desk Gallery* published by Zedcor, Inc.

.

ISBN: 0-9709433-2-6
Library of Congress Control Number: 2005902915

Cover illustration by: Alyssa Kosmer
Text designed and typeset by
Syllables Press, Mount Vision, NY, USA

Printed and bound in Canada by Webcom, Inc.

Editorial Sales Rights and Permission Inquiries should be addressed to:
Syllables Press, PO Box 674, Mount Vision, NY 03810
or contact Editor@SyllablesPress.com

Substantial discounts on bulk quantities are available to corporations, professional
associations, and other organizations. If you are in the USA or Canada, contact
Syllables Press, Special Sales Department, PO Box 672, Mount Vision, NY 13810; phone
1-888-463-1258 or e-mail: sales@SyllablesPress.com

10 9 8 7 6 5 4 3 2 1

Dedication

In memory of my beloved brother, Kenneth Allen Scruggs.

"Gentlemen, he was out because I said he was out."

Bill Klem, National League umpire, 1905-1941

*Food is our common ground,
a universal experience.*
JAMES A. BEARD

Table of Contents

Introduction

*O*n behalf of the farmers, the small businesses, the institutions and, as George Bailey would say in *It's a Wonderful Life,* for those who "do most of the working and paying and living and dying" in this area, I began writing *Home Plate: The Traveler's Food Guide to Cooperstown and Otsego County, NY.* What started as a fundraising project for two non-profit organizations became a discovery of my own backyard. If you live in Otsego County, or if you are a much-welcomed visitor, I hope that, through *Home Plate,* you find some of the same enriching and rewarding experiences.

Cornell Cooperative Extension of Otsego County sponsors 4-H Youth Development, Master Gardeners, and nutritional, agricultural, and many other family educational programs. The Walking Example Group advocates walking paths, bike trails, smart growth development and the preservation of open spaces. Both organizations work to improve the quality of life in Otsego County, and funding is always needed to enhance community programs.

With the help of Assemblyman Bill Magee, *Home Plate* got underway. Originally a cookbook to showcase and encourage the use of New York's diverse agriculture, *Home Plate* evolved into a travel guide and cultural roadmap of our very special part of Upstate New York. State Senator Jim Seward's support helped bring it to fruition.

Everyone represented in *Home Plate* plays a unique role in Otsego County. Some are directly involved in agriculture, others are on the periphery, and some create food for thought or a feast for the eye. All are paired with a delicious recipe featuring New York and Otsego County farm products. Since New York is second nationally in agricultural diversity, *Home Plate* offers a wonderful array of food.

I have lived in Otsego County for over seven years, but it was the research I did for *Home Plate* that truly illuminated this extraordinary area for me. I've met dozens of exceptional people who follow their passions, honor the land and their heritage, live their dreams, work hard, and look after one another. To all the people represented in this book, thank you for letting me get to know you and what you do with such devotion.

I am privileged to live among you.

Brenda Berstler

Commendations

*H*ome Plate: The Traveler's Food Guide to Cooperstown and Otsego County, NY was created with the support, the generosity, the vision and confidence of the following supporters. Their contributions have helped make this book possible.

NEW YORK STATE SENATOR JAMES L. SEWARD

NEW YORK STATE ASSEMBLYMAN WILLIAM MAGEE

THE COCA-COLA BOTTLING COMPANY OF NEW YORK, INC.

Syllables Press

Cornell Cooperative Extension of Otsego County

The Walking Example Group

Otsego County Tourism

TJ's Place The Home Plate

Otsego County Chamber

Price Chopper's Golub Foundation

NBT Bank

Wilber National Bank

Special Recognition

*T*he English language is so rich and diverse that is it the only language that needs a thesaurus. With all those words at my disposal, finding the right ones to say "thank you" with adequate sincerity and emotion elude me. The following people were essential to this project:

Alyssa Kosmer, whose artistic gifts beautifully illustrated my inarticulate ideas.

Richard Duncan, whose photography so poignantly captures Otsego County.

The National Baseball Hall of Fame and Museum, for their research assistance, their guardianship of the game, and for bringing me to Otsego County.

Our Celebrity Chefs for generously playing along with us.

All of the farmers, small businesses, artists, and institutions represented in *Home Plate,* for your hard work, dedication and collective stewardship of Otsego County.

Rich McCaffery for his unwavering confidence, encouragement and timely contributions of sanity.

Curt Akin, whose generosity and patient mentoring put these words on paper.

James Konstanty, Esq., for his reflections on his father and his steadfast expertise and guidance in this and so many other areas.

Elizabeth Berstler for her multifaceted editorial assistance, good humor, and endless patience with her sometime manic mother.

John Berstler for his quarter century of support of this project and every other endeavor, regardless of logic.

My mom, Marcella Steinman, who always let me use her kitchen as my playground.

And, always and forever, our New York State Farmers

Editor's Note

The author thanks the following people for their contributions to *Home Plate:*

Curt Akin, Melanie Crawford, Rich McCaffery, John Berstler, Elizabeth Berstler, and Christine Amos for their proof reading skills and gentle corrections.

John Boggs and Associates.

Steve Johnson, president of the Jack Graney chapter of the Society for American Baseball Research (SABR), for his research assistance.

The following writers and historians who generously shared their knowledge of their part of Otsego County:

        Jim Atwell (JimAtwell.com), Fly Creek
        Mark Simonson (www.oneontahistorian.com), Oneonta
        Marjorie Walters, Richfield Springs
        Sue Miller, Cherry Valley
        Nona Slaughter, Gilbertsville
        Barbara McCabe, Worcester

New York Farmers

Say "New York" and it usually conjures visions of neon, skyscrapers and bustling crowds. New Yorkers outside of Manhattan know that familiar picture as just one part of the Empire State, tucked into one small corner downstate.

Farming is the largest part of New York State's economy, a surprise to most visitors and many residents. Most of New York State is rural, with open pastures, green valleys, mountains and rolling foothills. Much of it is dotted with fish filled lakes and streams. In contrast to the frantic tempo of the Big Apple, nature sets a slower, more deliberate pace for our apple orchards, dairies, maple stands and the diverse family farms of the Upstate, Central and Western regions. The patience, skills and hard work of our farmers nurture a healthy and wealthy New York State.

Always an agricultural haven, Otsego County yields an abundance of farm products. Take a summer drive through our beautiful valleys and find farm stands selling just-picked corn, tomatoes, blueberries, or potatoes. Discover apple orchards and pumpkin patches during the gorgeous fall foliage season. Look for rhubarb, asparagus, and wild leeks in the spring; garlic fests in late summer, and fabulous pancake breakfasts featuring just tapped maple syrup in March. Our farmers' markets yield bushel baskets full of seasonal fresh greens, plump fruits, and colorful vegetables bursting with flavor and goodness. Tables are laden with organic meats, local herbs and homemade jams, baked goods, cheeses, flowers, and much more.

More than just buying fine food, a trip to the market means greeting friends and meeting the farmers who grow the spinach, keep the bees that make the honey, and know the chickens that lay the eggs you buy. We are proud of and grateful for the sustainable agriculture that nurtures us, preserves the earth and provides us with safe and delicious food.

> *Agriculture... is our wisest pursuit, because it will in the end contribute most to real wealth, good morals and happiness.*
> —THOMAS JEFFERSON TO GEORGE WASHINGTON, 1787

Home Plate Artists

Richard Duncan

Renowned photographer Richard S. Duncan was born in Catskill, New York. He spent his early childhood Upstate and has been back in Otsego County area for over seven years. His stunning photography has appeared in shows and books worldwide and is in private collections.

Look for Richard Duncan's work featured at Cooperstown's Fenimore Art Museum *Through the Eyes of an Artist: Photographs* by Richard S. Duncan, and his photo collection, *Mysteries of the Lake: Otsego Lake...Past and Present* at the Farmers' Museum. Find more of Richard's delightful area photographs in his book, *Cooperstown*.

Richard's extraordinary photography and books are for sale the Museum gift shops.

You may contact Richard Duncan at: PO Box 616 Cooperstown, NY 13326-0616.

Alyssa Kosmer

One of the brightest young art stars in New York today, Alyssa Kosmer is an illustrator currently attending college at The Cooper Union for the Advancement of Science and Art in New York City. A recent graduate of Cooperstown Central School in Cooperstown,

 NY and member of the National Honors Society, she attended the summer program of Interlochen Academy of the Arts where she won the award for exemplary ability in painting. Alyssa recently illustrated the 2005 annual holiday card for the nonprofit organization F.I.R.S.T. Alyssa created the cover for *Home Plate: The Traveler's Food Guide to Cooperstown and Otsego County, NY* and the gorgeous accompanying print, *Savor New York*.

Alyssa Kosmer may be contacted in care of the publisher (Syllables Press, PO Box 674, Mount Vision, NY, 13810).

IN THE KITCHEN

Haggerty Ace Hardware and Rental

A haven for do-it-yourselfers, professionals and gardeners, Haggerty Ace Hardware and Rental fills a wheelbarrow of needs.

Vegetable seedlings, blooming flowers and healthy plants announce the long awaited Otsego County spring. At Haggerty's, you'll find all you need for the growing season from fertilizers to garden tools to paint for the garden fence.

Haggerty's recently expanded house wares department includes canning supplies, small appliances and OXO kitchen tools to prepare and preserve the garden's bounty. Need a work shirt or protective pants? Find them in their wide selection of Carhartt and other work wear.

Haggerty's wide array of rental equipment takes the "chore" out of clearing, digging and tilling tasks, and other jobs, too.

Haggerty Ace Hardware personnel are well known in the Cooperstown area for their superior service and their starring roles in memorable commercials. Knowledgeable and friendly, the folks in the red vests can offer valuable advice for most home and garden projects to go with their quality products.

KNIVES SHARPENED HERE

Haggerty Hardware
5390 State Highway 28
Cooperstown, NY 13326
607-547-2166
haggertyhardware@stny.rr.com

Haggerty Rental and Repair
Maple Ridge Plaza
4773 State Highway 28
Cooperstown, NY 13326
607-544-1060

Kitchen Equipment

Well begun is half done.
—Mary Poppins

No artist or craftsman can work without the right tools. What you need in your kitchen will depend on what you like to cook and your personal style. An Aladdin's Cave of kitchen implements and gadgets are available and it's easy to clutter your kitchen with tools and machines you may rarely use. Keep in mind that most of the world cooks in a stone pot over an open fire. While you probably don't want to be that streamlined, avoid excess and, when it comes to what you truly need, get the best quality you can afford.

Good Knives

Knives to a cook are like paint to an artist. They are absolutely essential. You'll need a paring knife, at least one chef's knife (preferably two, in different lengths) a carving knife if you are a meat eater, and a long, serrated bread knife. Quality knives will last for decades, so splurge. Fifty or a hundred dollars may seem exorbitant, but it is not unreasonable for a good knife. The price per year of reliable service is great value. Take the time to hold the knife before you buy it and get a feel for the heft and balance.

No matter how expensive the knife, if it becomes dull it will be practically useless, if not dangerous. Learn to use a sharpening stone, invest in a good electric sharpener, or see if your local hardware store offers a sharpening service.

Good Pots

If knives are the paint, then pots are to the cook what the canvas is to the painter. Expensive pots aren't necessarily the best. Weight is a better guideline than price. For example, cast iron can be most reasonably priced and it is indispensable for some types of cooking, especially in the American South.

Stainless steel pots and pans with copper bottoms make good workhorse cookware. The steel lasts for years, it cleans well, you can cook anything in it (unlike aluminum cookware that cannot be used for anything acidic, such as tomato sauce,) and the copper bottoms ensure quick and even heat distribution. It is moderately priced new and sets are frequently available at our local auction house at great prices.

Baking Pans—Ovenproof glass baking dishes- the 9"x13" size is one of the most versatile baking dishes in the cupboard. An 8" or 9" square pan is handy, too.

Muffin Tins—a 12-cup tin is a great beginning. Get two if you make cupcakes. Consider using paper liners when making muffins. They are inexpensive, make washing the tins much easier and they keep muffins fresh longer.

Cookie Sheets—these are also indispensable in the kitchen. Even if you don't make cookies, you'll find multiple uses for one or two cookie sheets. Get heavy gauge ones so they will stand up to changes in heat and lots of use. Consider using parchment paper for the same reasons as paper muffin liners. Also, cookies do not stick to parchment, so you don't have to grease pans.

Cake Pans—this depends on how much you bake. Most cake recipes can be baked in muffin tins or the 9"x13" glass pan listed above. If you prefer layer cakes, you'll need 8" or 9" round pans. Again, get heavy gauge pans.

Pie pans—have pie pans on hand, even if you don't bake pies. They are handy for many uses, included marinating, breading cutlets and general baking.

MEASURING CUPS AND SPOONS

Dry weight and liquid volume are two different measures. They do not exchange equally. That is why there are graduated glass measuring cups for liquids and nested metal or plastic cups in increasing sizes for dry ingredients.

Liquid—Incredibly durable, microwave-safe glass graduated measuring cups come in a variety of sizes. The two-cup size is most useful, but get the one- cup and four-cup sizes as well.

Dry—Sets of four dry measure cups come in ¼, ⅓, ½ and one-cup units. If you do more than minimal baking, treat yourself and get a set of odd size cups and spoons, as well.

Lettis
Auction Service

*T*he Lettis Auction Room has been the place to gather on Thursday evenings in Oneonta for over fifty years. Peruse their ever-changing cache of fascinating inventory while enjoying a hot dog with New York sauerkraut from their in-house refreshment counter.

A playground for antique fanciers and estate sale fans, you never know what the Lettis team will offer at their weekly sale. Antique hunters' favorites in furniture, collectables, objet d'art, hardware, ephemera, Upstate New York and Native American goods might all be listed at any given sale.

Lettis Auction is the place to find kitchen goods and dinnerware at great prices. Revereware, Pyrex and cast iron cookware are frequently available, as well as fine china, baskets, linens and practical household goods.

If you're visiting Otsego County on a Thursday, or if you live in the neighborhood, plan to attend a Lettis Auction; take home something truly unique.

Auctions held Thursdays at 5:30PM, except some holiday weeks. Sale items available for preview beginning at 1PM the day of the sale.

The Lettis Auction Service never charges a buyer's premium. Cash, New York State checks and traveler's checks accepted.

Kevin Herrick, Owner and Auctioneer
23 Reynolds Street
Oneonta, NY 13820
607-432-3935

They will save a lot of redundant measuring. Odd size cups include ⅛, ⅔, ¾, 1½ and 2-cup volumes. The spoon sizes are 2 teaspoons, 1½ tablespoons and 2 tablespoons.

CUTTING BOARDS

Cutting surfaces are absolutely necessary unless you want to ruin your countertops. You'll need two types to keep meat and vegetables separate. Wood responds well to the knife blade, it absorbs heat and it's attractive. However, for poultry, meat or fish, plastic or glass is superior to wood because they can be thoroughly disinfected. Glass has its drawbacks because the knife blade slides a bit on contact and it is noisy.

WOODEN SPOONS

Time-honored and historically proven, wooden spoons don't scratch or transfer heat. They're quiet, beautiful and immeasurably useful. If they have any downside, it's that they should be hand-washed. Fine cherry or maple spoons are available at Todd's General Store at the Farmers' Museum in Cooperstown. Make sure the handles are long enough to allow stirring without risking steam burns.

HAND TOOLS

Ladles—perfect for getting soup out of the pot or pancake batter on the griddle.

Flexible Spatulas—these are practically indispensable. Make sure to get the type resistant to high heat, so you can use them either hot or cold.

Can Opener—a good manual kind is fine, unless you have a touch of arthritis.

Corkscrew—there is no other way to open a wine bottle.

Vegetable Peeler—economical and great for peeling carrots, cucumbers, zucchini, etc., and for shaving chocolate and hard cheeses.

Bottle Opener—most bottle tops these days twist off, but occasionally you'll still need the double-ended bottle opener. One end removes bottle caps, the other pierces cans of juice or evaporated milk.

Box Grater—the four-sided type will take care of most grating needs.

Colander—necessary for rinsing fruits and vegetables and draining pasta.

Whisk—indispensable for smooth sauces and gravies

MACHINES

Electric Mixer—not an absolute necessity, but if you've ever beaten egg whites into meringue by hand, you'll certainly appreciate one. Invest a bit on a heavy-duty electric mixer. Get one with enough power to meet the challenges of heavy batters and doughs.

Toaster—even the most basically equipped kitchen needs a toaster. Get one with slots wide enough to accommodate bagels and other thick breads.

Food Processor—whether or not you consider a food processor a necessity depends on how much you cook. They are wonderful work and time savers and do many laborious jobs in a matter of minutes or seconds.

Coffee Maker—for many, the morning pot of coffee is akin to the sun rising. There are lots of ways to brew coffee, including stovetop percolators, French presses, and electric coffee makers ranging from a few dollars to hundreds.
If you are a regular at the local gourmet coffee shop, think about investing in a coffee grinder, as well, and brewing at home. It is much more economical, even using brand name beans, and you can enjoy your favorite roast in your pajamas.

Microwave Oven—not absolutely necessary, but very convenient, especially for reheating foods and melting butter or chocolate.

Blender—great for smoothies and pureeing soups.

ALSO HANDY...

Kitchen Organization—save immeasurable frustration by keeping the most frequently used utensils in the same spot and within easy reach.

Your Imagination—it is absolutely your best asset in the kitchen.

Cooking versus Baking

> *Now, are we going to measure, or are we going to cook?*
>
> —FRANCES MAYES IN *UNDER THE TUSCAN SUN*

*A*lthough they happen in the same place, cooking and baking are distinctively different activities. Neither is superior to the other, and both are gratifying and more fun done with friends or family.

Cooking on the stovetop or grill is open to far more interpretation than the more exacting skill of baking. Baking allows for some substitutions and changes but, in general, measurement ratios and temperatures need to be respected for the best results.

Cooking, on the other hand, be it salads, soups, casseroles, pasta sauce, or dressings, invites creativity and the exhilaration of "making do" with whatever is in the pantry or the refrigerator. Creating new dishes from leftovers is not only resourceful and economical; it is an adventure to come up with a new favorite. Oftentimes, the Monday soup is as good as the Sunday dinner.

Baking can be more temperamental, but it is entirely worth the extra attention it demands. A well-made loaf of bread, scones from scratch or perfect oatmeal cookies are soul tending, evoking feelings of warmth and welcome and "home."

If you are unfamiliar with baking, start with quick breads, muffins, or cookies. They are easy successes and immediately gratifying. Work up to fancy cakes or intricate breads after you feel comfortable with oven temperature, leavening agents, the interaction of ingredients and the measuring skill that ensures successful home baking.

Kitchens are wonderful, inviting places, even a little magical. Where else are all your senses satisfied? Follow the wafting aroma of apple crisp or breakfast bacon, find a color spectrum in fruits and vegetables, from garnet red apples to deep green spinach, white onions to violet eggplant; delve into the diverse textures of creamy dairy goods, firm, but yielding fruits, crunchy nuts and nubby grains. The kitchen produces endless flavors, ready to dance on your taste buds. Sauces bubble, steaks sizzle, corn pops and coffee perks.

Kitchens are warm, well lit and their stocked shelves satisfy the basic human desire of freedom from want. Foods can rekindle warm memories of childhood and special times. The incomparable aromas of simmering soup and anything freshly baked can soothe jangled nerves and give a sense of safety.

Whether your preference is cooking or baking, enjoy being in the kitchen, and especially with people you love. Give everyone a task and revel in the kinship that comes from the celebration of food, friends and family. No matter how messy or crowded, you can always count on people to gather in the kitchen. It is truly the heart of the home.

Laughter is brightest where food is best.
—IRISH PROVERB

The Stocked Pantry

*I*f you cook for one or a crowd, or whether your kitchen is spacious or tiny, you need to keep essential ingredients on hand. You can make delicious and appealing meals surprisingly quickly when basic components are at the ready. Below is a list to help you create a variety of meals and avoid the frustration of finding yourself out of something critical in the middle of preparations. This is a good framework to get you started. Have fun tailoring it to fit your own tastes.

On the Shelves

Vegetable and/or Poultry Stock (in cans, boxes, concentrated paste, or bouillon cubes or granules)

Onions, Potatoes, Garlic—These three root crops are indispensable for a bounty of dishes. They prefer being stored in the dark and apart from each other.

Orzo Pasta	Spaghetti, or other pasta shapes
Rice, brown or white	Dried and/or canned beans
Canned tomatoes and tomato sauce	Olive Oil
Vegetable Oil	Mustard (lots of types to choose)
Ketchup	Peanut Butter
Canned Fruits and Vegetables (your preference)	
New York State Maple Syrup	New York State Honey
Chili Powder	Choice of Dried Herbs and Spices
Salt	Pepper

In the Fridge

Butter	Cheeses (New York Cheddar, mozzarella
Milk	and blue)
Apples	Eggs
Carrots	Spinach
	Celery

Seasonal Fresh Fruits, Vegetables and Herbs

In the Freezer

Ice   Vanilla Ice cream
Walnuts and/or pecans   Fruits and Vegetables

The Baking Corner

All Purpose Flour   Granulated Sugar
Maple Sugar   Oatmeal
Brown Sugar   Chocolate Chips
Unsweetened Baking Chocolate   Cocoa
Baking Soda   Baking Powder
Cornstarch   Cornmeal
Cinnamon

Down in the Country

Art and creativity flourish at Down in the Country. Located literally "down in the country" in Otsego County, artist Jacqueline Jones offers both tools for the fiber artist and her delightful and beautiful paintings.

Sheep and alpaca are commonly found in Otsego County, providing a local resource for their wool. If you are a beginning or master fibersmith, Down in the Country's Rakestraw Spinner is a wonder of spinning simplicity and efficiency. Unlike a vertical drop spindle, the Rakestraw Spinner works horizontally, eliminating the yarn dropping to the floor.

This ingenious hand spinner is portable and great for working while watching TV or visiting with friends. It is nicely travel-sized, perfect for spinning on road trips. Everything can be done on your lap!

The Rakestraw Spinner works well with wool, alpaca, silk, angora, man-made fibers and, with a little practice, even cotton. Ply Paddles, employing the Andean plying method, are also available. Watch the instructional videos for both tools at www.downinthecountry. com.

Jackie's artistic gifts also include fabulous, sometimes whimsical paintings of birds, animals and fantasy. She can also paint your house from your photograph. Call or visit the Down in the Country website for more information about artwork or spinning tools.

Jacqueline Jones
Mount Vision, NY
(607) 293-8333
www.downinthecountry.com

Deli Reuben Dunk
Down in the Country

A goodly amount of the cabbage produced in New York State (we are the top grower in the country) goes into sauerkraut. This easy recipe uses both sauerkraut and New York cheddar for a rich appetizer, low in carbohydrates and high in flavor.

Preheat oven to 350 degrees

1 pound sauerkraut, rinsed and well drained
1½ cups (6 ounces) shredded New York cheddar cheese
1½ cups (6 ounces) shredded Swiss cheese
6 ounces deli corned beef, chopped
1 cup mayonnaise or salad dressing

Put drained sauerkraut between several layers of paper towels to remove remaining moisture.

In a large bowl, combine the sauerkraut, cheeses, corned beef and mayonnaise. Place mixture in a 1½ quart casserole dish, spreading evenly. Bake, uncovered, for 20 to 25 minutes, or until hot and bubbly.

Serve dip warm with toast triangles, rye bread cocktail rounds or tortilla chips (regular or low-carb) or vegetable dippers- celery sticks, cauliflorets, bell pepper strips, etc. Or, stuff mixture into mushroom caps.

Glimmerglass Opera

~~~~~~~~~~~~~~~~~~~~~~~~~~~~~~~~~~~~~

*T*he world-renowned Glimmerglass Opera began its productions in 1975, with four performances of La Boheme staged in the Cooperstown High School auditorium. The four performances played to 1200 local residents.

The desire for world-class opera and the founders' belief "that a performing arts festival belongs here" has since seen the curtain rise on over thirty Glimmerglass seasons, drawing thousands of patrons worldwide. Glimmerglass now offers 43 performances of four different operas, all in new productions, each enchanting summer season.

Glimmerglass Opera moved to their permanent home in the Alice Busch Opera Theater in 1987. Splendidly situated on 43 donated acres on the northern end of Otsego Lake, the Glimmerglass home theater is the first American hall built specifically for opera since New York City's Metropolitan Opera House opened in 1966. This intimate venue seats 900 and its unique sliding side doors make a memorable impression. Opened before performances and during intermissions, patrons can enjoy the beautiful surrounding countryside while the dulcet tones of the orchestra and classic voices linger.

Opera at the Glimmerglass is unlike anywhere else, an opinion echoed by The Sunday Times of London, calling the Glimmerglass Opera's unspoiled rural surroundings "the most magical of settings."

PO Box 191
Cooperstown, NY 13326
607-547-2255
www.glimmerglass.org

Ticket Office:
18 Chestnut Street
Cooperstown, NY 13326

Back Yard Salsa

Glimmerglass Opera

〜〜〜〜〜〜〜〜〜〜〜〜〜〜〜〜〜〜〜〜〜〜

A simple and tasty mélange of great summer ingredients, Back Yard Salsa can be enjoyed with chips, western omelets, chili and gazpacho, etc.

3 large, ripe tomatoes, chopped
¼ green pepper, finely diced
¼ small red onion, finely diced
½ small Jalapeño pepper, finely diced
1 tablespoon balsamic vinegar
¼ cup fresh cilantro, chopped
½ teaspoon chili or Mexican spices
Salt and pepper to taste

Place all ingredients in a bowl and mix well. Let flavors mingle for 30 minutes. Serve with tortilla chips or other favorite crackers.

The ingredients can be adapted to your taste, but fresh cilantro is the key. Try growing it in your yard. It does very well in Otsego County.

Otsego County Fair

Spend the "best six days of summer" at the Otsego County Fair in Morris, NY. This old-fashioned county fair showcases Otsego County agriculture at its finest, complete with 4-H animals, garden produce, flowers and harness racing.

Plan to spend a full day at the Fair. Enjoy the rides, the shows, the shopping and the entertainment. Culinary competitions, fine needlework contests and livestock shows are still the main attractions. There is fun for everyone, strolling the midway, tasting the fair food, browsing the vendors or just relaxing on the many benches throughout the fairgrounds and watching the people.

An August tradition, the Otsego County Fair is set against the backdrop of the stunning Butternut Valley. Enjoy "the best six days" of fun, celebrating life in the country.

Otsego County Fair
Morris, NY 13808
607-263-5289
www.otsegocountyfair.org

Cheese Stuffed Baby Veggies

Otsego County Fair

*I*f you have a garden or a window box, reap the rewards of growing your own herbs. Having fresh herbs on hand makes creative, flavorful cooking easier.

⅓ cup ricotta cheese
2 tablespoons fat free cream cheese
2 tablespoons finely shredded radish
1 tablespoon snipped fresh chives
2 tablespoons snipped fresh basil
2 tablespoons snipped fresh cilantro
2 tablespoons snipped fresh parsley
⅛ teaspoon onion salt

20 cherry tomatoes
10-12 baby squash
Additional fresh herbs for garnish

In a small bowl, combine cheeses, radish, herbs and onion salt. Set aside.

Take a thin slice from the top of each tomato and scoop out pulp, using a small spoon.
Turn tomato shells upside down on paper towels and let drain.
Trim squash, cut in half and scoop out seeds. Invert on paper towels.

Stuff cheese mixture into veggies, garnishing, if desired, and serve immediately.
May be chilled, covered, up to two hours.

Ladybug

*D*iscover Ladybug, just down the stairs from Main Street, Cooperstown. Welcoming you with soft music, sweet smells and intriguing merchandise, Ladybug is a pleasant retreat. Set amid the rich baseball history that draws so many people to town, Ladybug offers a broad range of different types of items and gifts.

This family-owned and operated business includes fine articles for men, women and children. Local artisans' handcrafted items are showcased, as well as locally manufactured goods such as soap and maple syrup. You'll find unique women's clothing, quality jewelry and much more.

Ladybug's selections are constantly changing as they discover new and interesting items in the area and from around the world.

Stop by and make your own discoveries, or allow them to help you find the perfect gift. They gift-wrap for you as part of their complete customer service.

Doris Mark
108 Main Street
Cooperstown, NY 13326
607-547-1940

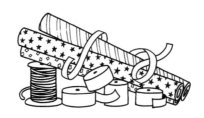

Purple Cow Shakes
Ladybug

~~~~~~

*T*his nostalgic favorite never loses its appeal. A delicious combination of dairy and grape, it is a nod to two of New York's leading products. It remains a favorite of kids and adults, alike.

3 cups vanilla ice cream or fat-free frozen vanilla yogurt
1 cup milk (whole, 2% or skim)
½ cup thawed Concord grape juice concentrate, undiluted
1½ teaspoons lemon juice

Place all ingredients in blender and process until smooth. Garnish with a sprig of fresh mint and a bit of whipped cream, if desired. Serve immediately and enjoy fully.

These shakes are the same pretty lavender shade as some of the lilacs at Bates Hop House, a *Home Plate* contributor.

Chutney Unlimited

Zing!

This is the most amazing stuff. Tanna's Garlic and Ginger Chutney is all vibrant flavors, dense textures and a satisfying finish sure to make you a devotee.

Stated as simply as possible, it's delicious. An out of the ordinary condiment, Tanna's Chutney enhances meats and fish and it is a knockout on New York State cheddar cheese. Serve it with rice or couscous or use it as a sandwich spread, especially on poultry. It's a great accompaniment to enliven eggs, on cheese and crackers, or just spooning it out of the jar.

Visit Tanna's website for recipes, serving suggestions and information about her chutneys and her garamasala, the "culinary aromatherapy." Lemon Fig Chutney is Tanna's newest addition. You'll want to keep her ordering information handy.

Tanna's products are available at *Home Plate* contributor Cooperstown Natural Foods, as well as many regional markets and shops. Don't leave Cooperstown without a few jars for yourself and friends.

"One taste is all it takes."

Tanna Roten
52 Pioneer Street
Cooperstown, NY 13326
607-547-7272

Order online at:
www.chutneyunlimited.com
E-mail: tanna@chutneyunlimited.com

Tanna's Sourdough Round

Chutney Unlimited

~~~~~~~~~~~~~~~~~~~~~~

*T*his may well be the world's easiest appetizer. It is delicious, simple beyond definition, and quick for impromptu gatherings.

Preheat oven to 375 degrees.

1 round loaf sourdough, rye, or your favorite bread
1 small wheel Brie cheese
Tanna's Garlic and Ginger Chutney

Hollow out the round loaf and reserve bread pieces. Drop in the Brie. Top generously with Tanna's Garlic and Ginger Chutney. Place loaf on cookie sheet and bake for 20-25 minutes. Serve with reserved bread pieces. Supplement with crackers, if necessary.

Tanna's Chutney is surprisingly tasty on vanilla ice cream. Don't think too long on this idea-just do it. Simply warm the Chutney, spoon over ice cream and let everyone guess!

---

*They dined on mince, and slices of quince,
Which they ate with a runcible spoon;
And hand in hand, on the edge of the sand,
They danced by the light of the moon.*
—EDWARD LEAR

Breezie Maples Farms

*I*f you are in Otsego County in the maple-sugaring month of March, pay a visit to Breezie Maples Farm. Take a deep, sweet breath and be grateful that you are in the only corner of the globe that produces maple syrup.

Breezie's is open year round and you can tour their production facility anytime. Take a drive up their hill and enjoy the views along the way. Be sure to call to arrange a visit.

Located in "Maple Valley", Breezie owners Rick and Nancy Newman are maple-producing partners with Larry Roseboom. Larry's ancestors were the original settlers of the first Westford, NY and the town of Roseboom, NY. His family's maple tradition dates back 250 years.

After several years of producing maple syrup on a hobby level, Rick and Larry toured the largest maple producers in the United States and Canada and transformed their operation to a state of the art facility. With 14,000 taps, Breezie Farms is one of the largest maple operations in the country. Their 40-year forest management plan as a dedicated sugar bush (a stand of sugar maple trees) will be the legacy of these two dedicated sugar makers.

Rick and Larry consistently produce award-winning syrup, earning more blue ribbons and Best in Show honors than any producer in Otsego County. Breezie's maple products are available online and at many retailers throughout the area.

To get to Breezie's, take Route 166 through Roseboom and turn right at the Pleasant Brook Hotel. Follow the La Fleure Road hill about 2.5 miles.

2269 County Highway 34
Westford, NY 13488
www.breeziemaples.com
607-638-9317
800-950-9676

Chin Drippin' Wings

Breezie Maples Farms

〰〰〰〰〰〰〰〰〰〰

*T*his is an easy and satisfying appetizer, perfect for ballgames and get-togethers. The two tablespoons of black pepper sounds like a lot, but Rick Newman swears by it; experiment to suit your own taste.

3 pounds chicken wings
1 15-ounce can tomato sauce
⅔ cup cider vinegar
⅓ cup dark maple syrup
2 tablespoons chili powder
2 tablespoons mustard
2 tablespoons black pepper
Combine all ingredients, except wings, and stir together.

Place wings in baking dish and pour tomato sauce mixture over all. Make sure sauce coats all wings. Cover and refrigerate. Allow wings to marinate overnight.

Preheat oven to 350 degrees. Bake wings about an hour, turning several times.

Maple syrup, like olive oil, comes in various grades. Like wine, it is sensitive to soil and climate and subtleties in flavor will vary from season to season. The lighter ambers are generally a bit more expensive and excellent for topping pancakes, waffles, ice cream, etc. Dark amber syrup has a bolder flavor that resists fading with heat. It is especially prized for baking and cooking. Medium amber falls between the two. Let your own taste be your guide and enjoy them all.

Brookwood Garden

*W*elcome to a world of history and horticulture, to the quiet inspiration of Otsego Lake views and trickling fountains. Welcome to a Cooperstown you never suspected.

Built on the site of one of the oldest summer estates on Otsego Lake, Brookwood Garden is alive with blooming colors and fragrances. This beautiful spot is ideal for summer picnics, a quiet stroll enjoying the flora, or just sitting and thinking by the lake. Brookwood is Cooperstown's very own "secret garden."

The first house on the Brookwood property pre-dates 1820 and the farm has known a succession of owners. Kathryn Jermain and her husband, landscape architect Frederick dePeyster Townsend, designed and built the garden and garden house between 1915-1920. In 1944, the estate was sold to J. Harry Cook, whose son Robert Wiles Cook created the Cook Foundation in 1985 to ensure the preservation of this unique property.

Brookwood Garden is open to the public. It is ideal for weddings, parties and receptions. Scheduled tours are available.

6000 West Lake Road (Route 80)
Cooperstown, NY 13326
607-547-2170
www.brookwoodgarden.com
info@brookwoodgarden.com

> *If of thy mortal goods thou art bereft, and from thy slender store two loaves along to thee are left, Sell one, and with the dole buy hyacinths to feed thy soul.*
> —MOSLIH EDDIN (Muslih-un-Din) SAADI (Sadi), GULISTAN (Garden of Roses)

Sam's Simply Sensational Tomatoes

Brookwood Garden

~~~~~~~~~~~~~~~~~~~~~~~~~~~~~

*O*nce you have transformed sun-dried tomatoes from tough, salty pieces of red leather into this utterly delicious combination, you can use them in countless recipes.

½ pound sun-dried tomatoes
1 cup virgin olive oil
4 to 5 cloves garlic, peeled and coarsely chopped
1 bay leaf, broken in two pieces
½ tsp. fennel seed, pounded in a mortar
Fresh and dried herbs (vary according to availability and preference):
Finely chopped oregano, thyme, marjoram, rosemary (use sparingly), basil

If whole, cut each dried tomato into strips, about an inch long. Soak tomato strips in very hot water for 20 minutes; drain. Soak another 20 minutes; drain a final time. Spread tomatoes on a cookie sheet. Dry in a 250-degree oven for 20 minutes. In a deep bowl, steep herbs and garlic in olive oil, while tomatoes are soaking and drying,

When oven drying is completed, add warm tomatoes to olive oil-herb mixture. Mix well, and add more oil to make sure all tomatoes are covered. Leave at room temperature while tomatoes absorb oil mix, adding more oil as needed. Tomatoes will last at least 2 weeks refrigerated (if you keep them well hidden)!

As a snack: simply scoop up tomatoes and oil from the bowl with a piece of good bread. As an appetizer: place a thin slice of mozzarella on bread, top with a fresh basil leaf and sun-dried tomato mixture.

As a quick main dish: combine about a cup of the tomatoes with a pound of blanched broccoli florets. Warm over low heat, adding more oil, if necessary. Add a handful of fresh chopped parsley just before spooning over one pound of hot, cooked pasta. Shower with grated Parmesan or Romano cheese.

Creek's Edge Elk Farm

~~~~~~~~~~~~~~~~~~~~~~~~~~~~~~~~~~~~~

C reek's Edge Elk Farm began raising elk in 2002 and now boasts a herd of 14 of these magnificent animals. The elk is available at their farm, in some farmers' markets and by mail within New York State.

Creek's Edge elk is flavorful and nutritious. High in protein, it is markedly lower in fat and cholesterol than many other meats, including beef, pork, chicken, bison and venison. Prized as gourmet meat, elk is equally versatile at barbecues and at formal dinners. Enjoy it grilled, fried, broiled or roasted.

Conveniently located just thirty minutes north of Cooperstown, Creek's Edge farm is nestled in the picturesque Mohawk Valley hills. Visitors are welcomed to view the elk grazing. Late spring is calving time and you can often spot baby elk frolicking in the pastures. Elk are well suited to Upstate winters. They are naturally hardy and grow a thick coat each winter to protect them from the elements.

Please call to arrange a tour or to inquire about elk availability.

Stacy Handy or Susan Keith
894 State Highway 80
Fort Plain, NY 13339
518-568-5476
518-993-4014 (Sue at the Farm)

A Member of the Cooperstown Farmers' Holiday Market

Elk Meatballs in Sweet and Sour Sauce

Creek's Edge Elk Farm

~~~~~~

*G*ive it a try; elk is flavorful and a pleasant alternative to beef.

Meatballs

2 eggs, well beaten
1 tablespoon parsley
2 cloves garlic, chopped
1 teaspoon salt
½ teaspoon pepper

½ cup milk
½ cup grated Parmesan cheese
1 cup plain breadcrumbs
1 pound ground elk burger

Preheat oven to 350 degrees
Combine first eight ingredients and then add elk burger, mixing well. Shape into walnut sized balls and place on well greased baking sheet. Bake for 15-20 minutes, or until centers are no longer pink. Do not overcook.

Sweet 'n' Sour Sauce

3 ½ cups tomato juice
1 cup brown sugar, packed
10 gingersnaps, finely crushed

¼ cup white vinegar
1 teaspoon onion salt

Combine all ingredients in saucepan. Bring to a boil over medium heat, stirring until cookie crumbs are dissolved. Add meatballs to sauce and bake for about 30 minutes, or until heated through. Meatballs may also be served plain or with your favorite sauce.

Cooperstown Wine and Spirits

~~~~~~

*W*hen looking for wine or spirits in Cooperstown, look no farther than this bright and tidy shop on Pioneer Street.

When browsing an amply supplied wine and spirits shop, a knowledgeable staff is your best tool to determine just the right selection for your taste and style. The team at Cooperstown Wine and Spirits can lead you on a "spirited" journey through their diverse inventory.

Cooperstown Wine and Spirits features a selection of New York State's finest wines along with excellent spirits and domestic and imported wines. They feature unique selections from the best vintners and distillers worldwide, handpicked for quality and value.

Conveniently located in the heart of Cooperstown, this friendly, well-stocked shop is open all year. Visa and MasterCard accepted.

Hours: Monday-Thursday 10AM-8PM
       Friday and Saturday 10AM-9PM
       Sunday 1-4PM
Ed Landers
45 Pioneer Street
607-547-8100
Cooperstown, NY 13326

In Vino, Veritas
In wine there is truth

Red Wine Cider Punch
Cooperstown Wine and Spirits

~~~~~~

A simple recipe that hails the first cider pressings of autumn. This versatile ruby-hued punch is red as sangria, but it's all New York, calling for New York cider and hearty New York red wine. It's perfect when autumn afternoons turn warm, when the leaves are raked, wood is stacked or you've finished the last round of golf of the season. It is equally good hot or cold.

The most complicated step in this recipe is making ice cubes. A day or so ahead, freeze one quart of the cider in ice cube trays. When served, the cider cubes will add flavor to the punch instead of diluting it.

2 quarts apple cider or apple juice
2 bottles dry red wine
2 tablespoons lemon juice
Sugar to taste
1 liter ginger ale (not entirely necessary, but it gives a nice spritzy lift)

Put all ingredients, except ice cubes and ginger ale, in a punch bowl and stir.
If making ahead, refrigerate mixture in a pitcher until serving time.

Just before serving, add ginger ale and cider ice cubes. Makes 30 (4 ounce) punch servings.

To make individual servings, keep wine-cider mixture refrigerated until desired. Pour over cider cubes in a glass and add a splash of ginger ale.

TO SERVE WARM: Heat wine/cider mix and add cinnamon sticks or mulling spices (a blend of cinnamon, ginger, cloves and nutmeg). Omit ginger ale. Sit by fire and enjoy.

Hilton Bloom
Art Studio

*J*ane Evelynne Higgins has traveled extensively, studying and creating art in Italy and Southern California. Still, it's the rolling dales of the Butternut Valley where she finds her most constant inspiration.

Jane's collages are stunning. Some are moving, some are humorous, and all are thought provoking. Drawing on diverse themes from Greek myths, the Bible, Shakespeare, modern pop culture and autobiographical elements she develops singular, wondrous pieces. What she does with an idea, a knife and scissors must be seen. None of her pieces are computer generated; her talented hands piece them all, deliberately and with inspiration.

Her Hilton Bloom Art Studio also generously showcases the abundance of artists and their creations in Gilbertsville. Jane's rotating displays of her fellow artists' works include collage, pottery, greeting cards, prints, painting and photography.

Take the beautiful drive to Gilbertsville and experience the contentment of this pleasant village. You're sure to find an enchanting memento from their bevy of local artists.

Open Memorial Day – Labor Day
Thursday – Saturday 1 – 5PM
Other times by chance or appointment

Jane Evelynne Higgins
24 Bloom Street
PO Box 12
Gilbertsville, NY 13776-0012
607-783-2779
www.gilbertsville.com
jane.al@frontiernet.net

Summer Strawberry Daiquiri Float
Hilton Bloom Art Studio

~~~~~~~~~~~~~~~~~~~~~~~~~~~~~~~~~~~~~~~

*T*his delightfully cool concoction is a perfect New York salute to end a summer meal or to enjoy on a hot August afternoon. New York strawberries, light dairy products and McCoy's honey combine in this attractive work. It's delicious with or without the rum.

2 cups frozen unsweetened strawberries
1 six-ounce container strawberry yogurt
½ cup milk
2 tablespoons New York State honey, or to taste
2 ounces light rum (optional)
2 scoops strawberry sorbet
Fresh strawberries for garnish
Sparkling sugar to decorate glass, if desired

Place sugar on a small saucer. Use plain or colored decorative crystals or regular granulated sugar. Wet the rims of two attractive glasses (such as margarita) and dip rims in sugar. Turn upright and set aside.

Process strawberries, yogurt, milk, and honey in a blender until smooth. Pour into prepared glasses and top with scoops of sorbet. Garnish with fresh strawberries and mint.

One must ask children and birds how cherries and strawberries taste.
JOHANN WOLFGANG VON GOETHE

The French Corner

*I*t's something special, the Continental fare at the French Corner. Their pan-continental menu features diverse and innovative recipes with European, Asian and American influences apparent.

Chef-owner Mark McCoy is an artist who has found his medium. He cooks for patrons individually, as if sharing his culinary talent as a gift, which indeed it is. Do not leave this Earth without first supping on his Mussels in Asian Lobster Broth.

In contrast to Cooperstown's pastoral country surroundings, The French Corner is sleek and urbane; its interior all clean lines of black, white and red. Their full bar features exceptional wines, talented mixologists and comfortable seating.

There are no processed shortcuts at the French Corner. You'll find only fresh, first-quality ingredients, memorable sauces and interesting accents. In short, real food prepared with genuine talent.

Reservations recommended.

161 Main Street (corner of Main and Chestnut)
Cooperstown, NY 13326
607-547-6106

One cannot think well, love well, sleep well, if one has not dined well.
—VIRGINIA WOOLFE

Ravioli Sacha

The French Corner

~~~~~~~~~~~~~~~~~~~~~~~~~~~~~~

This is one of The French Corner's amazing appetizer recipes, generously shared with *Home Plate*. It's a marvelous use of New York State's bumper crop of butternut squash.

Fresh pasta sheets for making ravioli (homemade, or purchased in larger markets)
1 butternut squash, cut in small dice
2 tablespoons goat cheese (plus more for garnish)
¼ cup unsalted butter
¼ cup hazelnuts, finely chopped

Melt half of the butter in large skillet. Sauté butternut squash until soft.

Transfer squash to food processor and puree with goat cheese and salt and pepper until smooth. Cool.

Cut fresh pasta into 3" squares. Spoon 1-2 tablespoons of squash filling onto square. Fold square into triangle, dab water on edges and press to seal. Trim raviolis, if necessary.

Bring a large pot of water to boil. Add raviolis to boiling water and cook 4-5 minutes. While they cook, melt the remaining butter. Swirl over low-medium heat until butter is browned. Add hazelnuts.

Drain pasta well and add to butter in pan. Coat raviolis with browned butter and hazelnut mixture and spoon onto plate. Sprinkle with goat cheese. Serve immediately.

The Rose and Thistle Bed and Breakfast

You'll enjoy a wonderful stay at this beautiful turn of the century Victorian bed and breakfast. Steve and Patti D'Esposito's warm welcome will make you feel instantly at ease and their attention to detail assures you that your comfort and satisfaction is their first priority.

Known to many returning guests for Steve's full country breakfasts and Patti's charming rose motif decorating, mornings at The Rose and Thistle start with good food and good conversation. After breakfast, lounge on the porch or get started discovering Cooperstown. You are walking distance to many village attractions and shops.

The Rose and Thistle offers comfort, convenience, and personable hosts to ensure a memorable stay.

Be sure to check their website for package specials and more information.

Steve and Patti D'Esposito
132 Chestnut Street
607-547-5345
Cooperstown, NY 1332

www.roseandthistlebb.com
stay@roseandthistlebb.com

Vegetarian Quiche

The Rose and Thistle Bed and Breakfast

~~~~~~

Quiches can be dressed up or down and served anytime of the day. They are perfect for brunch or as a light entrée for lunch or supper. Cut this quiche in thin slices, or bake in miniature tart or phyllo shells (available in the frozen food department), and serve as an appetizer.

Preheat oven to 350 degrees
Line a 9" pie pan with piecrust, purchased or homemade, or use miniature tart or phyllo shells

Whisk together in a bowl and set aside:
1 cup milk
4 eggs
½ teaspoon dry mustard
¼ teaspoon white pepper

Combine the following in a large bowl:
½ cup chopped red pepper
½ cup sliced mushrooms
½ cup canned artichokes, chopped
⅛ cup chopped scallions
¾ cup shredded New York cheddar cheese
¾ cup feta cheese
1 cup fresh or frozen chopped broccoli

Place vegetables and cheeses in prepared piecrust. Pour egg mixture over vegetables and cheeses. Bake 40-50 minutes, until a knife inserted into the center comes out clean. Cool five minutes. Slice and serve.

Cooperstown Baseball Bracelet

*T*he Cooperstown Baseball Bracelet is designed for women who are passionate about America's game. A sterling idea born on the tranquil and inspiring shores of Cooperstown's Three Mile Point, Cooperstown natives Anne Hall and Jennifer Stewart have created a classic piece of jewelry for female baseball fans.

Growing up in Cooperstown and in the shadow of baseball, Anne and Jennifer decided women needed a fashionable expression for their love of the game. Their simple and elegant bracelet fulfills the need.

Chic and stylish, the Cooperstown Baseball Bracelet is suitable for any of the baseball loving women in your life. Whether they play the game, cheer in the stands or drive the team, this tasteful bracelet is sure to please.

"Enjoy Baseball? Wear baseball."

Anne Hall and Jennifer Stewart
607-437-1492
www.cooperstownbaseballbracelet.com
cooperstownbaseballbracelet@yahoo.com

The first game played under lights in Wrigley Field was a contest of the All-Stars of the All-American Girls Professional Baseball League, July 1, 1943, 45 years before the August 1988 games between the Cubs and Phillies.

Mulligan Chutney

Cooperstown Baseball Bracelet

~~~~~~~~~~~~~~~~~~~~~~~~~~~~~~~~~

*T*he "sweet heat" contrast of these distinct ingredients combine for an easy chutney.

12 ounces apple jelly
12 ounces pineapple preserves
¼ cup dry mustard
⅓ cup prepared horseradish
1½ teaspoons black pepper

Put all ingredients in blender or food processor and mix until evenly combined.

This is a great enhancement to top cream cheese and crackers. Keep a jar in the refrigerator for easy, impromptu appetizers.

Three Mile Point is one of the many beautiful spots on Otsego Lake, and now the site of a popular Village public beach. There is also a Two Mile and Five Mile Point, the geographical distinctions used when mail was delivered by boat. For more views and history of Otsego Lake, look for Richard Duncan's breathtaking photographic homage in his book, Otsego Lake: Past and Present.

The Cherry Valley Museum

*L*ocated in the heart of the Village, the Cherry Valley Museum houses one of the finest collections of Early Americana in the New York State. Collections include early fire pumpers, Revolutionary War and Civil War artifacts, Victorian furniture, toys and clothing and a Revolutionary War diorama depicting the infamous "Cherry Valley Massacre." It is an ideal stop when getting to know Cherry Valley's rich history.

The Museum in located in the White-Phelon-Sutliff House, built by Jonathan Kinsbury in 1812-13 and is a fine example of Federal, Greek Revival, Italianate, and Colonial architecture.

The Cherry Valley Museum is a designated Heritage New York site, as well as being listed on the State and Federal Historic Registers.

Find the Cherry Valley Museum in the center of the Village of Cherry Valley, two miles south of Route 20 and 12 miles northeast of Cooperstown.

Open daily
Memorial Day - October 15 10AM- 5PM

49 Main Street
Cherry Valley, NY 13320
607 264-3303
607 264-3098

museum@HistoricCherryValley.com
www.cherryvalleymuseum.org

Rose Petal Drink

Cherry Valley Museum

~~~~~~

This gentle beverage evokes another era. Follow the floral theme and enjoy it with Lavender Cookies from *Home Plate* contributor, The Perennial Field.

Petals of three large organic roses, in full bloom (no sprays or powders!)
5 cups water
½ teaspoon lemon juice
3 tablespoons sugar

Bring water to a boil. Add rose petals and lemon juice, turn off heat and let stand 6-10 hours.

After steeping, strain into a pitcher and discard petals. Add sugar to the rose water and stir.

Refrigerate and serve chilled.

In the 19th century, Cherry Valley stood unique in its history and in its gardens, particularly its rose gardens. From Susan Roseboom-Belcher's "Roselawn", Dakin's "Woodlawn" and Hetheringtons's "Bee Haven", to the abundant wild roses that graced the fields and roadside, the wild roses of this scenic area reigned supreme. These gardens have all but faded into history, but the Cherry Valley Museum is creating a Heritage Rose Garden emulating some of the famous gardens that existed in Cherry Valley in the mid-nineteenth century. Wander through the garden and enjoy their historical love of roses.

The rose is the official flower of New York State.

New York State Historical Association (NYSHA)
The Farmers' Museum and Fenimore Art Museum

The Farmers' Museum and the New York State Historical Association (including Fenimore Art Museum) are hubs of constant activity and events. Set in one of the prettiest venues in Otsego County and just outside the Village of Cooperstown, both museums overlook Otsego Lake; the lake James Fenimore Cooper called "Glimmerglass".

As a living, working tribute to Otsego County agriculture, The Farmers' Museum is worth visiting time and again. The 19th century farm and village provides a view of the American life of our ancestors. A stroll around the grounds, a visit paid the animals, a bit of shopping in Todd's General Store or a conversation with one of the museum staff in period costume is not only informative, it's just plain fun and time well spent. Don't miss a ride on the fabulous Empire State Carousel!

Across the street is the Fenimore Art Museum. Housed in this handsome building's eleven galleries you'll find folk art, fine art and Native American collections honoring our American heritage. Enjoy food for the body and food for the soul at the Fenimore Café, overlooking Otsego Lake and the museum's gorgeous terraced gardens. Be sure to visit the Museum Shops for exceptional items and gift choices.
Please call or visit their websites for hours and admission.

The Farmers' Museum and Fenimore Art Museum
5775 State Highway 80 - Lake Road,
Cooperstown, NY 13326
607-547-1450
www.farmersmuseum.org
www.fenimoreartmuseum.org

Candlelight Evening Wassail

The Farmers' Museum

~~~~~~~~~~~~~~~~~~~~

Candlelight Evening is a much-loved tradition in Otsego County and not to be missed. Celebrated each December, this holiday celebration harkens back to a far less commercialized era.

For more annual NYSHA events, refer to *Home Plate*'s Food Events and Festivals.

4 spiced tea bags
1 quart water
1 gallon New York State apple cider
2 quarts orange juice
1 quart cranberry juice
1½ cups sugar
1 whole orange, unpeeled
12-15 whole cloves
4 cinnamon sticks
½ cup small cinnamon candies

Bring one quart of water to boil and add spiced tea bags. Steep for four minutes and remove and discard tea bags.

Put tea into large pot. Add cider, orange juice, cranberry juice and sugar. Bring to a boil and then reduce to a simmer.

Pierce orange with whole cloves, spacing them evenly. Make a design, if you like. Float orange in cider mixture. Add cinnamon sticks and candies and continue to simmer about thirty minutes.

Makes 2 gallons

A Rose is a Rose Flowers & Gifts

A Rose is a Rose Flowers & Gifts is a full service florist offering creative designs for the most intimate of gatherings to the most lavish affairs. Their professional staff will make your event one that's talked about for years to come.

A Rose is a Rose makes daily deliveries to Cooperstown, Richfield Springs and the surrounding areas, including service to Bassett Hospital, Glimmerglass Opera, accommodations, funeral homes and private residences.

Custom designs are A Rose is a Rose's specialty. In addition to fresh flowers and plants, you'll find also an array of dried floral creations, including wreaths and table arrangements. If you don't see what you're looking for, their artists will make it for you. A Rose is a Rose also offers interesting gift items, grapevine creations, and garden statuary.

A Rose is a Rose is located in an historic stone building (circa 1852) on Main Street in downtown Cherry Valley, New York. It is just minutes from US Route 20 (the old Cherry Valley Turnpike), an official New York State Scenic Byway.

Jackie Hull and her staff look forward to meeting you. Enjoy the beauty of quaint Cherry Valley and be sure to take home some flowers.

17 Main St.
Cherry Valley, NY 13320
607-264-3100
800-243-9501
aroseisarose17@hotmail.com

Horseradish Dip

A Rose is a Rose Flowers & Gifts

~~~~~~~~~~~~~~~~~~~~~~~~~~~~

You can keep these few simple ingredients on hand, for a quick appetizer for impromptu gatherings.

1 cup reduced-fat sour cream
¼ cup chopped fresh dill
3 tablespoons bottled horseradish
½ teaspoon salt

Combine all ingredients and refrigerate for 1 hour before serving.

Place in a pretty bowl and surround with raw, fresh New York State vegetables, bagel or pita chips.

Floral Tips

Adding bunches of fresh herbs to fresh flower bouquets lends interesting textures and fragrance.

Always cut flowers from your garden or roadside in the early morning or later in the afternoon and put in buckets of lukewarm water for longer lasting bouquets.

Never cut roses with scissors or a serrated knife. It pinches the pores closed and makes them hang their heads. A sharp, straight-edged paring or jack knife work best.

SOUPS
&
SALADS

The Otsego County Chamber

As with most elements of life, in business you need backup. Or, to borrow (liberally) from the poet John Donne, "no business is an island." Regardless of size and almost without exception, businesses need a support network, a collective voice to help further their business goals, so that they can best serve their customers, their employees and their communities. The Otsego Chamber is a singular resource for countywide contacts and business advice.

The Otsego County Chamber speaks for hundreds of Otsego County businesses and organizations, lobbying for their interests at the state and local levels. They work to improve the tangible business concerns of health insurance and energy costs. Their organization of focused committees works with the membership to improve the overall business climate in our region.

The Chamber strives to create an atmosphere that attracts investment and to build a positive, forward-thinking business community. If you are considering a move to Otsego County, call on the Chamber for relocation information.

"The Otsego County Chamber:
Your Business Voice!"

12 Carbon Street
Oneonta, NY 13820
607-432-4500
1-877-5-OTSEGO
www.otsegocountychamber.com
tocc@otsegocountychamber.com

Best Minestrone
Otsego County Chamber

*M*inestrone, like the Otsego County Chamber, is the collusion of distinct and colorful components complementing each other. Both of these collaborations arrive at successful conclusions. Each ingredient is individually valuable and, collectively, they are peerless.

4 cups vegetable or chicken stock
2 14-ounce cans stewed tomatoes (do not drain)
1 large potato, cubed
1 onion, chopped
2 stalks celery, chopped
2 carrots, chopped
1 large head cabbage, finely chopped
2 tablespoons Italian seasoning
1 15-ounce can kidney beans, drained and rinsed
3 cups fresh corn kernels (great use of leftover corn on the cob)
1 large zucchini, sliced
1 cup uncooked orzo pasta
Salt and pepper to taste

In a large soup pot combine the stock, tomatoes, potato, onion, celery, carrot, cabbage and Italian seasoning. Bring to a boil and reduce heat. Simmer for about 15 minutes, stirring occasionally.

Stir in the beans, corn, zucchini and pasta; simmer for 10 to 15 more minutes until the vegetables are tender and pasta is cooked. Add more stock or water as necessary, or a splash of dry white wine. Salt and pepper to taste.

NBT Bank

A familiar presence throughout Otsego County and Upstate New York, NBT Bank has been in business since 1856. Beginning in 1857 and continuing to the present, this independent community bank has made uninterrupted dividend payments, a testament of their commitment to success for their customers.

Believing that local enterprises are the lifeblood of communities, NBT works with small and large businesses to help them meet their goals. Their full line of banking services includes trust and investment services, financial consulting, retirement plan administration and cash management services. They are an excellent choice for businesses, municipalities and non-profit organizations to better manage their resources.

NBT Bank's personalized approach and focus on customer service, along with innovative products and services, makes them a superior choice for your banking needs.

Employees of the over 80 NBT Bank offices own approximately ten per cent of the company. NBT Bank is supportive of many Otsego County area programs and is a valuable community citizen.

Visit an NBT branch or ATM at many locations throughout Otsego County. Check www.nbtbank.com for a complete listing of locations.

One Wall Street
Oneonta, NY 13820
(607) 432-5800
www.nbt.com
1-800-NBT-BANK
Member FDIC

A fruit is a vegetable with looks and money.
　　　　　　　—P. J. O'ROURKE

Lentil Soup
NBT Bank

*I*t doesn't get much better than this. This soup is quick, hearty for chilly days, economical and it tastes wonderful. The spinach and carrots add beautiful color and an added nutritious kick. The cumin adds a bit of smoky wonder. It can be made vegetarian by omitting meat and using vegetable stock. It's delicious either way.

2 tablespoons olive oil
1 large yellow onion, chopped
1 teaspoon ground cumin
1 or 2 carrots, diced
2 cups lentils (any kind)
6 cups chicken or vegetable stock
2 cups (more or less) chopped fresh spinach
½ pound cooked, crumbled sausage or cubed kielbasa (optional, but really good.)

In large soup pot, sauté chopped yellow onion in olive oil over medium heat. Add cumin and carrots and continue cooking until onions begin to soften. Add lentils and stock and let simmer over low to medium heat for about 20 minutes.

Start testing lentils for doneness after twenty minutes. They should be ready in no more than thirty minutes.

Stir in spinach and let wilt. Stir in meat to heat through. Salt and pepper to taste. Add more stock or water, if necessary, to achieve desired consistency.

Top this soup with a dollop of sour cream and a bit of chopped parsley. Serve with crusty bread.

> *Only the pure in heart can make a good soup.*
> —LUDWIG VAN BEETHOVEN

The Walking Example Group
WE GO

*T*he Walking Example Group was founded in Otsego County to help create and maintain the healthy infrastructures that support healthy populations. WE GO encourages everyone to walk or bike to routine destinations and they work to ensure that safe and pleasant pathways exist.

Just as there are three legs on a milking stool, WE GO recognizes there are three components of a healthy mind and body. One is quality rest, a point too often overlooked in our hectic society; another is quality, nutritious food, such as that produced by Otsego County and New York State farmers. The third is routine physical activity, like walking to school or work, just like people did not so many years ago. If you remember the '60s, you probably recall when two-thirds of us were not overweight or obese.

Most people know that they need to stay active to stay healthy, but struggle with factors that work against daily activity, such as sedentary jobs and sedentary leisure. Many are frustrated with the lack of safe byways to go even short distances without using a car.

WE GO wants to see Otsego County accessible to non-motorized transportation—walking, cycling, snowshoeing, etc. Not just the recreational paths in our wonderful state parks, but dedicated destination trails that connect Otsego County towns and villages and paths that make walking and cycling safe within our communities.

Take a Walk. Put Your Heart In It.

Brenda Berstler
6 Westridge Road
Cooperstown, NY 13326
604-547-1870

www.walkingexample.org
A not-for-profit organization

Walking In Sunshine Apple Salad
WE GO

~~~~~~

*T*his salad is so easy and so good! It's a lighter alternative to the traditional Waldorf salad and it uses some of New York's finest ingredients. The vanilla yogurt and fruits makes it sweet enough to serve as dessert.

4 tart New York apples, unpeeled, cored and chopped
¼ cup toasted nuts (pecans, walnuts or slivered almonds)
¼ cup dried cranberries
¼ cup chopped dried cherries
1 8-ounce container low-fat vanilla yogurt

Combine all ingredients in a pretty bowl and toss to coat all ingredients with yogurt.

Appetizing additions: fresh blueberries, sliced strawberries, mandarin orange segments, granola, or whatever you find appealing. Add more yogurt as needed.

A vigorous five-mile walk will do more good for an unhappy but otherwise healthy adult than all the medicine and psychology in the world."
—PIONEERING CARDIOLOGIST PAUL DUDLEY WHITE

Dismal Inn
Sugar Company

*T*he Phillips' produce great stuff on their farm with the attention-getting name. Its derivation is immensely logical. The first few years Bruce Phillips tried farming were, by his own admission, "dismal."

Things have since improved considerably and now Bruce and Lucia Phillips produce a variety of goods on their land and in outbuildings built from Bruce's own lumber. The potting shed holds seedlings that become squash and heirloom pumpkins; the chicken house shelters hatchlings; Bruce makes custom shingles in the sawmill, and maple sap transforms into syrup in the sugaring house. Garlic, peas, gourds and vegetables sprout in their respective fields.

The Phillips' tap the maples up a steep hill on the family property near Hartwick, NY. The Dismal Inn Sugar Company practices state of the art maple production with their reverse osmosis process of separating water and maple sugar molecules. This method produces syrup using less heat and evaporation.

Lucia Phillips left a very different life on Wall Street to paint her wonderful primitives of rural life, landscapes, etc. and grow arugula, pumpkins and more. Her paintings are available at local art shows and may be viewed by appointment. Maple products, garlic and produce are available seasonally in regional shops. Call to place your order and the Phillips' will arrange a pick-up or delivery time.

Bruce and Lucia Phillips
Hartwick, NY 13348
607-293-6488
607-293-6164

Venison Stew

Dismal Inn Sugar Company

~~~~~~~~~~~~~~~~~~~~~~~~~~~~~~~~~~~~

Like most soups and stews, creating them is more art than science. The amounts given here are approximate and many of the ingredients only suggestions. Relax and enjoy culinary creating!

Almost all of these ingredients are produced on the Dismal Inn farms.

1 pound venison loin, cut in small pieces
½ cup flour   Salt
Black pepper   Red pepper (optional)
2-4 tablespoons olive oil   2 or 3 cloves of garlic
½ cup diced onions   ¼ cup diced peppers
Your choice of other vegetables: carrots, mushrooms, green beans, etc.
Water or broth to cover meat and vegetables
Red wine, to enhance the stew, or to enjoy while cooking it, or both
1 bay leaf   ⅛ cup maple syrup
1 tablespoon Worcestershire sauce or soy sauce
Fresh herbs

Combine flour, salt, black pepper in a lunch-sized brown paper bag, or a gallon-sized freezer bag. Add red pepper, if you like the heat. Shake venison pieces, coating with the flour mixture. Shake off excess flour.

Heat olive oil in a Dutch oven or soup pot and brown meat. Add onions, garlic and peppers. Mushrooms and carrots are good additions, too.

When meat is browned, cover with broth and/or water and about a glass of wine and let simmer. Add bay leaf. Add more liquid as needed. As meat and vegetables cook, add maple syrup, Worcestershire or soy sauce and whatever fresh herbs you fancy.

When meat and vegetables are tender, remove bay leaf and serve with rice, noodles or potatoes.

Cooperstown Chamber of Commerce

*W*here do we go, what shall we do, where will we stay, what's going on, where do we eat? A visit to Cooperstown generates a lot of questions.

Fortunately, The Cooperstown Chamber of Commerce is a boundless resource of information and advice. With so many options in this popular destination, any visitor might be a bit perplexed. The Cooperstown Chamber of Commerce represents over six hundred members, and their friendly and knowledgeable staff can answer myriad questions. Not only do they answer the usual inquiries of which restaurants serve late and where to find ATMs, but they can also tell you where to buy bait, get your car fixed or find fresh vegetables in season.

Stop by the Chamber's cheery yellow house on Chestnut Street, across from the Cooperstown Fire Station. You'll find a warm welcome and a helpful introduction to the wonders awaiting you in Cooperstown and the surrounding area.

Cooperstown Chamber of Commerce
31 Chestnut Street
Cooperstown, NY 13326
607-547-9983
www.cooperstownchamber.org
info1@cooperstownchamber.org

Spaghetti Salad
Cooperstown Chamber of Commerce

~~~~~~~~~~~~~~~~~~~~~~~~~~~~~~

Could cooking get any easier? Terrific as is, this versatile side salad serves as a great palette for your own creative additions; black olives, chopped onions, blanched broccoli florets, fresh herbs, etc. There are multiple possibilities, even grilled chicken or cooked shrimp to make a lunch or dinner salad. It's perfect when the summer tomatoes ripen.

2 pounds thin spaghetti, broken in half before cooking
1 jar McCormick Salad Supreme seasoning (half a jar does fine)
2 to 4 tomatoes, diced
1 or 2 cucumbers diced
1 green pepper, seeded and diced
1 16-ounce bottle Italian dressing

Cook spaghetti, drain and cool.

Place spaghetti in large bowl and toss in remaining ingredients. Cover and chill for at least 6 hours, allowing flavors to blend.

Toss again before serving, adding more dressing, if desired. Serve!

Siegfried Stoneware

*L*ike so many of our Otsego County farmers, business owners and artists, Alice Siegfried is passionate about her work. A talented and experienced potter, her gratification is in knowing that your hands use the pots she creates with her hands.

Her beautiful and functional pieces are perfect vessels to serve our locally produced food. They are dishwasher, oven and microwave safe and are fired using food safe glazes.

Beginning with a ceramics class she took at the State University of New York at Oneonta, Alice has been throwing, glazing and firing unique stoneware for forty years. Her remarkable pieces, pleasing to the eye and hand, are fired to an intense 2,381 degrees Fahrenheit in the catenary arch reduction kiln built by her late husband. Pottery is more art than science and Alice still revels in the surprise and reward of what awaits her when the kiln is opened.

Siegfried Stoneware is available at the Artisans' Guild, 148 Main Street in Oneonta and at the UCCCA Catskill gift shop, 11 Ford Avenue, Oneonta. Alice is also happy to show her pottery by appointment.

Alice Siegfried, Potter
Oneonta, NY 13326
607-432-8673

Alice's Raw Beet Salad

Siegfried Stoneware

*T*his is a vivid salad, versatile as a side dish or salad; it's open to your own creative additions. The colors and flavors collude wonderfully and it is bursting with great-for-you vitamins and antioxidants.

4 cups peeled and grated beets (about a pound)
1 orange, zested*, then peeled and cut into chunks
2 small or one large apple, unpeeled, cored and chopped
½ cup raisins
⅓ cup balsamic vinegar

Combine all ingredients, chill and serve.

Optional additions:
1 cup chopped celery
½ cup toasted nuts (walnuts, almonds, pine nuts)
1 cup grated carrots
1 cup shredded red cabbage
1 tablespoon chopped crystallized ginger

*Zesting tools are readily available in kitchen supply departments, such as *Home Plate* contributor Haggerty Ace Hardware. Take only the colored part of the peel; that's where the essential oils and flavors are. The white pith underneath is bitter. Zest the fruit first, and then peel it.

Glimmerglass Creative Learning Center (GCLC)

Home of Jilli's Gourmet Road Show

~~~~~~~~~~~~~~~~~~~~~~~~~~~~

*J*illi's Gourmet Road Show is a regional caterer that excels in providing the community with fresh, fabulous food. Jilli's is also the fundraising wheel of the Glimmerglass Creative Learning Center. All of the income from catering benefits this valuable not-for-profit organization.

Headquartered in Cooperstown, NY, The Glimmerglass Creative Learning Center is committed to nurturing each individual's creative potential by providing quality, affordable workshops and diverse learning experiences for people of all ages.

The Learning Center's motto is "JUST TRY IT!" Half of the fun is meeting new friends while exploring your creativity through classes and workshops offered throughout the year. Topics range from opera to yoga to leatherworking to cooking to soap making and on and on. Go to www.gclcenter.org for a current list of their eclectic and innovative curriculum.

For more information about the Learning Center or Jilli's Gourmet Road Show catering that supports it, contact them at the following:

PO Box 1105
Cooperstown, NY 13326

607-547-9988
www.gclcenter.org

607-547-8434 (kitchen)
www.gourmetroadshow.com
jillians@localnet.com

Asian Sweet Potato Salad

Glimmerglass Creative Learning Center

~~~~~~~~~~~~~~~~~~~~~~~~~~~~~~~~

*W*hat wonderful twist for sweet potatoes! These brilliantly orange tubers are remarkably good for you and this taste bud enticing recipe is a remarkable use for them.

4 pounds sweet potatoes, peeled and cubed
5 stalks celery, chopped
¼ cup dry roasted sunflower seeds
¼ cup dried cranberries
2 tablespoons Emeril's Asian spice seasoning
¼ cup mayonnaise (or preferred moistness)
¼ cup honey mustard

Boil sweet potatoes until tender, drain and cool. Do not overcook!
Whisk mustard and mayonnaise together.
Add the remaining ingredients to sweet potatoes.
Add mayonnaise blend and toss to coat.
Cover and chill at least one hour before serving.

The purpose of learning is growth, and our minds, unlike our bodies, can continue growing as we continue to live.
—Mortimer Adler

Cooley's Stone House Tavern

*I*f the dictionary were a subjective book, the word "pub" would be defined as "Cooley's."

This comfortable neighborhood bar offers a broad selection of cold brews, spirits and terrific casual food. Pulled pork and sweet potato fries are favorites, and Cooley's Turkey Chili was a Winter Carnival contender for Best Chili.

Don't miss the "Shotski," a wooden ski fitted with four shot glasses, ready to share an unforgettable experience with your three best friends, or the three you've just met. Four individual shots of your choice are downed simultaneously, to the clang of the Cooley's brass bell. Look for photos of Phil and Joe Niekro and Bruce Sutter partaking of the famous "Shotski."

Owner Tim Gould smartly renovated this building on Pioneer Street, with a beautiful three-sided bar, booths, pub tables and a comfortable big screen TV lounge. "Cooley's," is named in honor of the stoneworker and headstone maker whose business was there in 1872.

Open Seven Days a Week
Sunday-Thursday 11:30AM to 1AM (kitchen closes at 10PM)
Friday and Saturday 11:30AM to 2AM

Tim Gould
49 Pioneer Street
Cooperstown, NY 13326
607-544-1311
www.cooleystavern.com

Cooley's Turkey Chili

Cooley's Stone House Tavern

~~~~~~~~~~~~~~~~~~~~~~~~~~~~~

Don't let the number of ingredients put you off; the components are easily available and the result is worth the measuring. Grandma's Baked Beans are a New York favorite, available at *Home Plate* contributor Price Chopper supermarkets and most local general stores.

2 pounds ground turkey, or cubed skinless turkey breast
1 tablespoon olive oil
1 large onion, diced
1 red bell pepper, diced
1 green bell pepper, diced
2 16-ounce cans diced tomatoes
1 tablespoon tomato paste
1 tablespoon chopped garlic
1 tablespoon Worcester sauce
2 tablespoons chipotle Tabasco sauce
3 tablespoons chili powder
½ tablespoon cumin
1 tablespoon oregano
½ tablespoon black pepper
½ tablespoon salt
1 16 ounce can kidney beans
1 16 ounce can Grandma Brown's Baked Beans

In good-sized soup pot, brown turkey in olive oil. Add onions and bell peppers, sautéing until tender. Add all remaining ingredients, except beans, and simmer on low heat for about an hour, stirring occasionally. Add beans and simmer another half hour. Great served on cold days.

Recipe by Chef Glenn Lane

Artisans' Guild

~~~~~~~~~~~~~~~~~~~~

A gorgeous collection of local talent, the Artisans' Guild represents about 50 area artists and crafts people who work in paint, pottery, wood, glass, jewelry, fiber, wax, even soap and chocolate. This non-profit, cooperative shop is unique in our region. Ninety per cent of all proceeds go directly to the artists.

This is a wonderful place to shop, not only for inspired, original articles and gifts, but also to get a feel for the creative energy that powers Otsego County. New artists with quality products are always welcomed to join the Guild.

At least one of the Guild's artists is always on hand to share information about the one-of-a-kind pieces and the processes that made them, or to help you choose just the right item to enhance your home or please a lucky gift recipient.

The Artisans' Guild uses many of New York's non-edible agricultural products. Wood, flowers, wool, and beeswax are used in a number of the exceptional products found here. The Artisans' Guild should be a sure stop in your discovery of Otsego County.

Hours: Monday – Saturday 10AM- 6PM
Also Sunday Noon- 4PM during summer and holidays,

Deborah Blake
148 Main Street
Oneonta, NY 13820
607-432-1080

ART and GIFT SHOP

Artisans' Celebration Salad
Artisans Guild

~~~~~~~~~~~~~~~~~~~~~~~~

*T*ap into your creative side when making this salad. There are no hard and fast rules. Vary the ingredients as you like, allowing taste, color and texture be your guide. Let the art flow.

A farmers' market in summer will have lots of greens and herbs to choose. Organic veggies are available at larger markets and health food stores.

Salad
Mixed greens- red and green romaine, leaf lettuce, spinach etc.
Fresh herbs- parsley, chives, dill, cilantro
One New York apple, diced
New York State cheese- cheddar or jack, cut in bite sized pieces
Almonds or walnuts (optional)
Sunflower seeds
Edible flowers (optional, but very attractive)

Vinaigrette
Olive oil and vinegar in a 1:1 ratio. Vary the ratio as your taste dictates.
A smidge of New York State mustard
A few drops of New York State maple syrup

Place greens and herbs in a large bowl. A large pottery bowl from the Artisans' Guild is highly recommended.
Top with apple, cheese, nuts and seeds.
Drizzle vinaigrette over all and festoon with edible blossoms.

Enjoy!

Cooperstown Winter Carnival

The Cooperstown Winter Carnival (CWC) is one of Cooperstown's most endearing traditions. Winter can drag a bit in Otsego County and, for over forty years, this February celebration has enlivened our Upstate snow season with three days of celebrations. Local restaurants and individuals compete for the honor of the best chili or chowder, cheesecake, cocktail, wings, or most decadent chocolate creations. A host of great events include a polar bear jump, ghost walking tours, a pub crawl, winter sports and hikes, snow sculptures, parties, music and much more.

Enjoying broad-based community support, The Cooperstown Winter Carnival invites everyone to take part in the festivities. Anticipating any weather related contingencies in mercurial February, the CWC volunteers plan a balance of indoor and outdoor activities. The CWC brings new events to the Carnival each year and continues with old favorites.

Look for the Cooperstown Winter Carnival the second weekend in February (the week before Presidents' Weekend). Visit their website for information and a schedule of events.

1-800-843-3394
www.cooperstowncarnival.org
Cooperstown, NY 13326

Spicy
Corn Chowder
Cooperstown Winter Carnival

~~~~~~~~~~~~~~~~~~~~~~~~

*T*his wonderful chowder is perfect to warm you on a winter's day. It is adapted from the 2006 winner of the Cooperstown Winter Carnival Chili/ Chowder Contest.

1 cup heavy cream
1 cup chicken broth
4 slices bacon
1 large baking potato (Russet), diced
½ of one Habenero* pepper, minced
2 tablespoons butter

4 cups whole milk
½ cup each diced red, yellow and green bell pepper
1 cup frozen corn kernels

2 tablespoons flour.

In soup pot, dice bacon and fry until cooked. Drain all but about a tablespoon of fat.
Sauté bell peppers and habanero pepper in bacon fat until they begin to soften.
Add potatoes and corn to peppers. Stir together, and then add chicken stock. Simmer until vegetables are tender.
While vegetables simmer, melt butter in a saucepan. Add flour to make a roux. Gradually whisk in milk and simmer until slightly thickened. Add thickened milk to vegetables, and then stir in cream.
Season to taste with salt and pepper.

*The Scoville scale measures the heat of peppers. Habaneros rank #1, so handle them with care. Wear rubber gloves when handling and be careful not to get your hands anywhere near your eyes or nose.

*Chowder breathes reassurance.
It steams consolation.*
—CLEMENTINE PADDLEFORD

Hoffman Lane Bistro

~~~~~~~~~~~~~~~~~~~~~~~~~~~~~~~~~~~~~~

*O*ne of the most casually classy, dependable restaurants in Cooperstown, the Hoffman Lane Bistro offers first-class fare in a relaxed and chic atmosphere.

This sophisticated, yet comfortable eatery has been a favorite of both locals and visitors since it opened in 1999. Tuna au Poivre and their knockout meatloaf are signature favorites. Owner Mark Loewenguth, his capable staff and superb food provide a memorable evening.

Hoffman Lane Bistro frequently features live entertainment to complement their tantalizing menu, full bar and wine selection. Reservations are, of course, recommended.

Hoffman Lane Bistro is handily located in the center of Hoffman Lane, between Otsego Lake and the National Baseball Hall of Fame and Museum.

Be sure to view their lovely espaliered tree growing on the Hoffman Lane side of the restaurant.

Mark Loewenguth
2 Hoffman Lane
Cooperstown, NY 13326
607-547-7055
www.hoffmanlanebistro.com
mark@hoffmanlanebistro.com

> *Dining is and always was a great artistic opportunity.*
> —FRANK LLOYD WRIGHT

Chopped Iceberg Salad

Hoffman Lane Bistro

~~~~~~~~~~~~~~~~~~~~~~~~~~~~~~~~~~

*T*his surprising salad melds a diverse selection of components. The ingredients are individually tasty and the whole is greater than the sum of its parts. It is a sure hit.

Salad
½ head iceberg lettuce
½ cup sun dried tomatoes, sliced thinly
1 cup candied walnuts
½ cup crumbled blue cheese
1 Granny Smith apple, cored, cut in thin slices
    and chilled with lemon to prevent browning

Dressing
⅓ cup sherry vinegar
¼ cup walnut oil
½ cup olive oil
¼ cup diced shallot
⅛ cup New York maple syrup
Salt and freshly ground pepper to taste

Whisk all dressing ingredients together and salt and pepper to taste.

In a large bowl, combine lettuce, sun dried tomatoes, walnuts and blue cheese. Toss with dressing. Divide onto four chilled plates. Garnish with apple slices. Top with freshly ground pepper, if desired.

Recipe compliments of Chef Eric Swart

Stella Luna Ristorante

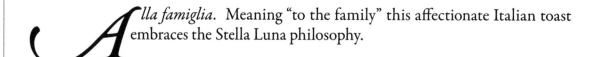

A lla famiglia. Meaning "to the family" this affectionate Italian toast embraces the Stella Luna philosophy.

At Stella Luna, brothers Antonio and Vincente Avanzato have created the beauty and ambience that makes warm memories possible. Exceptional food and attention to detail are Stella Luna hallmarks. From Vinny's hand selected wines and premium spirits to Aunt Ruth's tiramisu to Giuseppa Avanzato's portrait gracing the bottles of olive oil at every table, Stella Luna brings old world style and relaxed elegance to dinner.

Stella Luna invites you to slow down. Savor the food, savor the moments and enjoy the wine. Relax and engage in the kind of conversation that draws new friends close and brings dear ones closer.

Enjoy the warmth, superb food and *la dolce vita* (the sweet life) that make Stella Luna singular in a hectic world.

Stella Luna is located in the impressively renovated Market Street train station.

Hours: 5-9PM Tuesday, Wednesday and Sunday
           5-10PM Friday and Saturday
           Closed Sunday

Antonio and Vincente Avanzato
58-60 Market Street
Oneonta, NY 13820
www.stellalunas.com
607-433-7646
Fax: 607-433- 9623

Stella Luna
Sicilian Salad
Stella Luna Ristorante

~~~~~~~~~~~~~~~~~~~~~~~~~~~~~~~~

*T*his salad may be Sicilian at heart, but it translates beautifully using New York State ingredients. Make it when the tomatoes are at their peak.

Vary the proportion of the ingredients to taste and availability. Cut all ingredients about the same sized dice.

2 big, beautiful, luscious locally grown tomatoes
1 garden fresh cucumber
About half of a good sized sweet onion
¼ cup fresh mozzarella cheese (available in cheese departments or delis)
A healthy pinch of chopped fresh oregano
Salt and pepper
Extra virgin olive oil

Dice all ingredients and place in an attractive serving bowl. Add oregano and salt and pepper to taste. Drizzle extra virgin olive oil over all. Toss and serve. Great bread and wine are perfect companions to this deceptively simple salad.

> *It takes four men to dress a salad: a wise man for the salt, a madman for the pepper, a miser for the vinegar, and a spendthrift for the oil.*
> —*ANONYMOUS*

Sidney Federal Credit Union

~~~~~~~~~~~~~~~~~~~~~~~~~~~

The Sidney Federal Credit Union in Oneonta is a community based credit union, serving the financial needs of residents and newcomers to Otsego County and our neighboring Delaware and Chenango Counties. They are an all-inclusive financial institution, offering a broad range of services at their branches and online. Services include Share Accounts, Share Draft Accounts, Term Share Certificates, IRA's, Loans, Visa Cards, Debit Cards, Kid's Accounts and more.

With two convenient Oneonta locations they are easily accessible from Interstate 88 or within town. Both branches have ATMs and drive-up windows.

You'll receive courteous and professional customer service at each of the Sidney Federal Credit Union eight branches, in the tri-county area of Otsego, Chenango and Delaware Counties and the Town of Colesville.

Sidney Federal Credit Union...There is a Difference.

Otsego County Branches

53 Market St.
Oneonta, NY 13820
1-877-642-7328
www.sfcuonline.com

75 Oneida St.
Oneonta, NY 13820
1-877-642-7328

Potato Leek Soup
Sidney Federal Credit Union

~~~~~~~~~~~~~~~~~~~~~~~~~~~~~~

*T*his tempting soup is terrific! It's easily made, quick and a reliable favorite. The recipe can be varied to dress it up or down and it cannot be made wrong. New York wild leeks are especially good, but the garden variety is also excellent.

¼ cup unsalted butter
2 pounds leeks
6 cups chicken or vegetable stock or water
2 pounds baking potatoes
Salt and pepper
2 tablespoons snipped fresh chives

Carefully wash and trim leeks. Slice white portions only, thinly.
Peel potatoes, quarter lengthwise and slice thinly.

Melt butter in a large saucepan. Add leeks and sauté over medium heat until they begin to soften, 3-5 minutes.
Add the stock and potatoes and bring to boil. Reduce heat to low. Cover and simmer until potatoes are tender, about 20 minutes.

Salt and pepper to taste. Garnish with chives.

Variations:
- Puree soup in blender. Return to pot and add one cup of light cream.
- Serve the creamed soup chilled as vichyssoise.
- Served hot, the creamed version is good with Swiss or Cheddar cheese stirred in immediately before serving.

Riverwood

Riverwood carries an eclectic and fascinating inventory. This gem of a shop is a browser's haven. Starting with the river otter that greets you at the entry to the Toyland in the rear, Riverwood is a magical stroll through the intriguing, the original and the beautiful.

Owner Rick Gibbons, a leather artist and a confessed puzzle and gadget guru, chooses every clever and curious piece in the Riverwood repertoire. His splendid taste has filled his shop with an irresistible array, ranging from Tibetan singing bowls to locally made Soap Rocks, sushi sets to American Fine Crafts including jewelry, pottery, photography, blown glass, woodcrafts and metal sculpture.

Discerning shoppers will appreciate Rick's large selection of Brighton leather goods and accessories. The Bats baseball dice game and Cooperstown custom slate home plates are sure to win a fan's heart.

Looking for something special? You're sure to find it here and, at Riverwood, the fun is in the discovery.

88 Main Street
Cooperstown, NY 13326
607-547-4403
www.riverwoodgifts.com
riverwood@verizon.net

Pumpkin Apple Soup
Riverwood

~~~~~~

Two of New York's most important crops are highlighted in this fabulous autumn recipe. It's perfect for Halloween, Thanksgiving or just because evenings are cool and the leaves are vivid. The sweet/smoky contrast is enticing.

4-6 strips of bacon, diced
1 large onion, chopped
1 15-ounce can pumpkin
2 cups apple cider
1 cup water
¼ cup brown sugar
4 chicken bouillon cubes
1 large apple, peeled, cored and chopped
1 to 2 teaspoons white pepper (to taste)
Salt to taste
1/3 cup crystallized ginger, finely chopped
Sour cream and chopped fresh herbs for garnish

Sauté bacon and onion in a soup pot. Drain fat. Add remaining ingredients and simmer in a covered pot for about half hour, until onions and apples are soft and liquid reduces. Stir frequently.

When soup is done, puree in batches in blender, or in the soup pot with a stick blender until smooth. Serve with a dollop of sour cream and a sprinkling of fresh chopped herbs.

This soup is beautifully presented in a hollowed out pumpkin. Remove the strings and save the pumpkin seeds to roast for a snack. After enjoying the soup, rinse and carve the pumpkin for autumn décor.

SnowFest

February is Otsego County's coldest, snowiest month. In the face of nature's extremes, The Cooperstown Chamber of Commerce has the only logical response: they throw a three-day festival celebrating the season.

Celebrated on Presidents' Weekend, SnowFest accentuates the delights of the Otsego County winter. Massive blocks of snow sculpted into magnificent works of art make Cooperstown an outdoor museum. Well-shod crowds walk the solidly frozen Otsego Lake, taking in unique shoreline views as they "Walk on Water" toward hot cider and chili. You can cross country ski in the moonlight along the Cooperstown shores of Otsego Lake and enjoy winter sports at Glimmerglass State Park. The Poker Walk is a fun introduction to Cooperstown merchants and horse drawn wagon rides are available throughout the Village.

Time to warm up? You'll find a variety of great food, great music and terrific entertainment at the indoor celebrations. Dances, dinners, movies, puppetry, art exhibits and more offer something for all ages.

Make plans to attend these wonderful days of winter merrymaking. Contact the Chamber for more SnowFest information and to make reservations.

Cooperstown Chamber of Commerce
31 Chestnut Street
Cooperstown, NY 13326
607-547-9983
www.cooperstownchamber.org
info1@cooperstownchamber.org

Southwest White Chili
Cooperstown Chamber of Commerce

~~~~~~~~~~~~~~~~~~~~~~~~

*I*f there is someone who doesn't like this light version of classic chili, they've yet to surface in Otsego County. Even if that statement is a slight exaggeration, this chili is superb. It's a perennial favorite at the Walk on Water event of SnowFest.

2 tablespoons olive oil
2 pounds boneless, skinless chicken breasts, cut into cubes
½ cup chopped cooking onion   2 cups chicken broth
2 4-ounce cans chopped green chilies
2 19- ounce cans white kidney beans (cannellini), undrained

Spice blend:
2 teaspoons McCormick California Style Blend Garlic Powder
2 teaspoons ground cumin   1 teaspoon dried oregano leaves
1 teaspoon dried cilantro leaves   ¼ to ½ teaspoon ground red pepper

Toppings: Shredded Monterey Jack cheese, snipped green onions, fresh cilantro

Mix spice blend ingredients together; set aside.
Heat olive oil in a 3-quart saucepan over medium heat. Add chicken and cook for 4-5 minutes, stirring often. Remove chicken with a slotted spoon, cover and keep warm. Add chopped onion to saucepan and cook for two minutes. Stir in the chicken broth, green chilies and the spice blend. Simmer mixture for 30 minutes.
Stir in cooked chicken and kidney beans and simmer for ten minutes. Garnish with cheese and onions. Chow down.

> *Wish I had time for just one more bowl of chili.*
> THE DYING WORDS OF KIT CARSON

BREADS

Liberty Market

~~~~~~~~~~~~~~~~~~~~~~~~~~~~~~~~~~~~

Yoga instructor Bonnie Fayssoux finds contentment in baking. She's perfected her recipes and techniques by baking for some pretty tough critics- her own six children.

Liberty Market's signature desserts and bakery favorites are the delicious results. Bonnie bakes to order multiple varieties of yogurt muffins for breakfast, knockout cookies for snacks, silky cheesecakes for dessert and delectable pies or cobblers to finish dinners and special holiday meals.

Bonnie uses only the best, wholesome ingredients available and the quality shines through. Otsego County farm fresh eggs, real butter, fine chocolate and fruit fillings create her irresistible favorites. Sugar substitutes are available at your request.

Liberty Market's enticing baked goods are made fresh to order and delivered to you, or pick up arrangements made. Shipping is available. Please give them a day or two notice so that they may make your order to your satisfaction. Allow a week during the holidays.

Muffins • Cookies • Cobblers • Cheesecake

"Relax and enjoy"

Bonnie Fayssoux
187 Joe Chamberlain Road
Cherry Valley, NY 13320

To order call:
518-234-9642 or
607-264-8327
www.libertymarket.net

Honey Rolls
Liberty Market

~~~~~~

*T*hese rolls are a joy to make. Bonnie, admirably, makes them by hand at double the volume. This is the bread machine adaptation of her recipe. The honey makes these rolls slightly sweet and delicious. The dough is elastic and a pleasure to work with, allowing you to make whatever shape you desire.

LIQUID INGREDIENTS
½ cup New York State honey, heated
½ cup milk
½ cup water
4 tablespoons butter, melted
1 egg

DRY INGREDIENTS
4 cups bread flour
1 tablespoon ground flax seed
2 teaspoons yeast

Heat honey in microwave or on top of the stove until just boiling. Remove from heat and stir in milk and water. Add melted butter and stir thoroughly. Beat in egg. Put mixture in bread machine bucket.

Put flour on top of honey mixture. Make a well in center of flour.
Put flax seed and yeast in well.

Set bread machine to dough setting. When dough cycle is complete, remove dough to a floured board. Easily shaped, this dough makes 12 to 18 of your favorite rolls, i.e. knots, cloverleaf, crescent, etc. Any shape will work.

Place rolls on greased pans. Cover with a clean towel and put in a warm place to rise a bit, but not doubled, 30-45 minutes.

Preheat oven to 350 degrees. Brush rolls with an egg wash (one egg beaten with 1-2 tablespoons water). This makes them golden brown, glossy and gorgeous. Bake for 15-25 minutes, depending on shape and size.

BlueStone Farm

*I*n the middle of April the BlueStone Farm family begins preparing the soil for planting their organic vegetable gardens. They first sow seeds for lettuce, carrots, beets, zucchini, corn, potatoes and squash. Next, they plant locally grown seedlings such as broccoli, cabbage, heirloom tomatoes, and an array of herbs including parsley, basil, thyme and rosemary. You'll find their fresh produce available on summer Saturdays at the Cooperstown Farmers' Market.

Regular weeding and watering is vital to caring for and maintaining the BlueStone Farm gardens. They use water from their own wells and only organic fertilizers such as kelp, dried fish emulsion and other natural fertilizers.

A baking day at BlueStone Farm begins by picking garden fresh zucchini and carrots for their Zucchini Carrot Granola Muffins. They use only the finest fresh, natural ingredients in their muffins, including free range chicken eggs. Look for BlueStone Farm granola, produce and baked goods and bring a little of the country into your home.

Marty Bernardo
Bissell Road
Cooperstown, NY 13326
www.bluestonefarm.org
bluestone@capital.net
607-547-8227

Zucchini and Carrot Granola Muffins
BlueStone Farms

W ow! These wonderful muffins are a great wake up, afternoon snack or served with meals. Packed with vitamins and fiber, they are moist and delicious. From our granola making friends at BlueStone Farms.

Preheat oven to 375 degrees.
Prepare 12-cup muffin tin. Spray with no-stick spray, grease and flour, or line with paper liners.

1½ cups flour
¾ cup light brown sugar
1½ teaspoons baking powder
½ teaspoon baking soda
¼ teaspoon salt
½ teaspoon cinnamon
2 eggs, beaten
¼ cup vegetable oil
½ cup grated carrots
1¾ cups grated zucchini
1 cup BlueStone Farm Granola, plus more for sprinkling

Combine flour, brown sugar, baking powder, baking soda, cinnamon and salt in large mixing bowl. Beat eggs and oil together in small bowl and add to dry ingredients, stirring until just combined.
Fold in carrots and zucchini and BlueStone Farm granola.
Fill muffin cups half full and sprinkle each with additional granola.
Bake 15-20 minutes, or until golden brown.
Remove from oven and allow to cool 5 minutes. Remove muffins from tin and let cool on wire rack.

Worcester Historical Society

Worcester, NY fits the idyllic definition of the American "home town." A walk through The Worcester Historical Society Museum chronicles the evolution of this peaceful town with its broad Main Street and stately school. Stories of Worcester's past include the history of the Waterman Pen Company, Abram Garfield, the father of President James Garfield, Civil War generals, Ulysses Grant's bugler, Seth Flint, Underground Railway stops and major league baseball great, Jim Konstanty.

Worcester history is reflected in the Victorian furniture and clothing housed in its Museum; in the books, photos and ephemera on the shelves and on the walls. The antique popcorn cart recalls countless parades, ball games and festivals.

The Worcester Historical Society has kept the annals of Worcester events since 1970. A disastrous fire in 1994 destroyed three Main Street buildings and heavily damaged the Museum. After three years and countless hours of restoration, the Museum re-opened its doors with more than 300 members and many rooms of priceless local artifacts.

The empty space next to the Museum, where the buildings stood prior to the 1994 fire, is destined to be a community heritage park, designed by *Home Plate* contributor Walker Planning and Design.

The Worcester Historical Society Museum is open June through September, Wednesday, Thursday and Friday from 1-3PM.

144 Main Street
Worcester, NY 12197
607-397-1700
www.worcesterhistoricalsociety.org

Irish
Soda Bread
Worcester Historical Society

~~~~~~~~~~~~~~~~~~~~~~~~~~

*I*rish Soda Bread began as a plain loaf containing no enhancements such as sugar or caraway seeds. Raisins are considered traditional and, if they are included, your bread becomes a "Spotted Dog." Soda Bread became popular in the 1840's with the commercial availability of baking powder and baking soda used as leavening agents in place of yeast. It must be made with buttermilk or sour milk (1 cup of milk mixed with 1 tablespoon of vinegar or lemon juice).

A significant percentage of Worcester residents are of Irish descent.

Preheat oven to 350 degrees

3½ cups all-purpose flour
2 teaspoons baking powder
¼ teaspoon baking soda
½ cup sugar
¼ teaspoon salt
1 stick butter
2 teaspoons caraway seed (optional)
1½ cups buttermilk
1 cup raisins

Stir flour, baking powder, baking soda, sugar and salt together. Cut butter into flour mixture, using a pastry blender or a food processor using short pulses.

Add caraway seeds to flour/butter mixture. Stir in buttermilk, and add raisins.

Form into a round loaf. Place in pie plate and cut an X on top. Bake for about an hour.

The Taste of Britain

~~~~~~~~~~~~~~~~~~~~~~~~~~~~~~~

Perry Owen is the British Baker. Since 1993 Perry has introduced Yanks to the glories of sausage rolls, tea cookies, meat pies and English breads and dainties at the Cooperstown Farmers' Market.

Perry wasn't always a baker. After a corporate life spent in England and the United States, he retired and then quickly became bored. That was when he decided to bring his passion for baking to the Cooperstown Farmers' Market.

However, English and American ingredients and methods don't readily translate. They are two cuisines separated by common ingredients. After much trial and error, Perry achieved the authentic British taste for his baked goods.

Perry prefers farmers markets for their direct link between producers and consumers, an increasingly unusual relationship in today's marketplaces. Every Saturday during their season you'll find Perry and the best of Britain at the Cooperstown Farmers' Market.

A Member of the Cooperstown Farmers' Market

Perry Owen
Norwich, NY 13815
607-336-3333
pvowen@cnyconnect.net

England and America are two countries separated by a common language.
—GEORGE BERNARD SHAW

Cheese and Herb Loaf
The Taste of Britain

~~~~~~~~~~~~~~~~~~~~~~~~~~~~~~~~~~~~~~~

*T*his savory loaf is quick to make and the aromas of warm cheese and fragrant herbs baking make the kitchen smell wonderful.

Preheat oven to 350 degrees

Stir together:
1 ½ cups flour
2 teaspoons baking soda
Generous pinches each: dry mustard, chopped parsley, chopped chives and
      rosemary
½ cup shortening
¾ cup whole milk
1 egg
½ cup grated New York Sharp cheddar cheese

Stir together flour, baking soda, dry mustard and herbs. Cut in shortening with a pastry blender or in a food processor using short pulses. Add milk, egg and cheese and stir together.

Place in greased loaf pan (or, line the pan with parchment paper) and bake 20-30 minutes, or until a toothpick inserted into center comes out clean.

Daylily Dreams Bed and Breakfast

After a day of exploring the cultural richness of the Upper Susquehanna Valley, relax with a cool drink in Daylily Dream's screened gazebo. Overlooking their lush perennial gardens, only Rae's wonderful cooking rivals this welcoming "food for the soul".

Rae and Bob serve full home made breakfasts featuring the bounty of our local dairies and farms. Their warm hospitality and sumptuous breakfast fare make Daylily Dreams an easy choice.

Daylily Dreams Bed and Breakfast offers four tastefully appointed guest rooms, each equipped with a queen sized bed, private bath, AC and cable TV. A three-minute drive will take you into the Village; an eight-mile scenic drive takes you to the Glimmerglass Opera.

You'll find genuine country charm and hospitality at Daylily Dreams Bed and Breakfast.

Rae and Bob Consigli
1599 County Route 33
Cooperstown, New York 13326
Toll free 866-547-1888

www.daylilydreams.com
info@daylilydreams.com

Zucchini Cheddar Cheese Loaf
Daylily Dreams Bed and Breakfast

What a great use for the ever-plentiful summer zucchini! This dense bread is excellent with meals, even as a savory breakfast bread. Enjoy it toasted and spread with butter or cream cheese.

2½ cups flour
4 teaspoons baking powder
1 tablespoon sugar
1½ teaspoons salt
½ teaspoon freshly ground black pepper
1 cup sharp NY State cheddar cheese shredded
½ cup freshly grated Parmesan cheese

2 cups coarsely shredded zucchini
   (one medium to large)
3 green onions finely chopped
2 large eggs
¾ cup whole milk
⅓ cup olive oil

Sift together flour baking powder, sugar, salt and pepper.

Combine ¼ cup cheddar and 6 tablespoons Parmesan cheese into flour mixture. Add zucchini and green onions.

In medium bowl, beat eggs with a fork or whisk; stir in milk and oil. Add egg mixture to flour mixture stirring until dry ingredients are moistened. Batter will be very thick.

Scrape batter into greased loaf pan. Spread evenly. Sprinkle with remaining cheese mixture. Bake 55-60 minutes. Cool loaf in pan 5 minutes. Remove from pan and cool on wire rack.

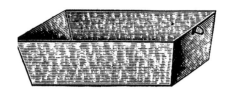

Stannard's Maple and Elk Farm

The Stannards have been making maple products on their pretty–as-a-picture farm for four generations. Their years of experience are evident in their first-rate maple syrup, maple cream, candy and jelly. Be sure to try their granulated maple sugar. It's a scrumptious alternative to white sugar and great on hot or cold cereal, in tea, topping muffins, etc.

Visitors are always welcomed. If you're here during maple season (March to the first days of April) look for the old fashioned bucket hanging from the large maple tree in the front yard. The Stannard's production system has been updated to modern techniques, but traditional implements such as wooden buckets, wooden spiles (the "tap") and antique drills are still on display.

The Stannard's also offer elk, from the herd they pasture on a neighboring farm. Elk is flavorful meat, much lower in fat than beef, pork or chicken. Mary can tell you how to cook it and she has lots of recipes for both elk and maple in their farm shop.

Roseboom is just twelve scenic miles from Cooperstown. Give a call ahead to see what's going on at the farm the day you want to visit.

Maple makes everything taste better!

Warren, Mary and Julie Stannard
166 Stannard Hill Road
Cherry Valley, NY 13320
stannardsmaple@msn.com
607-264-3090

Maple Bran Muffins
Stannard's Maple and Elk Farm

~~~~~~~~~~~~~~~~~~~~~~~~~~~~~~~~~~~

*B*ran muffins are so easy to make and delicious, with lots of important fiber and vitamins. Be sure to use a darker maple syrup for baking.

Preheat oven to 400 degrees.

1½ cups flour
1 tablespoon baking powder
¾ teaspoon salt
1 ½ cups All Bran cereal
1 cup milk
½ cup maple syrup
1 egg
⅓ cup oil
½ cup raisins (optional)

Combine cereal and milk in a large bowl. Let sit for three minutes.
In a separate bowl, combine flour, baking powder and salt.
Add egg, syrup and oil to cereal mixture and beat well.
Add flour mixture and stir until all ingredients are combined

Grease or line a 12-cup muffin pan. Fill all cups evenly and bake for about 20 minutes.

Always buy Pure Maple Syrup. It has 32% fewer carbohydrates than that brown sticky stuff sold as pancake topping. Real New York Maple Syrup contains calcium, potassium, iron, phosphorous and B vitamins. There is, of course, no comparison in flavor.

TePee Pete's Chow Wagon

T his is not your ordinary snack stand. Pete Latella serves terrific casual fare at his Chow Wagon, right next door to his sisters' enterprise, The TePee.

Enjoy the outside seating, take in the breathtaking view of the Mohawk Valley and delve into Pete's mouth-watering creations. His "nearly famous" chili varieties include 7-Pepper, Hot, Mild, Garlic and Vegetarian. Pete also serves buffalo and elk burgers, veggie wraps, freshly made nachos, taco salads, fried bread and more. He has an out of the ordinary selection of salsa flavors, including apple, cherry, mango, peach, garlic, black bean and cranberry. Salsas are available for sale.

As Pete says, he's "just a guy with a pot of chili and a dream". Don't miss this place, not only for the food, but also for the sheer fun of it.

"Great food with a view"

Hours:
July and August: Open seven days a week, 10AM-6PM, Sunday closing at 5PM
May – October: Same hours, closed Tuesdays

Pete Latella
7632 US Highway 20
Cherry Valley, NY 13320
607-264-3987
www.thetepee.net
thetepee@capital.net

> *Thanks to the Interstate Highway System, it is now possible to travel across the country from coast to coast without seeing anything.*
> —CHARLES KURALT,
> ON THE ROAD WITH CHARLES KURALT

Hot Apple Fried Bread
Tepee Pete's Chow Wagon

~~~~~~~~~~~~~~~~~~~~~~~

*R*ich and indulgent, this bread is, of course, delicious.

3 cups flour
¾ cup sugar
3 tablespoons shortening
2 tablespoons baking powder
1 tablespoon salt
2 cups diced apple
½ cup minced jalapenos
¾ cooked and crumbled bacon
1½ cups lukewarm water

Mix flour, sugar, baking powder and salt in large bowl. Cut in shortening
    Add diced apples and bacon mix well.
    Add 1 cup of water and stir into mixture. Slowly add remaining water until a soft ball forms and a pulls away from the side of the bowl.

You may have to add a bit more water to achieve the right "feel". Add more flour if dough seems too sticky, but be careful not overwork dough. Fold in jalapenos.

Cover dough with damp cloth and refrigerate for 2 to 3 hours. When ready to fry, take dough out and let stand at room temperature for about 10 minutes.
    Divide dough into four quarters.
    Stretch or roll each quarter of dough on floured surface until it is 6"-8" in diameter.
    Heat vegetable oil in large frying pan until hot. Add dough round and fry till golden brown on each side. Drain on paper towels and enjoy with shredded New York cheddar or cheese sauce for dipping.

Wilber National Bank

One of the many outcomes of the huge influence of hops in 19th century Otsego County was the formation of Wilber National Bank. David Wilber began his financial institution in Milford, NY to aid his prospering hops business. With the arrival of the railroad in Oneonta, Mr. Wilber decided to move his operation to the bigger town. By 1874 he and his son, George, had commenced the banking business at the corner of Main and Dietz Streets.

From a start of $300,000 in assets, Wilber National Bank now counts more than $750 million. They provide financial answers to thousands of customers in their 20 full-service offices in six Upstate Counties, including Otsego and the surrounding region.

Wilber National Bank offers a complete range of financial services including checking, savings and retirement plans, loans and trusts and investment services. They are a leader in financial trends and offer consumers the latest in banking technology.

Wilber National Bank consistently provides high quality service and innovative products. They continually renew their commitment to enhanced relationships with their customers.

Call or visit Wilber National Bank at www.wilberbank.com for a complete list of Wilber National Bank locations.

"Providing money management solutions with new ideas and old-fashioned service."

Main Office
(24 Hour ATM)
245 Main Street
Oneonta, NY 13820
(607) 432-1700 or
1-800-374-7980
www.wilberbank.com

How To Preserve Children

Wilber National Bank

Be as creative as you like with this recipe!

INGREDIENTS

1 large grassy field
1 half dozen children
2 or 3 small dogs
A pinch of brook
Small amount of pebbles
Add: Flowers, sun and sky

Mix the children and dogs together well and put them in the grassy field. Stir constantly. Pour the brook over the pebbles. Sprinkle the field with flowers, spread under a deep blue sky and bake in hot sun. When children are thoroughly heated, remove and set to cool in a bathtub.

BREAKFASTS & BRUNCHES

Sunny Slope Farm
Bed and Breakfast

What a beautiful place. Sunny Slope is a working dairy farm, complete with a big old barn, tidy farmhouse, a well-loved family dog and, of course, milk cows. The Brunner family has produced milk since 1933.

Milk produced by the Sunny Slope Holsteins, Jerseys and the colorful crossbreeds that give award winning "super milk" is marketed for Cabot and McCadam Cheese and other Agri-Mark companies. The cows are pastured in nearby fields and create a lovely rural landscape.

The Brunners expanded their business to welcome overnight guests in 1986. Guests stay in the 1820's farmhouse and experience, if only for a few hours, "life on the farm." Mornings feature hearty breakfasts that may include milk, bacon, sausage, eggs and maple syrup, all produced on Sunny Slope Farm.

Plan a stay at Sunny Slope for the natural beauty and the Brunner's sincere hospitality. Glimpse what life was like for most Americans, not so many years ago, when most of us lived on farms. Walk the pastures and woods, learn how milk is produced or crops planted and harvested. Or, just swing on the porch and watch the birds.

Cliff and Patti Brunner
211 Brunner Road
Cooperstown, NY 13326
607-547-8686
sunnyslope@mymailstation.com

Blueberry Stuffed French Toast
Sunny Slope Farm and Bed and Breakfast

10 slices good quality French or Italian bread, cut into 1" cubes
1 8-ounce block cream cheese, cubed
¾ cup blueberries, fresh preferred
8 large eggs
¼ cup maple syrup
1¼ cup milk
Cinnamon

Sauce:
½ cup sugar
1 tablespoon cornstarch
½ water
½ blueberries
1 tablespoon butter
½ cup New York State maple syrup

Preheat oven to 350 degrees.
Butter a 13"x9" baking dish. Put half of bread cubes evenly in pan. Scatter cream cheese cubes over bread, then blueberries. Top with remaining bread cubes.

Whisk eggs, milk and syrup together; pour over bread. Sprinkle, as desired, with cinnamon. Cover with foil. (Dish may be refrigerated overnight at this point).

Bake covered for 30 minutes. Uncover and bake another 30 minutes until lightly browned.

While French toast bakes, make sauce. Whisk sugar, cornstarch and water together until dissolved. Cook over medium heat for five minutes, stirring constantly. Stir in blueberries and simmer until they pop. Add butter and maple syrup. Serve over baked French toast.

Glimmerglass Opera

*M*ention "Cooperstown" in many circles and thoughts turn to batons rather than bats and Puccini instead of pitching. Glimmerglass Opera has brought worldwide artistic acclaim to the Cooperstown area through their innovative and inspiring productions of familiar and rarely performed works.

Glimmerglass Opera is the second largest summer opera festival in the country.

The Glimmerglass Opera is strongly associated with New York City music, including their informal partnership with the New York City Opera. After seventeen years as Glimmerglass General Director, in 1996 Paul Kellogg was named General and Artistic Director of The New York City Opera. He remains Artistic Director of Glimmerglass Opera, providing a creative alliance and foundation of co-productions. As noted by *Newsday,* "Glimmerglass has become the source of a river of ideas that flows toward Manhattan."

Glimmerglass also continues their collaborations with other companies such as the Boston Lyric Opera, Houston Grand Opera, Opera North, UK and the Florida Grand Opera.

Plan an idyllic musical experience on scenic Otsego Lake. Visit the Glimmerglass Opera website for summer festival schedules.

PO Box 191
Cooperstown, NY 13326
607-547-2255
www.glimmerglass.org

Ticket Office:
18 Chestnut Street
Cooperstown, NY 13326

Cinnamon Thyme Poached Pears
Glimmerglass Opera

T hese mouth-watering pears are equally at home as a dessert, with a bit of whipped cream. Although the Emerson quote below exaggerates, keep careful watch to catch pears at their peak of flavor, fragrance and firmness.

4 large New York State pears (Bosc or Bartlett) ripe, but still firm
1 cup pear nectar
1 cup water
¾ cup New York State maple syrup
2 stick cinnamon, slightly crushed
1½ teaspoons thyme leaves
4 strips lemon peel

Peel and core pears from bottom, leaving stems intact. Cut a thin slice off the bottom of each pear to provide a flat, even bottom. Set aside.

In a medium saucepan, add remaining ingredients. Bring mixture to a boil. Add pears and arrange standing with stems pointing up. Reduce heat and simmer, covered, 20-30 minutes until pears are tender.

Remove pears from saucepan. Continue to cook liquid until reduced to ¾ cup, about 15 minutes. Serve pears drizzled with sauce.

There are only ten minutes in the life of a pear when it is perfect to eat.
—RALPH WALDO EMERSON

Daylily Dreams
Bed and Breakfast

~~~~~~

Daylily Dreams means comfortable accommodations, wonderful food and hospitality, all with the recurring theme of their spectacular lilies. Modern day conveniences such as high-speed Internet access and cable TV are available, but your surroundings are set to yesteryear's less frantic pace.

They also offer Special Packages, just to entice you a little more. Holiday and theme packages are available, including Golf Outings, Mother-Daughter Getaways, the Leatherstocking Quilter's Shop Hop and more. Call or visit their website for more information.

Make the most of your stay in Otsego County. Rae and Bob can suggest places to visit, to shop and to eat. Their package deals make it easy for you to linger and truly enjoy Cooperstown and our fascinating area at a leisurely, satisfying tempo.

Rae and Bob Consigli
1599 County Route 33
Cooperstown, New York 13326

Toll free 866-547-1888
www.daylilydreams.com
info@daylilydreams.com

Life, within doors, has few pleasanter prospects than a neatly arranged and well-provisioned breakfast table.
—NATHANIEL HAWTHORNE,
THE HOUSE OF SEVEN GABLES

Not So
Eggs Benedict
Daylily Dreams Bed and Breakfast

~~~~~~~~~~~~~~~~~~~~~~~~~~~~~~~~~~~~~

Some mornings are just meant to be enjoyed. Kick back, relax, work the crossword and let the morning slip by while you enjoy this satisfying dish.

2 English muffins, split and toasted
4 poached eggs
4 thick slices tomato (or sautéed mushrooms, asparagus, etc.)
1 package 10 ounce frozen chopped spinach, thawed and drained
¼ cup snipped parsley or dill
1 small shallot, finely chopped
1 teaspoon butter + 1 teaspoon olive oil
1 cup whole milk
2 tablespoons Knorr's cream of spinach soup mix
Fresh baby spinach leaves for garnish
Sprinkle of paprika

Split and toast English muffins, butter lightly and place in serving dish.

In medium frying pan, heat butter and oil and sauté shallot. Add drained spinach and warm through. Stir in chopped parsley or dill.

Bring milk to a simmer in a small saucepan. Add cream of spinach mix to milk and stir constantly until sauce thickens.

Place spoonfuls of spinach on top of each buttered English muffin half. Place tomato slice on top of spinach, followed by a poached egg.

Cover with about 2 tablespoons spinach sauce. Sprinkle tops with a paprika. Serve with baby spinach leaves for a garnish, and country ham slice on the side.

Makes four servings and multiplies easily.

Bryn Brooke Manor

T his gracious bed and breakfast sits magnificently on a hill overlooking Otsego Lake in Cooperstown. "Bryn" is the Welsh word for "hill", "Brooke" is the owner's daughter, and "Manor" because this beautiful, rambling house is reminiscent of an English manor house.

The architecturally significant 1884 shingle-style home has been carefully restored with beautiful details, fine wood and Victorian furnishings. Tastefully decorated guestrooms, spacious common areas, inviting twin porches, a flower-encircled swimming pool and numerous guest amenities keep Bryn Brooke Manor in demand with discriminating guests.

Your breakfast is cooked to order and features fresh produce, fresh local eggs, quality meats, from-scratch biscuits, muffins, scones and other delicious baked goods. Sweet dreams are encouraged with homemade Bryn Brooke Bedtime Cookies.

Brenda Berstler is especially well-versed in Otsego County attractions and hidden gems. She is happy to offer suggestions to help you make the most of your visit.

John, Brenda, and Elizabeth Brooke Berstler
6 Westridge Road
Cooperstown, NY 13326
607-544-1885
607-287-0162

www.brynbrookemanor.com
brookebb@stny.rr.com

"Vaffles" Ulrike

Bryn Brooke Manor

~~~~~~~~~~~~~~~~~~~~

*T*his fabulous waffle breakfast was named for a favorite guest. Originally from Frankfurt, Germany, Ulrike suggested it one fine August morning when the Bryn Brooke kitchen was full of just-picked Otsego County blueberries. Use cookie scoop-sized balls of ice cream, fresh blueberries and genuine maple syrup.

Waffles

2 cups all-purpose flour
3 teaspoons baking powder
½ teaspoon salt
3 eggs, separated

1¾ cups milk
4 tablespoons butter, melted
3 tablespoons sugar

Toppings

New York State maple syrup
Best quality vanilla ice cream

Fresh blueberries

Stir dry ingredients together in a large bowl. In another two bowls, separate eggs. Beat eggs yolks in one bowl; add milk and butter. Add milk mixture to dry ingredients and stir until smooth. With an electric mixer, beat egg whites until stiff peaks form. Gradually add sugar to egg whites, beating constantly. Gently fold egg whites into waffle batter. Spread batter on hot, oiled waffle iron and bake waffle until golden.

Serve waffles topped with small scoops of ice cream, generously scatter fresh blueberries and pour maple syrup over all. A brilliant way to start the day.

> *'When you wake up in the morning, Pooh,' said Piglet at last, 'what's the first thing you say to yourself?' 'What's for breakfast?' said Pooh. 'What do you say, Piglet?' 'I say, I wonder what's going to happen exciting today?' said Piglet. Pooh nodded thoughtfully. 'It's the same thing,' he said.*
> —A. A. MILNE,
> *THE HOUSE AT POOH CORNER*

The Inn at Cooperstown

*I*n a Village that prizes its porches, The Inn at Cooperstown has a beauty. Their expansive veranda extends across the Inn's entire façade, welcoming guests to relax and enjoy the view of Cooperstown.

The Inn at Cooperstown is an excellent example of Second Empire architecture. Henry J. Hardenbergh, the noted designer of New York City's Dakota Apartments and Plaza Hotel, designed the building in 1874. It was extensively restored in 1985 and, as The Inn at Cooperstown, it has since welcomed 150,000 guests.

Conveniently located near the intersection of Main and Chestnut, (where you'll find Cooperstown's only traffic light), the Inn at Cooperstown is an easy walk to most Village attractions. It is also near a trolley stop.

Rest well in one the Inn's seventeen lovely rooms, all with private baths and the amenities expected at a premium accommodation. Professional service, attention to detail and a courteous staff are always the order of the day. Gift certificates are available.

The Inn at Cooperstown was placed on the Select Registry of Distinguished Inns of North America in 1999.

Marc and Sherrie Kingsley
16 Chestnut Street
Cooperstown, NY 13326
607-547-5756

www.innatcooperstown.com
info@innatcooperstown.com

Asparagus and Sweet Pepper Frittata
The Inn at Cooperstown

Frittatas are the Italian cousins of quiche. These classic egg pies can be simple, with just one or two additions to the egg base, or as enriched and colorful as this one.

Preheat oven to 350 degrees

12 ounces red potatoes, thinly sliced and blanched
8 asparagus spears, top 3 inches only, steamed al dente
4 ounces red pepper, diced and sautéed
8 ounces sour cream
7 eggs
4 ounces cheddar cheese, shredded (reserve 2 tablespoons)
4 tablespoons fresh parsley, chopped
1 tablespoon olive oil
Salt and freshly ground pepper to taste

Whisk eggs until frothy and stir in sour cream, red pepper, cheese, salt and pepper.
Coat a 10" glass pie pan with cooking spray. Place potatoes in bottom of pan, overlapping slightly. Pour egg mixture over potatoes.
Arrange asparagus spears on eggs and sprinkle with parsley and reserved cheese.
Bake until knife inserted comes out clean, 35-40 minutes.
To make frittata puffed and crispy, broil the last 5 minutes.

Recipe courtesy of Jilli's Gourmet Road Show
and the Glimmerglass Learning Center

The Rose and Thistle Bed and Breakfast

Steve and Patti D'Esposito welcome you to their tastefully colorful Victorian home. With its broad front porch, the Rose and Thistle is a lovely spot to sit and plan your day in Cooperstown, or to rock and relax after a day full of activity.

You're sure to sleep well in one of their beautifully decorated rooms and awake to a delicious breakfast. There is a reason why "homemade" food is so prized and Steve and Patti's breakfasts illustrate the point. Start your day in Cooperstown on a high point with a grand breakfast at their big Square Table in their cozy dining doom.

Enjoy the good company at the Rose and Thistle. Steve and Patti's valuable ideas will help you get the most from your stay in Cooperstown, and you can compare experiences with their other guests. Even Molly, the guard cat, makes you feel at home!

The Rose and Thistle Bed and Breakfast
132 Chestnut Street
607-547-5345
Cooperstown, NY 1332

www.roseandthistlebb.com
stay@roseandthistlebb.com

Apple Puff Pancake
The Rose and Thistle

~~~~~~~~~~~~~~~~~~~~~~~~~~~~~~~~~~~~~

This "pancake pie" is equally as good for dessert as for special breakfasts and brunches.

Preheat oven to 400 degrees

3 New York State tart cooking apples, pared, cored and sliced
2 tablespoons butter, melted
1 cup flour
1 cup milk
New York State honey
1 teaspoon baking soda
1 teaspoon baking powder
3 eggs, beaten

Topping: 2 tablespoons sugar mixed with 1 teaspoon cinnamon.

Spray sides of a glass 9" pie plate with cooking spray. Put butter in bottom of pan. Place apple slices on bottom of pie plate, overlapping. Drizzle honey over apples.

In a separate bowl, combine flour, milk, sugar, baking powder, baking soda and beaten eggs. Mix well, to pancake batter consistency. Pour over apples. Sprinkle sugar/cinnamon mixture on top of batter. Bake for 25-30 minutes.

Serve immediately with New York State maple syrup.

New York produces dozens of apple varieties; Check with an orchard, farmers' market or produce department about which ones are best suited to baking, eating fresh or both. When baking, Cortland and Macintosh are reliable favorites.

The White House Inn

*T*he White House Inn is one of Cooperstown's finest bed and breakfasts. Welcoming and comfortable, Ed and Margie Landers get your day started perfectly with full breakfasts featuring local products and wonderful baked goods.

The White House Inn is close to just about everything. Walking a minute or two puts you in the heart of the village and at the door of restaurants, shopping and the National Baseball Hall of Fame and Museum.

It feels like coming home when you stay at the Landers' Greek Revival style house. Enjoy the seclusion of the garden and swimming pool. On cool evenings, relax by the fireplace in the gathering room, or in the parlor with a good book. You'll rest well in your tastefully appointed room and private bath.

The White House Inn is on the National Historic Registry.

The White House is open year round. Children are welcomed and television, air-conditioning and telephones are available. Regretfully, they cannot accept pets. Smoking permitted outdoors only. Major credit cards accepted. For rates and reservations, call or write your hosts Ed or Marjorie Landers.

46 Chestnut Street
Cooperstown, NY 13326
607-547-5054
607-547-1100 fax
www.thewhitehouseinn.com
stay@thewhitehouseinn.com

The Official New York State Apple Muffin

The White House Inn

Apples are part and parcel of our New York identity. New York is the second largest producer of apples in the United States and the apple is our state fruit. The Apple Muffin is, of course, the state designated muffin.

Preheat oven to 375 degrees

Muffin Topping

½ cup chopped walnuts
½ cup brown sugar
¼ cup flour

1 teaspoon cinnamon
1 teaspoon grated lemon peel
1 to 2 tablespoons melted butter

Combine all topping ingredients and set aside.

Muffin Base

2 cups flour
¾ cup brown sugar
½ cup granulated sugar
2 teaspoons baking soda
½ teaspoon salt
1½ teaspoons cinnamon
½ teaspoon cloves

2 cups NYS cooking apples, coarsely chopped
4 ounces cream cheese, cut into small cubes
½ cup raisins
½ cup chopped walnuts
3 eggs, slightly beaten
½ teaspoon vanilla
⅛ teaspoon nutmeg

In a small bowl, make muffin topping. In a large mixing bowl, combine the first eight ingredients, flour through nutmeg, and set aside. In a separate bowl, stir remaining ingredients, apples through vanilla, together. Mix wet and dry ingredients just until combined. Do not overbeat. Portion batter into greased or lined muffin pans, sprinkle with topping and bake 20-25 minutes. ENJOY!

Harmony House Café and Harmony House Antiques and Home Furnishings

*T*his is a great place to sit, relax and let Fly Creek surround you. The Harmony House offers phenomenal food, good coffee (and the best iced tea) and Internet access through one door and antiques and home furnishings through another.

Harmony House owner Richard Votypka has tastefully renovated the copious space that throughout its history has housed a grocery store, a glove factory, a girls' finishing school and Oddfellows Hall and put it to outstanding use. Historic photos of those bygone days adorn the café walls along with local artists' works. Enjoy terrific casual dining from 7AM to 3PM, seven days a week.

Right next door, find traditional and country wares filling corners and shelves of Harmony House Antiques and Home Furnishings. Enjoy this charming shop and its ever-changing inventory Monday – Saturday 9AM to 5PM and Sunday 9AM to 4PM.

Homemade food and great coffee in relaxing, country surroundings together with interesting shopping is time well spent.

The Harmony House is at Fly Creek's country crossroads. Look for the blinking traffic light.

Richard and Mary Lou Votypka
6208 State Highway 28
Fly Creek, NY 13337

Harmony House Café: 607-547-5077
Fax: 607-547-6011
Harmony House Antiques: 607-547-4071

Apple Scones with Maple Cream Sauce

Harmony House Café and Antiques

~~~~~~~~~~~~~~~~~~~~~~~~~~~

Scones:

Preheat oven to 375 degrees

2 cups all purpose flour	¾ cup cream
4 teaspoons baking powder	1 egg
¾ teaspoon salt	1 teaspoon vanilla
1/3 cup sugar	1 cup finely chopped tart apple
6 tablespoons butter	

In large mixing bowl, stir together flour, baking powder, salt and sugar. Cut in butter as if making a pie crust.

In a separate bowl, beat egg and cream together. Stir into dry mix, along with chopped apple.

Turn mixture out onto floured surface and knead until liquid is evenly absorbed.

Pat dough about an inch thick and cut into triangles.

Brush scones with an egg wash (1 egg, beaten with 1 or 2 tablespoons water) and sprinkle with sugar.

Bake about 15 minutes, or until golden brown.

Maple Cream Sauce:

1 tablespoon butter	1 cup pure New York maple syrup
½ teaspoon cinnamon	½ cup heavy cream
Pinch of nutmeg	

In small saucepan, melt butter and add spices. Add syrup and bring to gentle boil. Slowly whisk in cream and whisk constantly until the syrup is reduced by about a third. Serve over hot, split scones. This rich sauce is also delicious on pancakes and waffles.

Cooperstown Brewing Company

~~~~~~~~~~~~~~~~~~~~~~~~~~

The Cooperstown Brewing Company is a standing celebration of Otsego County's rich brewing heritage and company president Stan Hall's family legacy.

In the 1800s, the United States depended on Otsego County and the surrounding area for beer. Our part of New York produced most of the hops crucial to American brewing at the time. Stan Hall's grandparents were hop farmers, their farm just three miles from where the Cooperstown Brewing Company is now located. Drawing on his family tradition, hops still grown at the Brewery are used to finish their Back Yard Pale Ale.

The Cooperstown Brewing Company maintains the tradition of the classic English breweries found in nineteenth century Cooperstown. They use the finest barley malts, hops and yeast in their award winning ales, porters and stouts. Enjoy Old Slugger Pale Ale, Nine Man Golden Ale, Benchwarmer Porter, Strikeout Stout, Back Yard India Pale Ale and Pride of Milford Special Ale.

Tours and tasting are available daily year round. Located just ten minutes south of Cooperstown, off State Route 28 at Milford, NY. Turn onto Route 166.

Stan Hall
110 River Street
PO Box 276
Milford, NY 13807
E-mail: taproom@cooperstownbrewing.com
Website: www.cooperstownbrewing.com
607-286-9330 or 1-877-FINE ALE

> *He was a wise man who invented beer.*
> —PLATO

Golden Buck

Cooperstown Brewing Company

Reminiscent of Welsh rarebit, this warm and luscious dish makes a memorable brunch, or an easy supper. Use New York State cheddar, fresh eggs from the farmers' market, slices of just picked tomato and one of Cooperstown Brewing Company's best brews to create an incomparable meal.

3 cups New York State cheddar cheese, grated
1 tablespoon butter
¾ cup Nine Man Golden Ale or one of Cooperstown Brewing Company's
    other fine brews
1 egg yolk, slightly beaten
Cayenne pepper, paprika, and/or freshly chopped herbs for garnish
One each per serving:
Tomato Slices
Poached Eggs
Toasted English muffin halves or toast points

Gently melt butter in top of a double boiler or in a saucepan over low flame. Add cheese. When cheese begins to melt, add half of the ale. Cook, stirring constantly. Add egg yolk to remaining half of ale and whisk together. Slowly add to melted cheese, stirring constantly until smooth and thick.

To Serve:
Spoon a bit of the cheese sauce onto the muffin halves. Top with tomato slices and poached eggs. Ladle cheese sauce over all and finish with a sprinkle of cayenne pepper or freshly chopped herbs. Steamed broccoli or asparagus spears may be used in place of or in addition to the tomatoes. Serves 4.

HERE'S TO HEALTH ...And Happiness

The Barnwell Inn

Located in the heart of Cooperstown, The Barnwell Inn is a beautiful, welcoming bed and breakfast. Dating from 1850, this well-kept yellow Victorian is furnished with rich colors and antiques. A cozy stay awaits you at the elegant Barnwell Inn.

Experienced innkeepers Mark and Tara Barnwell will make you feel at home with their hospitality and gourmet breakfasts. New York products are frequently featured in their egg dishes, fresh fruits and juices, breakfast meats, breads and Mark's own "dessert for breakfast" sweets.

You'll rest well in one the four beautifully appointed guestrooms, each with a private bath, cable TV and air-conditioning.

Convenient to just about everything, Cooperstown's attractions are just a short stroll from the Barnwell Inn. Come relax in their comfortable surroundings and warm welcome.

Mark and Tara Barnwell
48 Susquehanna Avenue
Cooperstown, NY 13326
1-607-547-1850
Barnwellinn@aol.com
www.Barnwellinn.com

Tampa Eggs
The Barnwell Inn

~~~~~~

*T*ravel is great for generating new culinary ideas. A trip to the famous Gasparilla Invasion celebration held annually in Tampa, Florida inspired Mark and Tara's Tampa Eggs. This is a frequently requested favorite of Barnwell Inn guests. The Barnwell's serve it for breakfast with their Baked French Toast, and note that it is just as good for lunch or dinner.

Preheat oven to 350 degrees

1 package flour tortillas
1-2 cups Monterey Jack cheese, grated
1-2 cups cooked breakfast sausage, crumbled
3 tablespoons chunky salsa
8 eggs
3 cups half and half
Salt and pepper

Coat a 9" baking dish with cooking spray. Line with tortillas.
Cover tortillas with Monterey Jack cheese, sausage and salsa.

Beat eggs with half and half and season with salt and pepper. Pour beaten eggs over base ingredients. Bake about 50 minutes, until the casserole rises and browns. Top casserole with more cheese and return to the oven for a few minutes until cheese melts.

Serve immediately and savor with much joy.

> *Never work before breakfast; if you have to work before breakfast, eat your breakfast first.*
> —*Josh Billings*

Natura Productions

*O*tsego County is home to some of the thousands of lakes and waterways that beautify New York. Natura Productions exists to protect them and extol the essential human connection to water. Scottie Baker offers evocative art, graphics and nature-themed products celebrating this basic premise of life.

Scottie is committed to water preservation. A portion of the profits from Natura Productions benefit organizations that protect the environment and groups that preserve and use traditional wooden watercraft.

Natura has ideal products for water lovers, canoeists, the conservation-minded and outdoor folks. Choose from art prints of painted canoes and painted paddles, nature graphics, the Still Point Collection of water themed photography, Sweetwater soaps and balm, charming Canoemates note cards, and Painted Paddle apparel.

Scottie Baker
PO Box 77
Fly Creek, NY 13337
607-547-5356
www.naturaproductions.com
scottieb@naturaproductions.com

Wild Leek
and Cheese Tart
Natura Productions

*O*n woodland walks during late April and early May, wild leeks provide much welcomed green on our deciduous slopes. Also called ramps and wild onions, they have two or three broad, smooth onion scented leaves and a white, more strongly onion flavored bulb underground. All parts of the wild leek are edible. Harvest them with a dandelion digger and garden trowel. Yes; they are worth the effort.

Preheat oven to 400 degrees
2-3 cups chopped wild leeks*
2 cloves New York garlic, minced
2 tablespoons unsalted butter
Sauté leeks and garlic lightly in butter. Spread them evenly in the bottom of a buttered 8" or 9" deep-dish pie pan or 8"x 8" square baking pan.

½ pound New York State cheddar cheese, grated
4 farm fresh eggs, beaten
2 cups milk
1 cup Bisquick
2 tablespoons chopped parsley
Combine all ingredients and pour over leeks. Bake for 35-40 minutes, until a knife inserted in the center comes out clean.

* If using domestic leeks, add a minced shallot to intensify flavor. The broad leek leaf resembles a lily of the valley leaf.

Cooperstown Book Nook

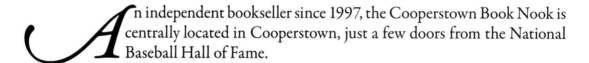

An independent bookseller since 1997, the Cooperstown Book Nook is centrally located in Cooperstown, just a few doors from the National Baseball Hall of Fame.

Bestsellers, local interest books and books of every genre fill the Book Nook's shelves. They are happy to fill your custom requests, including out of print books. The Book Nook's special children's section features books and toys for the short set.

This is a great browsing shop. You never know what special book or item you'll find tucked away in the Book Nook.

Monday-Saturday 10AM-5PM
Sundays Noon-3PM
Open extended hours in the Summer

61 Main Street
Cooperstown, NY 13326
607-547-2578
bnook@aol.com

> *I cannot live without books.*
> THOMAS JEFFERSON, 1815

Sunday Morning Apple Pancake

Cooperstown Book Nook

To enjoy while reading the *New York Times Book Review.*

Serves one.

1 large New York State apple of your choice, peeled and chopped
2 farm fresh eggs
2 tablespoons flour
2 tablespoons milk
1 tablespoon fresh butter

Melt butter in frying pan, over medium heat.

While butter is heating, whisk eggs in bowl. Whisk in flour and milk. Add to hot pan with melted butter. Scatter chopped apples on top. Gently brown on one side, then flip and brown on the other.

Serve with powdered sugar and New York State maple syrup. Enjoy!

Gilbert Block Quilt Shop

*T*his amazing shop is located in the heart of Gilbertsville. In fact, it may be the heart of Gilbertsville. Owner Nona Slaughter is the "go-to" person for just about everything going on in this agreeable historic New York town. She even hosts a morning radio program, *Nona Knows,* at 8AM every Saturday morning on WRFG 99.3 FM, Gilbertsville Community Radio.

True to its name you'll find beautiful quilts, wall hangings, table runners and bolts and bolts of colorful fabrics and quilting supplies in the Gilbert Block Quilt Shop. It is also filled with "you just never know what you might find" wonder. Hand made doll clothes or Philippine fish traps, unique, custom made rakes and Nona's sister's exquisite baseball calligraphy are just a few of the rare finds here. Need a chair caned or repaired? Ask Nona.

Gilbertsville is home to a significant artists' community, and Nona's shop also offers handcrafted items from local artists. You'll find this charming place on Commercial Street in the century old Gilbert Block.

Open Monday-Friday 10AM-6PM, Saturday 9AM-6PM, Sunday 1PM-4PM

Nona Slaughter
9 Commercial Street
PO Box 351
Gilbertsville, NY 13776
607-783-2872

Farmers' Breakfast Cookies
Gilbert Block Quilt Shop

~~~~~~~~~~~~~~~~~~~~~~~~~~~~~~~~~~

When you visit her shop, be sure to ask Nona how one of these cookies from 1920 was placed among the objects in the Gilbertsville Historical Society.

These traditional cookies were baked early in the mornings for farmers who spent long days in the fields.

1 cup shortening
2 cups sugar
2 eggs

4 ½ cups flour
1 teaspoon nutmeg
½ teaspoon salt

1 cup buttermilk
1 tablespoon baking soda

Cream shortening and sugar together. Beat in eggs
In separate bowl, stir dry ingredients together.
Mix baking soda into cup of buttermilk.

Add buttermilk mixture and dry ingredients, alternately, to sugar mixture.

Cover dough and let sit overnight, or at least three hours in refrigerator. Roll on floured board and cut with large round cutter. Place a raisin in the center of each cookie and sprinkle with sugar. Bake at 350 degrees for 8-10 minutes.

Plow fields and tend cows.

BlueStone Farm

~~~~~~~~~~~~~~~~~~~~~~~~~~~~~~~~~~~~~

CREATIVE BAKING WITH BLUESTONE FARM GRANOLA

BlueStone Farm Granola's versatility extends well beyond breakfast. The BlueStone staff has created dozens of recipe using their plainly delicious granola. A variety of muffins, pancakes, apple crisp, even cheesecake are made more appetizing with the multiple ingredients in BlueStone Farm Granola. Find great suggestions in the Recipe section at www.bluestonefarm.org.

BlueStone Farm Granola enhances almost any cookie, muffin, hot or cold cereal, or pancake recipe. Try it as a topping for your favorite fruit crisp. It makes a terrific ingredient in the BlueStone pie crust recipe.

Look for BlueStone Farm Granola throughout the Otsego County area, at retailers and served in accommodations. It is available at the Cooperstown Farmers' Market, and at *Home Plate* contributors The Fly Creek General Store and Bassett Healthcare, among others.

Shipping is available. Call or visit their website and make BlueStone Farm Granola both a breakfast tradition and a unique addition to baking.

Marty Bernardo
Bissell Road
Cooperstown, NY 13326
www.bluestonefarm.org
bluestone@capital.net
607-547-8227

Granola Scones
BlueStone Farms

~~~~~~~~~~~~~~~~~~~~~~~~~~~

Scones just say, "Good Morning!" They are fairly easy to make and incomparable with rivulets of melting butter. To be completely British Isles, serve them with clotted cream. Add strawberry jam and you can conquer the world on them.

Preheat oven to 400 degrees.
1½ cups flour
¼ cup brown sugar
2 teaspoons baking powder
¼ teaspoon salt
½ cup (one stick) real butter
2 cups BlueStone Farm Granola
¾ cup buttermilk

Cinnamon sugar: 1 tablespoon sugar mixed with ¼ teaspoon cinnamon

Mix dry ingredients together in large bowl. Cut in butter, by hand with a pastry blender or in a food processor using short pulses. Return to bowl and stir in granola and buttermilk.

Turn out onto lightly floured surface and knead briefly. Pat out into a circle in a greased deep-dish pie pan. Cut into 12 wedges with a pizza cutter. Or, pat dough on floured surface to a 1" to 1½" thickness and cut with a biscuit cutter. Sprinkle scones with cinnamon sugar. Bake for 15-17 minutes on greased or a cookie sheet lined with parchment, or until golden brown.

Bates
Hop House

George Alverson loves lilacs. The beautiful, fragrant blossoms are his passion and he knows them as well as anyone in a 200-mile radius of Otesgo County. He offers 150 varieties amongst his 4000 lilac plants.

Lilacs come in colors beyond the well-known lavender, deep purple and white. The yellow, pink and magenta varieties are especially appealing. With his broad knowledge of this lovely plant, George can direct you to hedge varieties, the headiest perfumes, early and late bloomers, and the most appropriate colors to fit your needs.

Located in the Bates Hop House, this sturdy stone building warehoused hops at the beginning of the Civil War. The space is now well used as the headquarters of the Alversons' lilac operation.

Like the Otsego County spring, George Alverson's lilacs are highly prized and their availability temporary. Open only from May to mid-July, a visit to his Cherry Valley gardens is well worth the trip to enhance the beauty and perfume of your own garden.

George Alverson
54 Lancaster Street (just up the street from *Home Plate* contributor The Rose
     and Kettle Restaurant)
Cherry Valley, NY 13320
607-264-3450

Alicemae's Recipe for a Beautiful Spring Garden
Bates Hop House

~~~~~~~~~~~~~~~~~~~~~~

Watching spring unfold in Otsego County is like enjoying a leisurely meal after fasting over the winter. The spirit-lifting snowdrops, crocus and lily-of-the-valley are served first, with following courses of daffodils, hyacinth and tulips. Then come the magnificent, redolent lilacs, scenting our valleys with every breeze. Behind them are the irises and peonies and then we know it's summer.

New York State is significant producer of floriculture, ranking fifth nationwide. Our growers maintain almost 25 million square feet of greenhouse and temporary growing facilities.

Follow Alicemae Alverson's directions and delight in a fragrant and fine-looking landscape.

Scatter bright daffodils and colorful tulips among lilacs, lilacs, and lilacs.

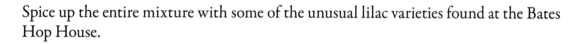

Contrast dark purple Ludwig Spaeth, blue President Lincoln, magenta Charles Joly and blue and purple Nadezhda with delicate pink and white Beauty of Moscow and yellow Primrose. Add a selection of the many sparkling white lilacs.

Spice up the entire mixture with some of the unusual lilac varieties found at the Bates Hop House.

Sit back and revel in Spring. Enjoy the beauty and perfume of these prized blooms.

ENTRÉES

Leatherstocking Massage

~~~~~~~~~~~~~~~~~~~~~~~~~~~~~~~~

Nurturing food, routine activity and rejuvenating relaxation enhance good health. After a stressful week, a professional massage can work wonders. Nationally certified massage therapist Robert Fiorentino offers the positive effects of Swedish, deep tissue, sports or hot stone massage at his studio or in your home.

Massage therapy is widely respected for its benefits in reducing stress, improving circulation and easing accumulated tensions. An hour of experienced hands-on therapy releases knotted muscles and it's a valuable addition to a fitness program or physical or chiropractic therapy.

Massage therapy is especially beneficial for people who stress their bodies in daily activity, such as construction workers, musicians, healthcare providers, teachers and anyone who spends long hours at a desk or traveling.

Located just ten miles from Cooperstown, Leatherstocking Massage offers a variety of therapeutic services in a comfortable, home-like atmosphere. Visits in your home and out-calls are available by appointment.

"Experience health, wellness of mind and body through massage."

Robert Fiorentino
180 Smith Road
PO Box 213
Springfield Center, NY 13468
315-858-9486
315-868-2119
rfmassage@usadatanet.net

Rob's Favorite Chicken and Pasta
Leatherstocking Massage

*T*his dish is best made with homemade pesto and alfredo sauce and fresh mushrooms. It's still delicious, even if you take a few shortcuts.

The night before:
Marinate two large, boneless and skinless chicken breasts in a small amount of olive oil and Italian seasonings. Refrigerate.

The rest of the ingredients:
8 ounces whole-wheat ziti pasta
8 ounces alfredo sauce
4 ounces pesto (more or less, to taste)
6 ounces artichoke hearts
6 ounces sun dried tomatoes
7 ounces mushrooms

Making dinner:
Bake or grill chicken breasts and cut into chunks. Set aside.

Cook pasta al dente, or to your preference; drain. Place in large serving bowl.

Heat Alfredo sauce, pesto, artichoke hearts, sun-dried tomatoes and mushrooms until heated through. Add sauce and chicken pieces to pasta and toss to coat.

Serve with fresh tossed salad, garlic bread, your favorite wine, candlelight and...

Mickey's Place

*I*n a village teeming with baseball memorabilia, Mickey's Place is a must stop.

Owner Vin Russo fills requests from the ordinary to the unusual. Need a genuine Louisville Slugger, a reproduction vintage Indians jacket, a Willie Mays autograph or a Mets cap inscribed in Hebrew? This is the place.

You'll find baseball cards (just like the ones Mom threw away), regulation and reproduction jerseys, Louisville Slugger bats engraved on premise, and an inventory sure to make a baseball fan's heart quicken.

Mickey's Place sells the largest selection of current, old-time and minor league baseball caps anywhere. All autographs are certified genuine. Mickey's sell only Major League Baseball licensed apparel.

A Baseball and Sports Emporium

Vin Russo
74 Main Street
Cooperstown, NY 13326
607-547-5775
800-528-5775
Fax: 607-547-6212
www.mickeysplace.com
info@mickeysplace.com

Vin's Rice Balls
Mickey's Place

~~~~~~~~~~~~~~~~~~~~~~~~~~~~~

These rice balls make a hearty main dish from ingredients you can keep on hand. Like Mickey's Place's owner, they are very Italian.

3 cups cooked rice
1 pound lean ground beef
Italian seasoning
4-inch stick pepperoni, chopped
¼ pound butter, softened
3 eggs, separated
8 ounces shredded mozzarella cheese
1 cup grated Parmesan cheese
1 small can of peas, drained
1 small can of mushrooms, drained

3 egg whites and enough milk, flour, and breadcrumbs to coat balls, set up in four separate stations.

Vegetable oil for deep-frying.

Brown beef in olive oil, adding a generous sprinkling of Italian seasoning.

Microwave or sauté chopped pepperoni briefly and drain on paper towels to render fat.

In large bowl, combine cooked rice, browned ground beef, drained pepperoni, peas, mushrooms and both cheeses. Stir in butter and egg yolks to bind mixture.

Shape mixture into balls. Roll in milk, then flour, then egg whites and, finally breadcrumbs. Deep fry rice balls in vegetable oil until golden brown.

SweetTooth SchoolHouse

*T*his little slice of culinary perfection near Roseboom is the captivating result of Harriet and Richard Sessler's vision. After buying the Pleasant Brook Greek Revival schoolhouse and church, they transformed the buildings into a bakery, café and tearoom called the SweetTooth SchoolHouse.

Offering brilliant, handcrafted food for lunches, brunches, theme dinners and authentic afternoon teas, they also host dress-up parties for little girls (of all ages) and make the meticulously renovated church available as a unique and elegant venue for your special event or country wedding. The SweetTooth SchoolHouse is unlike anything in Otsego County.

Harriet's specialties star fresh New York ingredients, as well as fine imported goods. Enjoy savory homemade soups and quiches and a wide array of cakes, pastries, tarts and cheesecakes.

The SweetTooth SchoolHouse is located 14 beautiful miles from Cooperstown in the hamlet of Pleasant Brook (Town of Roseboom).

Open Tuesday – Sunday 10AM - 5PM. Reservations recommended.

540 State Highway 165
Pleasant Brook, NY
607-264-3233
www.sweettoothschoolhouse.com

Chicken and Biscuits
SweetTooth SchoolHouse

*I*n some parts of the country church suppers and firehouse fundraisers feature chili or spaghetti. In Otsego County, it's Chicken and Biscuits. Harriet's recipe is easy and delicious.

Chicken Gravy
3 or 4 boneless, skinless chicken breasts cut in bite-sized pieces

¼ cup melted butter
1 small onion, chopped
1 cup potatoes, peeled and diced
1 cup chopped celery
1 cup water
1 cup chicken broth

1 cup frozen peas
1 cup frozen chopped carrots
1 can cream of potato soup
1 can cream of chicken soup
2 cups canned chicken gravy
½ cup milk

Poach chicken pieces, onion, celery and potatoes in water and broth until tender. Reduce liquid to about a half cup.

Add peas, carrots, soups, gravy and milk. Bring to a simmer. When hot, spoon over split biscuits.

Buttermilk Biscuits
2 cups all purpose flour
1 tablespoon baking powder
1 teaspoon salt

⅓ cup shortening
1 cup buttermilk
1 tablespoon white sugar

Preheat oven to 425 degrees. In large bowl, stir dry ingredients together. Cut in shortening until mixture resembles coarse meal. Stir in buttermilk.

Turn dough onto floured board and knead 15-20 times. Pat or roll dough to 1" thickness. Cut into large biscuit shapes, brush off excess flour and bake on an ungreased cookie sheet 13 to 15 minutes.

The Wieting Memorial Association

~~~~~~~~~~~~~~~~~~~~~~~~~~~~~~~~~~

This is how we should all get to enjoy the movies! The Wieting Memorial Association maintains a beautiful, traditional theater. They show one quality film at a time on a big screen, over a stage that once hosted vaudevillians. You can even get a seat in the balcony. Located right on Main Street, the Wieting is an easy walk from anywhere in Worcester.

Hellen Wilder Wieting built The Wieting Memorial in 1910 (for $15,000) to honor her husband Philip, the third president of the Bank of Worcester. She intended that the stately colonial building be a community center. The building originally housed a gymnasium and bowling alley in the cavernous basement, along with the theater and auditorium on street level. Upon completion, the building was deeded to The Wieting Memorial Association. The Wieting Memorial is held in trust for the people of Worcester and managed by the Association.

In 1922, the East Wing was added to house the Iroquois Chapter of the D.A.R. and to enlarge the Worcester Free Library.

Take a stroll through Worcester. Embrace this classic American small town and treat yourself to what "going to the movies" once meant.

Movies are shown on weekends from mid-June to mid- September, as well as the last weekend of school vacations. The theater boasts a new screen, projector and sound system. A family of four can enjoy the film, popcorn and drinks for about $20.

To find the Wieting Memorial, take exit 18, off of Interstate 88. Follow Route 7 to Worcester.

The Wieting Memorial
168 Main Street
PO Box 472
Worcester, NY 12197
607-397-7309

Otsego County Pot Roast

The Wieting Memorial Association

*T*o many people, this satisfying meal defines the term "Sunday dinner."

2 ¼ pounds boneless beef roast (New York raised)
2 cups spicy tomato juice
2 cups chopped onions (New York grown)
1 clove New York garlic, minced
6 potatoes (New York grown) cut into large chunks
3 cups New York carrots, cut into 2-inch pieces

Lightly coat a Dutch oven with cooking spray and heat over medium heat about a minute. Add roast and sauté 2-3 minutes on each side, or until browned.

Add 1¾ cups tomato juice, onion and garlic to the meat.

Season to taste with salt and pepper and bring to a boil. Reduce heat to low, cover and cook for an hour.

Add potatoes and carrots; cover pot and cook another 45 minutes. When done, transfer roast and vegetables to a platter.

In a small bowl, combine flour and remaining ¼ cup juice. Stir into pan drippings over medium heat for 3 to 4 minutes, or until thickened. Serve gravy over meat and vegetables.

> *Strange to see how a good dinner and feasting reconciles everybody.*
> —SAMUEL PEPYS (1633-1703)

Bassett Healthcare

~~~~~~~~~~~~~~~~~~~~~~~~~~~~~~~

A HISTORY OF CARING

Founded in 1922, Bassett Healthcare is named in honor of Dr. Mary Imogene Bassett, a compassionate and skillful physician who devoted herself to the sick and underprivileged people of Cooperstown and the surrounding area. Since then, Bassett has made major contributions in the field of medicine, primarily by establishing new methods of providing high quality, affordable healthcare to rural populations.

EXCELLENCE YOU CAN TRUST

Bassett continues to invest in and expand its services and programs, and remains dedicated to its threefold mission of excellence in patient care, medical education, and medical research. Affiliated with Columbia University, Bassett provides a unique environment to educate new physicians – creating sophisticated "big city" healthcare in a rural setting.

BASSETT HEALTHCARE: RIGHT WHERE YOU NEED US

One Atwell Road
Cooperstown, NY 13326
1-800-BASSETT (1-800-227-7388)
1-607-547-3456
www.bassett.org
Public.Relations@bassett.org

Sun-dried Tomato Crusted Chicken

Bassett Healthcare

A food processor makes this dish a snap.

Preheat oven to 375 degrees
2 boneless, skinless chicken breast halves (8 ounces each)
1 teaspoon black pepper
½ teaspoon kosher salt
4 cups cubed French bread
½ cup oil-packed, sun-dried tomatoes, drained and sliced
4 large garlic cloves, peeled
½ cup all-purpose flour
2 eggs
2 tablespoons water
2 tablespoons olive oil
2 tablespoons fresh Parmesan cheese

In a food processor, make coarse breadcrumbs from French bread.

Trim fat from breast halves. Slice each breast in half lengthwise and pound each half to ½" thickness. Season, as desired, with pepper and salt.

In a food processor, pulse breadcrumbs, tomatoes, Parmesan cheese, and garlic. Transfer to a shallow dish.

Place flour in a second shallow dish. Blend eggs and water with a fork in a third shallow dish.

Dredge chicken in flour, dip into egg wash to coat, and then press into the crumbs.

Heat oil in an ovenproof nonstick skillet over medium-high heat. Sauté chicken 3 minutes or until golden brown. Carefully flip chicken, then place pan in oven. Roast 8-10 minutes, or until cooked through. Rest 5 minutes before serving.

Lake Clear Wabblers

*E*nter the fisherman's world when you enter the Delaney's shop. The vernacular is all spoons and spinners, flutter weights and fluted skinner blades. This dedicated father-son duo has an inside track on what fish strike. Their hand finished casting and trolling lures have a proven record of catching the big ones.

For over eighty years, Lake Clear Wabblers has made lures to catch trout, walleye, muskie, northern pike and other game fish. Their experience shows in the quality, success record and outright beauty of their product. The brass, chrome and copper wabblers, Geneva spoons, skinner spoon bait and spinning lures could be mistaken for jewelry. Their light absorbing glow spoons are as pretty and vivid as fruit sherbet and irresistible to sport fish.

For fast or slow water, clear or murky conditions, bright or cloudy days, Lake Clear Wabblers has just the lure or trolling rig you need to catch the whoppers.

Please call to arrange a visit. Order a free catalog at the contacts below.

"Quality is our standard"

Tom Delaney
PO Box 301
10 Spring Street
Gilbertsville, NY 13776
Phone: 607-783-2587
Fax: 607-783-2538
www.lakeclearwabbler.com
lcwabbler@stny.rr.com

Brook Trout in Brandied Butter

Lake Clear Wabblers

*T*he brook trout is the state fish of New York.

2 cups all-purpose flour
1 tablespoon chopped fresh thyme
1 tablespoon chopped fresh rosemary
4 brook trout, cleaned (other trout work as well. Fish should be about 10-12 ounces each)
Salt and freshly ground pepper
3 tablespoons butter
2 tablespoons olive oil
¼ cup brandy
Lemon wedges and 2 tablespoons chopped fresh Italian parsley for garnish

Season the trout well inside and out with salt and pepper.

Combine flour, thyme and rosemary in a strong plastic bag. Shake each trout in the herbed flour, then remove, and shake off excess.

In a large skillet, heat the butter and oil together over medium-high heat. The two fats combine for great flavor and the olive oil stands a higher heat than the butter alone.

Add trout and brown each side for 1-2 minutes, until skin is brown and crisp.

Add the brandy and cover the skillet. Cook fish another 5-6 minutes over moderate heat. Uncover and continue cooking until the flesh is opaque. Be careful not to overcook. Pour the hot pan juices over the fish, and garnish with lemon wedges and chopped fresh parsley.

The Oneonta Elks Lodge BPOE 1312

The Benevolent and Protective Order of Elks is the largest and most active fraternal organization in the United States, numbering over a million members. The Elks is a community service organization founded on the principles of charity, justice, brotherly love and fidelity. The Oneonta chapter's members and their good works benefit local programs and residents.

Centrally located and professionally equipped, The Oneonta Elks Lodge is a perfect setting for events or meetings. The Lodge features one of the largest banquet rooms in the area, capable of seating 200 guests. They offer a full catering service and room rentals. The Elks' lower level bowling alley is also available for rent for special theme parties and events.

For catering, room and banquet reservations, contact Bryan Bennett.

Bryan Bennett
Oneonta Elks Lodge
82-86 Chestnut Street
Oneonta, NY 13820
607-432-1312

Veal Française

The Oneonta Elks Lodge BPOE 1312

New York State produces a significant amount of veal and this simple and delicious recipe uses it in grand style. Accompany with fresh New York vegetables. Serves two.

10 ounces veal medallions
Flour for dredging
½ cup olive oil
3 eggs
2 tablespoons fresh chopped parsley
A handful of grated Romano cheese
Black pepper to taste
½ teaspoon chopped garlic
Lemon to taste
¼ cup white wine
1 tablespoon butter

Beat together eggs, half of parsley, Romano cheese and black pepper. Pour into shallow pan (a pie pan works well).

Heat oil in sauté pan over high heat, being careful not to let it burn. While oil heats, dredge the veal medallions in the flour; dip in egg mixture. Shake off excess egg. Cook veal in hot oil about two minutes on each side, until golden brown. Drain on paper towels and keep warm.

Pour residual oil from pan and turn off heat. Add butter to the still warm pan, sprinkle or grind some pepper and add parsley. Turn the heat to low-medium and add the chopped garlic. Sauté gently and add wine, simmering about two minutes, until wine reduces by about half. Serve medallions and sauce over pasta or rice.

Cooperstown/Otsego County Tourism

Cooperstown/Otsego County Tourism welcomes you to this beautiful part of the Empire State. Their office is honored to act as the destination marketing organization for Otsego County, the "catalyst" that pulls our wonderful attractions and events together for you to enjoy.

Everyone knows Otsego County as the Birthplace of Baseball, but here are some "curious facts" about our area. For more (useful!) information, click on VisitCooperstown.com.

- Otsego County is located within a 750-mile radius of 50% of the North American population.
- Our region boasts an internationally acclaimed opera, an emerging performing arts center, several summer theater production companies and festivals, and one of the country's top folk art collections.
- James Fenimore Cooper, son of Cooperstown founder William Cooper, immortalized our area in his great American novels, The Leatherstocking Tales.
- Cooperstown is located at the southern end of Otsego Lake, known in Cooper's novels as "Glimmerglass." Otsego Lake is the headwaters of the Susquehanna River.
- Boy Scout Troop #1 in Unadilla is the longest chartered troop in the US.
- The National Baseball Hall of Fame opened its doors June 12, 1939; the first sports Hall of Fame in America. The Museum has drawn more than 13 million visitors since opening.

Contact them for more information and get the most from your visit!

Deb Taylor
242 Main Street
Oneonta, NY 13820
Phone: 800-843-3394
Fax: 607-432-5117
www.VisitCooperstown.com
info@visitcooperstown.com

Quick and Easy Capellini with Sausage Spinach

Cooperstown/Otsego County Tourism

~~~~~~~~~~~~~~~~~~~~~~

This recipe is quick to make, very tasty and it reheats easily.

1 tablespoon olive oil
1½ pounds Italian sausage (sweet or hot) cut into one-inch pieces
1 large onion, chopped
Several large garlic cloves, chopped
Pinch of crushed red pepper
1 14-ounce can chicken broth
¼ cup water
4 ounces (half a box) capellini or vermicelli pasta, broken in half
2 ten-ounce bags fresh spinach, coarsely chopped
Salt and pepper to taste

Heat oil in Dutch oven or stockpot over medium-high heat; add sausage and cook for 3 to 4 minutes, turning as it browns. Add onion, garlic, crushed red pepper, and cook 2 to 3 minutes, until onions and garlic are browned.

Add broth and water to pot; cover and bring to a boil. Add pasta and cook 3 minutes, stirring frequently. Add spinach and cook, stirring spinach into the pasta and sauce for 2 to 3 minutes more until pasta is al dente and spinach is wilted.

Serve immediately, with salt and pepper.

Fox Hollow Nursery

Experience the bounty and welcome at Fox Hollow Nursery. This family-owned and operated farm offers summer vegetables, autumn pumpkins and squash, Christmas trees and wreaths in the winter and year-round lawn care.

The Monzeglio family came to Otsego County from Long Island, NY in 2001, after finding and falling in love with the old farm. Their new neighbors told them stories of the once successful farm and farm stand. The Monzeglios have since worked constantly to restore Fox Hollow to its original glory.

The farm stand offers fresh produce from July through Thanksgiving. In October stop by for a family photo among the pumpkins, gourds and squash and take home a few, too! For the holidays, you'll find beautiful trees, wreaths and evergreen roping. The Monzeglios are proud members of the Otsego County agricultural community. They believe this is a great place to live and raise a family.

Neil and Bonnie Monzeglio
2751 State Highway 23
West Oneonta, NY
(Between Oneonta and Gilbertsville)
607-263-5764
bmonzeglio@stny.rr.com

Spinach and Bowties
Fox Hollow Nursery

~~~~~~~~~~~~~~~~~~~~~~~~~~~~~~~

*E*asy, quick, delicious and so good for you, this recipe makes great use of two of our favorite Otsego County crops- spinach and garlic.

8 to 10 ounces bow tie noodles (farfalle)
5 cloves garlic, finely chopped
2 tablespoons olive oil
10 to 16 ounces fresh spinach
4 ounces feta cheese, crumbled
Parmesan cheese
Salt and pepper to taste

Cook pasta according to package directions.

While pasta is cooking, wash and sort spinach, removing stems.

Heat olive oil in large skillet and sauté garlic over medium heat about a minute.

Add spinach, cover and cook over medium high heat 8-10 minutes, tossing frequently. Add a small amount of water, if necessary, so spinach steams but does not burn.

Add hot spinach to cooked bowties and toss with feta cheese. Top with Parmesan cheese and serve on warmed plates. Serves 4.

Washing the sand from spinach or leeks can be a pain. Instead of endless rinsing, fill a clean sink, large pan or bowl with cold water. Swish the leaves in the water and let float for a few minutes. After the sand and dirt has drifted to the bottom, fish out the leaves and let drain in a colander. Much easier and more effective!

The Konstanty Law Office

~~~~~~~~~~~~~~~~~~~~~~~~~~~~~~~~~~~~~

*W*ith nearly forty years experience, the Konstanty Law Office offers professional legal services in multiple specialties, together with counseling for a wide range of legal questions.

Consult the Konstanty Law Office for business litigation, real estate transactions, estate planning, matrimonial law, and general legal counsel and advice. A respected local firm throughout central New York, the Konstanty Law Office has handled litigation from coast to coast, as well as county, state and federal appeals courts.

Like a medical check-up is necessary to maintain your health, legal check-ups are necessary to maintain your legal affairs in good condition. Konstanty Law's experience and skill assures you that the decisions you make regarding your will, estate plan, or health care proxy will be respected.

For routine legal issues to the most challenging life situations, consider the expertise and assurance of the Konstanty Law Office.

James Konstanty
Stephen Baker
252 Main Street
Oneonta, NY 13820
607-432-2245
866-432-2245
www.konstantylaw.com
law_info@konstantylaw.com

Sauerbraten
The Konstanty Law Office

~~~~~~~~~~~~~~~~~~~~~~~~

*T*his traditional German roast is exceptionally tender and the sauce is delicious. It is an easy recipe, but does require a bit of planning. Begin marinating the roast three days before you intend to serve it.

One 3 to 5 pound beef roast (round, chuck or similar cut), trimmed of excess fat.

MARINADE
1 cup red wine
5 cups water
5 cups vinegar
2 onions, sliced
2 bay leaves
3 tablespoons pickling spice
6 peppercorns

SAUCE
14 crumbled gingersnaps
Sour cream

Combine all ingredients, except roast, in a large pot. Bring to a boil; reduce heat and simmer for 5 minutes. Cool marinating liquid to room temperature. Add meat to marinade and refrigerate. Let stand for three days.

When ready to cook, preheat oven to 350 degrees. Strain marinade and add 2 cups back over meat. Bake, covered, for 2-2½ hours.

When meat is tender, remove to a platter. To make sauce, stir crumbled gingersnaps into meat broth and add enough sour cream to achieve desired consistency.

Serve sauerbraten with noodles, boiled potatoes or dumplings.

Recipe courtesy of Beth Adams

TJ's Place
The Home Plate

TJ's Place is Americana. Baseball merchandise and autographed memorabilia, Coca-Cola décor, cheeseburger platters, apple pie baked on the premises and a friendly staff make TJ's welcoming, vibrant and satisfying.

Known by the locals fondly as "Ted and Diane's," this fun, family restaurant offers the largest menu in Cooperstown. With special menus for kids and seniors, plus vegetarian selections, TJ's offers something for everyone.

Wake up with omelets or pancakes, stop midday for great hot deli sandwiches or Caesar salads and relax at dinner with homemade soup and a steak cut to order.

TJ's also offers a large screen TV and a full bar with frosted mugs ready for your favorite brew.

Bring the team! TJ's can accommodate parties up to 50 for breakfast, lunch or dinner. A mainstay of Cooperstown's Main Street for seventeen years, TJ's Place The Home Plate is the all-American restaurant for a very American village.

Ted Hargrove and Diane Howard
124 Main Street
Cooperstown, NY 13326

607-547-4040
800-860-5670
Fax: 607-547-4042
www.tjs-place.com

Need a place to stay? Call TJ's about The Stables, their overnight accommodation next to TJ's Place the Home Plate.
thestablesinn@yahoo.com

TJ's Famous New York Turkey

TJ's Place The Home Plate

A quick raid of your spice cabinet enlivens this traditional roasted turkey and flavors delicious gravy.

Preheat oven to 370 degrees

1 turkey
Olive oil
Seasonings: Garlic salt, onion salt, finely ground black pepper, Spanish paprika, Bell's Turkey Seasoning, poultry seasoning and a small amount of thyme.

Remove neck and giblets from turkey and place in roasting pan. Add water to pan, filling about half way. Rub turkey breast and legs with olive oil.

Sprinkle turkey with a generous amount of all seasonings and rub into skin.
Cover turkey and pan with aluminum foil and roast until a meat thermometer reads 160 degrees (about 20 minutes per pound).

After turkey is roasted, remove from pan and place on platter. Let turkey set two hours. Let turkey broth cool to 160 degrees and then refrigerate. Remove fat when solidified and reserve turkey broth. This turkey "essence" is like gold for dressing and gravy.

Dressing: Season bread cubes with Bell's Turkey Seasoning and moisten with reserved turkey broth. Use about 1 cup cubes per serving. Bake in oven at 375 degrees until toasty brown.

Gravy: Put 4 cups turkey broth in deep saucepan and bring to a boil.
Put 4 tablespoons flour in glass measuring cup and stir in enough cold water to make a smooth paste. Slowly whisk into broth and simmer gravy to desired thickness. Add more broth if too thick; let cook down if too thin.

Serve turkey, dressing and gravy with cranberry sauce and enjoy completely.

The National Soccer Hall of Fame

From Greenland to Madagascar to Patagonia, soccer is the world's most popular sport. The National Soccer Hall of Fame keeps the most extensive and important collection of soccer history, housing over 100,000 artifacts, photographs, displays and video of America's brightest soccer moments.

Established in 1979 in Oneonta, New York, this distinguished institution is a 40,000 square foot interactive museum, so bring your sneakers! The museum's Kick's Zone Game area challenges visitors of all ages to test their skills on unique games created exclusively for the Hall. The Power Shot tells you how hard you can kick, and Speed Dribble tests your ability to score around life-size MLS players impeding your progress. There are 12 different games for everyone to enjoy, and a mini indoor field for 3–on-3 competitions.

The soccer fields surrounding the museum's modern, angular building have been rated #1 in the nation. These fields host youth and adult tournaments, scholastic and college matches, and games between professional teams with international players. Over 60,000 people a year visit the National Soccer Hall of Fame campus to play and watch the world's most popular game.

The National Soccer Hall of Fame and Museum hosts many special events throughout the year. Visit www.soccerhall.org for details. The museum is open seven days a week year-round, with the exception of New Years Day, Thanksgiving and Christmas. Please call or check their website for hours and the dates of their annual Hall of Fame Induction.

18 Stadium Circle
Oneonta, New York 13820
(607) 432-3351
Website: www.soccerhall.org
E-mail: nshof@soccerhall.org

Pam's Mom's Famous Meatballs

The National Soccer Hall of Fame

Make these meatballs smaller and use them for appetizers, served with your favorite marinara, sweet and sour, barbeque or Asian sauce. Double this recipe and keep half of the cooked meatballs in the freezer for quick meals. If using fresh herbs, triple the amounts given.

2 tablespoons olive oil
1 medium onion, chopped fine
2 cloves garlic, crushed
1 pound hamburger
½ pound ground pork
½ pound ground veal
3 eggs
1 cup breadcrumbs
¼ cup grated Parmesan or Romano cheese
1 teaspoon oregano
1 tablespoon parsley
Salt and pepper

Sauté onion and garlic in olive oil until soft. Put all ingredients in large bowl and mix well using a large wooden spoon or just washed hands.

Form meat mixture into 2-inch balls and place in microwave safe dish. Cover and microwave on high for four minutes. Turn meatballs over and microwave another four minutes. Microwave power differs; be sure to check for doneness. Add to your favorite pasta sauce.

Price Chopper Supermarkets

P rice Chopper Supermarkets has supported New York agriculture almost from the beginning. Immigrant brothers Ben and Bill Golub set up the Empire State Red Label Egg Program in 1933, the year their Central Markets opened. Working with Cornell University and the New York State Department of Agriculture, they established a market for local farmers and ensured their customers of the best quality eggs. At that time most eggs were shipped from the Midwest. They were up to month old by the time they reached the consumer.

Long a trendsetter in the grocery business (including being among the first to introduce S&H Trading Stamps), in 1957 Central Markets created the Grower-Producer Program, helping many small family farms develop modern business methods and new farming techniques.

In 1973 Central Markets became Price Chopper Supermarkets. They are located in six Northeastern states, including over 60 stores in New York. In Otsego County, find Price Chopper Supermarkets in Oneonta and Richfield Springs. Price Chopper supermarkets still proudly support local farmers. They offer the best in produce, meat, bakery and groceries in these clean and friendly markets. Many stores have a full selection of organic goods.

Price Chopper Supermarkets are still under the watchful care of the Golub family. The 20,000 employees own 55% of the privately owned stock. Each employee is valued and his or her contributions recognized. Since they began in 1932, the company has never lost a day to labor disputes.

The Golub Foundation, established in 1981, is Price Chopper's parent company and the philanthropic branch of the corporation. Through their belief in good corporate citizenship they work to enhance the quality of life in Price Chopper communities.

Summer Supper Garden Pie
Price Chopper Supermarkets

*T*ake a stroll through the produce department and come home with the fixings for a terrific main dish. This satisfying combination of New York's finest vegetables and cheese makes a wonderful entrée that just happens to be vegetarian. If using fresh herbs, multiply the amount by 3.

Preheat oven to 425 degrees
1 medium eggplant, cut in ½" cubes
1 large onion, sliced
1 zucchini, sliced
¾ teaspoon oregano
½ teaspoon salt
2 9" unbaked pie crusts
(Available in the refrigerated or frozen foods department)
½ cup grated Parmesan cheese

8 ounces shredded mozzarella cheese

¼ cup olive oil
1 green pepper, seeded and cut into strips
2 cloves garlic, minced
¾ teaspoon basil
¼ teaspoon black pepper

2 medium vine-ripe tomatoes, cut into eighths
1 tablespoon milk

Sprinkle eggplant cubed liberally with salt; place between paper towels and weigh down with a heavy cutting board for 30 minutes to remove excess moisture.

Heat half of the olive oil in a large skillet. Add eggplant and sauté in hot oil, stirring constantly for about 5 minutes. Remove eggplant and set aside.

Pour remaining olive oil in skillet. Sauté onion, green pepper, zucchini and garlic until just tender, about 5 minutes. Add cooked eggplant, oregano, basil, salt and pepper. Set aside.

Line a 9" pie pan with one of the crusts. Sprinkle with half the Parmesan cheese. Spoon half of the eggplant mixture on top of the cheese. Top with half the tomatoes and half the mozzarella. Repeat layers and top with all but 1 tablespoon of the Parmesan.

Cut remaining piecrust into lattice strips. Weave the strips on top of the vegetables, brush with milk and sprinkle with the remaining Parmesan. Bake pie for 25 minutes. Let stand for 15 minutes before cutting.

Recipe courtesy of Cornell Cooperative Extension-Otsego County

Syl•la•bles Media Group

*B*ridging the time of typewriters and when "cut and paste" literally meant scissors and rubber cement, to the current lightning speed of publication and communication, Syllables makes your words come alive, in print and on the Web.

Attractive, effective websites are the mark of talent and experience. Syllables bring the tools necessary to create a website that trumpets your product or interest, reflects your personality and gets your word out.

Drawing from a seemingly bottomless well of practice and skill, Syllables addresses your website needs, from development to continued updating. They have their own hosting services to ensure satisfactory response times. Their enhanced capabilities and special programs can make your website stand out in a sea of others. On-line credit card processing is available.

Honing their publishing proficiency during years of providing trade typesetting to New York City publishers, Syllables now serves only individuals and small private presses. They offer a combined 45 years of professional computing experience and 30 years in the business of type. Syllables does the line and content editing, manuscript preparation, etc., that brings brilliant, but sometimes jumbled, ideas into sensible print.

Call or visit Syllables at www.syllables.com for more information about publishing projects or website construction, hosting, and maintenance.

"Where Words are Treated With the Utmost Care"

Curt Akin
Mount Vision, NY
www.syllables.com
607-293-8202

Shepherd's (Cottage) Pie

Syllables Media Group

Sometimes, when either the weather is cold or the world has been, it's comforting to tuck into the warmth and substantial simplicity of meat and potatoes. Traditional Shepherd's Pie is made with lamb or mutton. When made with beef it becomes a Cottage Pie. To make this recipe even easier, use leftover mashed potatoes, or purchase them ready-made in the refrigerated section.

2 pounds potatoes, peeled
½ cup milk   2 tablespoons butter
Salt to taste
(Or, make your favorite mashed potatoes)

1½ pounds ground beef   1 large onion, peeled and chopped
2 tablespoons vegetable oil   1 to 2 cups frozen mixed vegetables
                                          (corn, peas, carrots, etc)
2 tablespoons flour   2 cups beef stock
Butter and/or shredded cheese

Boil potatoes in salted water until tender, 15 to 20 minutes. When cooked, drain and mash with milk and butter. Salt to taste.

While potatoes cook, brown ground beef in a large frying pan. When no longer pink, drain fat. Put two tablespoons vegetable oil in the same pan and sauté onions until they begin to soften. Add the mixed vegetables and cook over medium heat 1 to 2 minutes, until they begin to defrost. Sprinkle flour over the meat mixture; stir and cook another 2 minutes. Add beef stock and bring to a boil. Simmer until thickened, stirring occasionally.

Preheat oven to 375 degrees. Spoon the meat mixture into an ovenproof dish and top with mashed potatoes, spreading evenly. Make designs with a fork for more interesting browning. Dot with butter or sprinkle with shredded cheese, if desired. Bake for 25 to 30 minutes, until top is brown and gravy bubbles.

CELEBRITY
CHEFS

Assemblyman William Magee

*I*t's easy to find Assemblyman William "Bill" Magee's office in Albany. The Holstein figure at the door and the rows of milk bottles inside tell you that you have found the Chairman of the Agriculture Committee.

Assemblyman Magee has represented his constituency in Otsego, Madison and Oneida counties since 1990. A small businessman and auctioneer, he was elected to the Assembly after serving 19 years on the Madison County Board of Supervisors, representing the Town of Nelson.

Assemblyman Magee is a tireless supporter of the 111th District's economic revitalization. He has supported numerous proposals to reduce taxes, energy costs and bureaucracy. In addition to chairing the Agriculture Committee, Mr. Magee serves on the Aging, Banking, Higher Education and the Committee on Local Governments.

He is an ardent advocate for the state's volunteer fire and ambulance services and for funding and financial aid so that all may have a college education. Assemblyman Magee sponsored and won approval for the Northeast Interstate Dairy Compact to ensure stable milk prices for New York dairy farmers and he worked for passage of the Farm Viability Act. Assemblyman Magee works diligently with farmers, producers, wholesalers and retailers to sell more New York products in New York.

Assemblyman Magee sponsored the legislation that resulted in the designation of New York State Route 20 as a Scenic Byway.

He and his wife, Jeanette still live in his life-long home of Nelson, NY.

Assemblyman Magee was the initial supporter of *Home Plate: The Traveler's Food Guide to Cooperstown and Otsego County, NY.*

New York Maple Dried Cherry Syrup

Assemblyman Bill Magee

*I*ncorporating several of New York's finest crops, this versatile topping beautifully enhances pancakes and waffles, and also ice cream, bread pudding, rice pudding and oatmeal.

¾ cup New York maple syrup
½ cup firmly packed brown sugar
¼ cup New York honey
Juice of one orange, plus one teaspoon orange zest
Juice of ½ lemon, plus ½ teaspoon lemon zest
1 tablespoon butter
½ teaspoon cinnamon
½ cup chopped dried New York tart cherries

Combine syrup, brown sugar, honey, juice and zest, butter and cinnamon in a medium saucepan. Stir well and bring to a boil over medium heat, stirring occasionally. Reduce heat to a simmer and gently cook for ten minutes. Add New York cherries and cook an additional minute.

Makes 1½ cups.

State Senator James L. Seward

A life-long resident of Otsego County, James L. "Jim" Seward has served Otsego County in the New York State Senate since 1986. He also represents the residents of Herkimer, Schoharie, Greene, Cortland and parts of Tompkins and Chenango counties in the 51st Senatorial District.

Long a champion of the interests of his constituency, Senator Seward is chair of the Senate Majority Task Force on Volunteer Emergency Services and of the Senate Standing Committee on Insurance. He was named as chair of the Senate Energy and Telecommunications Committee in 1986. After the 9-11 terrorists' attacks on the World Trade Center, Senator Seward was appointed to head a special Senate review panel on State and local emergency preparedness

Senator Seward has fought for and won state commitments to tax relief, economic development, education, and the state's paid and voluntary fire departments. He continues to champion health insurance for the uninsured and to reduce health insurance costs.

Always community and civic minded, Jim is on the board of directors of *Home Plate* contributors Wilber National Bank and the Glimmerglass Opera. He is also a board member of Pathfinder Village and the Catskill Symphony.

Senator Seward and his wife Cindy reside in Milford, NY. They have two children.

Summer Squash & Cheese Casserole

Senator James L. Seward

New York is fifth in nationwide squash production and Otsego County usually produces a bumper crop. Make the most of these versatile, prolific, vegetables while they are at their summer peak. They are, of course, wonderful if purchased from an Otsego County farm stand.

Preheat oven to 350 degrees

2 or 3 small yellow or zucchini squash, sliced
¼ to ½ cup butter
6-8 New York Sharp Cheddar cheese slices
13 round butter crackers, crushed (Ritz, or similar)

Cook squash in boiling salted water until soft; drain and mash with potato masher or process lightly in food processor. Put a layer of squash in ungreased 1-quart baking dish. Add a layer of sliced cheddar cheese. Dot with pats of butter and top with crushed crackers. Repeat layers, ending with cracker crumbs. Bake uncovered 20-30 minutes. Enjoy.

The trouble is, you cannot grow just one zucchini. Minutes after you plant a single seed, hundreds of zucchini will barge out of the ground and sprawl around the garden, menacing the other vegetables. At night, you will be able to hear the ground quake as more and more zucchinis erupt.

—DAVE BARRY

Assemblyman Marc W. Butler

*A*ssemblyman Marc Butler has represented the central New York area in the Assembly since 1995. His current district includes the eastern portion of Otsego County and the entirety of Herkimer and Fulton counties.

Mr. Butler serves on the Agriculture, Insurance and Higher Education Committees. He is the ranking minority member on the Assembly Economic Development Committee.

Assemblyman Butler conceived and created legislation that resulted in the Southern Adirondack Trail Scenic Byway, stretching for 76 miles between Herkimer and Hamilton counties. He was also an initial sponsor of the legislation that lead to the STAR program for school property tax relief.

Marc and his wife, Susan, are the volunteer chairs for the Herkimer Area Resource Center (HARC) Annual Wine Auction, benefiting people with disabilities, and others in the Herkimer community, to achieve full potential and enriched lives. He is also a board member and the former chairman of the Valley United Way.

Assemblyman Butler is a lifelong resident of the Mohawk Valley and resides in the Village of Newport.

Ratatouille
Assemblyman Marc Butler

~~~~~~~~~~~~~~~~~~~~~~~~~~~~~~~~~~~~~~

*T*his delicious recipe sings of summer. It's a great way to use the garden harvest and get five servings of vegetables everyday. Low in fat and calories, it bursts with flavor. This is a flexible recipe. Be creative with the choices and amounts of herbs and vegetables.

2 to 4 tablespoons olive oil
I yellow onion, chopped
2 bell peppers, any color, sliced or diced
2 small or medium zucchini, cubed
1 small eggplant, cubed
4 cloves garlic, crushed
2 medium tomatoes, chopped in large chunks
1 bay leaf
1 teaspoon each basil and marjoram (if using fresh herbs, increase to one tablespoon)
½ teaspoon oregano
Rosemary to taste
¼ cup dry red wine
½ cup tomato juice
2 tablespoons tomato paste
2 teaspoons salt
Black pepper to taste
Chopped fresh parsley

In large frying pan, heat olive oil and sauté garlic. Add bay leaf and onion; salt lightly. Add eggplant, wine and tomato juice. Add herbs. Stir well and simmer 10-15 minutes over low heat. Add squash and peppers. Cover and simmer 10 minutes. Add salt, pepper, tomatoes and tomato paste.

Stir in parsley just prior to serving. Serve over rice and/or with good bread. Top with grated cheese (Parmesan or Romano) and olives, if desired.

James Fenimore Cooper

urely the most omnipresent influence in Cooperstown and the surrounding area, the works and characters of James Fenimore Cooper enliven street names, businesses, signage and much more.

The eleventh of twelve children of Cooperstown founder William Cooper, James Fenimore Cooper is one of America's first novelists. Born in New Jersey in 1789, he spent his formative years in the "western wilderness' that is now Otsego County. Cooper was educated by tutors and, for a time, at Yale. There he admittedly learned little and was eventually expelled for, among other practical jokes, teaching an ass to sit on his professor's chair. Cooper's early adulthood was spent at sea where he gained experiences that would later appear in his novels.

Still not of the literary life at age 30, he reportedly began writing at the urging of his wife, heiress Susan Augusta De Lancey. Supposedly upon reading a disappointing novel, he announced that he could write a better story. His wife challenged him to do so and thus *Precaution* was born. An unsuccessful first effort, it led to a prolific career nonetheless. His five Leatherstocking novels include *The Pioneers,* set in frontier Cooperstown and introducing his American hero, Natty Bumpo; *The Last of the Mohicans,* widely considered his best work, *The Prairie, The Pathfinder,* and *The Deerslayer.*

Although a successful writer, he was personally controversial and encountered much derision from contemporaries in Cooperstown and abroad. Writers Honore de Balzac and Victor Hugo admired him, but later in the nineteenth century, Mark Twain took Cooper's writing to task in his amusing *Fenimore Cooper's Literary Offences.*

James Fenimore Cooper's statue is in Cooper Park next to the National Baseball Hall of Fame and Museum. He is buried, with his family, in Cooperstown at Christ Episcopal Church.

A Crookneck, or Winter Squaſh Pudding

The era of James Fenimore Cooper

~~~~~~

This recipe is borrowed from what is recognized as the first American cookbook, *American Cookery* by Amelia Simmons. It was first published in 1796, a few years after James Fenimore Cooper was born.

The recipe is written verbatim and looks completely misspelled. In colonial English, the letter "f" was generally used where we would now use the letter "s".

The squash, apples and "Pompkins" (pumpkins) are definitely found in Otsego County. The jury is out on "whortleberries".

Home Plate sincerely hopes that this recipe would meet Mr. Cooper's approval.

"Core, boil and ſkin a good ſquaſh, and bruize it well; take 6 large apples, pared, cored and ſtewed tender, mix together; add 6 or 7 ſpoonfuls of dry bread or biſcuit, rendered fine as meal, half pint milk or cream, 2 ſpoons of roſe-water, 2 ſpoons wine, 5 or 6 eggs beaten and ſtrained, nutmeg, ſalt and ſugar to your taſte, one ſpoon flour, beat all ſmartly together, bake.

The above is a good receipt for Pompkins, Potatoes or Yams, adding more moiſtening or milk and roſe water, and to the two latter a few black or Liſbon currants, or dry whortleberries ſcattered in, will make it better."

> *The Americans are the grossest feeders of any civilized nation known. As a nation, their food is heavy, coarse, and indigestible, while it is taken in the least artificial forms that cookery will allow. The predominance of grease in the American kitchen, coupled with the habits of hearty eating, and the constant expectoration, are the causes of the diseases of the stomach which are so common in America."*
>
> —JAMES FENIMORE COOPER

Yogi Berra

*Y*ogi.

There are names that simply mean "baseball." "Yogi" means not only baseball, but American culture: his colorful persona, his exuberant leap into Don Larsen's arms after catching the only perfect game in World Series history, the cartoon classic Yogi Bear named after him and, of course, his "yogi-isms." Yogi's malapropisms are so ingrained in American vernacular that people who have no idea of the source often quote him. "It ain't over 'til it's over," "it's déjà vu all over again" and "when you come to the fork in the road, take it" all have the same sage source in Yogi.

A native of the "The Hill" Italian area of St. Louis, MO, Lawrence Peter "Lawdie" Berra was nicknamed "Yogi" because a childhood friend thought he resembled a yogi (a Hindu holy man) seen in a movie. His major league career began in 1946 after serving in the US Navy. During his 19-year career with the New York Yankees he was a 3-time Most Valuable Player and he appeared on 15 All-Star teams. He played in 14 World Series, hitting the first pinch-hit homer in Series history in 1947. As manager of the Yankees and the Mets, he led both American and National League teams to the World Series.

Yogi Berra was inducted into the National Baseball Hall of Fame in 1972, the same year the Yankee's retired his number 8. He is number 40 on The Sporting News' list of 100 Greatest Baseball Players and fans elected him to the Major League Baseball All Century-Team. Visit the Yogi Berra Museum on the campus of Montclair State in Montclair, NJ.

Yogi. That's all you have to say.

> *Williams was the most natural hitter, but Berra was the most natural ballplayer.*
>
> —CASEY STENGAL

Yogi Berra's Tripe Dinner

*T*ripe is considered a delicacy in many parts of the world. It takes some time, but to tripe connoisseurs like Yogi, it's worth the wait. It gets better as it sits, so you may want to cook it one day and serve it the next.

5 pounds fresh tripe (it will cook down considerably)
10 tablespoons salt
3-4 red potatoes
1-2 cups fresh or frozen lima beans
1-2 large carrots
2-3 celery ribs
1 large Empire Sweet onion
Basil and oregano

Wash tripe in cold water. Cut in 1" pieces and place in good-sized pot. Cover with cold water and 5 tablespoons of salt. Bring to a boil and cook for two hours. After two hours, pour water off, cover with fresh cold water, another 5 tablespoons of salt and boil for another two hours. After two hours, take off heat and rinse in cold water. Return tripe to pot, cover with fresh cold water and cook for another hour, this time without salt.

Cook vegetables in a separate pot during the tripe's last cooking hour. The vegetables are versatile; use more or less to your taste. Cut potatoes and carrots into good-sized chunks. Dice celery and onion. Boil with a pinch of basil and oregano. When potatoes and carrots are al dente (cooked, but still firm), remove from heat. DO NOT DRAIN vegetables.

Drain cooking water from tripe. Add tripe to vegetables and vegetable broth. Stir in one teaspoon chicken stock granules. Salt and pepper to taste.

Serve with good bread and cold beer.

Recipe courtesy of TJ's Place The Home Plate

Paul Blair

Arguably the best centerfielder to play the game in the late 1960s and early 1970s, Paul Blair was known for playing the position shallow. His speed and uncanny knack for judging the hitter's ability and a hit ball's trajectory determined how he played centerfield. You can't dispute the results. During his seventeen-year career, no ball hit over his head went out of the park. He made it look simple; if a ball was hit in Paul Blair territory, he caught it.

"If a ball went over my head, it was a souvenir." Paul Blair made no fielding errors during his entire career, posting a .988 fielding percentage.

Though his style may have been unorthodox, it worked, earning him eight Gold Gloves. He holds the American League record for the most Gold Gloves awarded to any centerfielder. He is the only Baltimore Orioles outfielder ever to win the honor.

His quickness, intuitive play and bunting ability extended his major league career to seventeen seasons, playing with the Baltimore Orioles, the New York Yankees and the Cincinnati Reds. Paul Blair appeared in six World Series, four with the Baltimore Orioles and two with the New York Yankees. His home run in Game 3 of the 1966 Series provided the only run in the Orioles 1-0 win over the Los Angeles Dodgers, in the Series the Orioles would go on to sweep.

Paul Blair was elected to the Baltimore Orioles Hall of Fame in 1984.

> *I never saw Paul Blair's first step.*
> —EARL WEAVER,
> ON PAUL BLAIR'S REMARKABLE FIELDING

Sure Catch Blueberry Pancakes

Paul Blair

~~~~~~~~~~~~~~~~~~~~~~~~~~~~~~~~~~~~~~

Separating the egg and folding in the beaten egg white makes these pancakes especially light. Their airy texture makes them absorb lots of maple syrup. This recipe multiplies easily.

1 cup all purpose flour
2 tablespoons sugar
2 tablespoons cornmeal
½ teaspoon baking soda

1 egg, separated
2 tablespoons butter
1 to 1½ cups buttermilk
½ cup fresh blueberries

Stir dry ingredients together in large bowl and set aside.

Melt butter in glass measuring cup in microwave or over low heat on top of stove. Add cold buttermilk to the hot butter and stir thoroughly. Add egg yolk and stir together.

In a separate bowl beat egg white to soft peaks and set aside.

Add buttermilk mixture to dry ingredients and stir just until combined. If necessary, add more milk to achieve desired consistency (buttermilk or plain milk may be used to thin batter). Gently fold in beaten egg whites and blueberries.

Ladle batter onto hot, oiled griddle. Cook on one side until bubbles appear and start to break. Flip and cook on the second side about a minute. Serve with New York maple syrup or farmers' market jam.

Recipe courtesy of Bryn Brooke Manor

Bill
Madden
New York Daily News

When Billy Joel croons longingly for The *Daily News* in his aching, reflective favorite *A New York State of Mind,* surely Bill Madden's baseball column is what he's missing.

Bill Madden has written about and embraced the boys in pinstripes for over a quarter century. Covering the Yankee beat for the *New York Daily News* from 1978, he became their national baseball columnist in 1989. Bill Madden's affection for the Yankees began much earlier, including witnessing Don Larsen's perfect game as a fifth-grader in 1956.

His book, *Pride of October: What It Was to Be Young and a Yankee* profiles various Bronx players from across generations, eloquently crafting multi-layered and very human looks at Yogi Berra, Phil Rizzuto, Reggie Jackson, Don Mattingly and other Yankees.

Bill Madden also penned Don Zimmer's bestselling autobiography *Zim- A Baseball Life* and co-authored *Damned Yankees* with Moss Klein.

Bill Madden is a supporter of the Baseball Assistance Team (B.A.T.) the non-profit organization that provides life assistance to members of the extended baseball family.

Broccoli and Leek Sauté

Bill Madden

~~~~~~~~~~~~~~~~~~~~~~~~~~~~~~~~~~~~~

Simple, delicious, gorgeously green, with a pleasant little kick from the red pepper. This is the easiest of side dishes, and an excellent accompaniment to most entrées. *Home Plate* thanks Lillian Madden for this contribution on Bill's behalf.

2 tablespoons olive oil
4 cloves garlic, sliced
2 leeks, white and pale green parts
1 bunch fresh broccoli
¼ teaspoon red pepper

Thoroughly rinse leeks and broccoli. Thinly slice leeks and cut broccoli into florets. Trim and chop broccoli stems, using the tender parts.

Heat olive oil in large frying pan. Add sliced garlic and leeks and sauté until soft. Add broccoli and cover pan. Cook over medium heat until broccoli is tender but still bright green. Sprinkle with pepper and toss just before serving.

One pound of trimmed spinach may be substituted for broccoli. Cooking time will be a bit less.

> *Nothing flatters me more than to have it assumed that I could write prose- unless it be to have it assumed that I once pitched a baseball with distinction.*
> —ROBERT FROST

Bob Feller

*P*itcher "Rapid Robert" Feller is the senior living member of the elite few elected to the National Baseball Hall of Fame. Elected in 1962, he spent his entire 18 year career with the Cleveland Indians, amassing 266 victories. His total wins may have been as much as 100 more, but for the four peak seasons he spent serving his country in the Navy during World War II. Enlisting after Pearl Harbor, he was decorated with five campaign ribbons and eight battle stars. He said of his time in uniform, "Baseball in the Navy always was much more fun than it had been in the major leagues."

A native of the farming region of Van Meter, Iowa, Bob Feller's father, in what must have inspired a famous scene from the film *The Natural,* built a backstop to encourage his son's gift and strong arm. At the age of 17, Bob Feller made his major league debut with the Indians, striking out 15 batters. After that season, he returned to Van Meter to graduate from high school. The ceremony was covered on NBC Radio.

A dominating pitcher, Bob Feller has a bounty of awards and records to his credit, including three no-hitters. He is the only pitcher ever to throw a no-hitter on opening day (April 16, 1940 at Comiskey Park). He is the winningest pitcher in Cleveland Indians history. His number 19, retired in 1957, was the first they so honored. His statue stands at the entry to Cleveland's Jacob's Field.

Bob Feller explains the method behind his remarkable pitching ability like this: "I just reared back and let them go."

You may visit the Bob Feller Museum in Van Meter, Iowa.

The rewards of an outing to one of the many farmers' markets in Otsego County.

Nothing says summer like tomatoes ripening on the vine.

Photos by Richard Duncan

Everything here is good and good for you. Even the tablecloth looks scrumptious!

You're on your honor- Help yourself!

Below: *Look closely- the roses in this bouquet are radishes and the lilies are zucchini*

SELF SERVE
$3.50 DOZ.
THANKS

Some of Otsego County's more important residents

Kisses from Otsego County!

Bounty!!

Look for farm stands like this throughout Otsego County

Slow down!

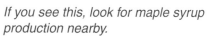

If you see this, look for maple syrup production nearby.

Not a steam bath, but maple sap transforming to maple syrup

The promise of a great breakfast.

Healthy chickens—healthy eggs.

Rolling hills and vast pastures are the signature of Otsego County. We treasure our dairy and produce farms and our precious open spaces. We pass the love of our land on to future generations, to their stewardship and safekeeping.

Bob Feller
Chili
Bob Feller

~~~~~~~~~~~~~~~~~~~~~~~~~~~~~~

*A*s simple and straightforward as a Bob Feller fastball, everyone can make and enjoy this chili.

1 tablespoon oil
½ cup chopped onion
¼ cup chopped green onion
1 pound lean ground beef
2 8-ounce cans tomato sauce
1 16-ounce can kidney beans
1 teaspoon salt
Chili powder

Heat oil in two quart saucepan. Cook onion, pepper and beef until lightly browned. Add tomato sauce and cook over low heat for five minutes. Add the kidney beans and salt. Stir in one tablespoon chili powder, adding more to taste.

Serve topped with chopped onions, shredded New York cheese, diced tomatoes and sour cream, if desired.

Recipe courtesy of TJ's Place The Home Plate

> *In his day, Bob Feller was the best pitcher living.*
> —JOE DIMAGGIO

Carl Erskine

Fondly known as "Oisk" to Brooklyn Dodger fans, Indiana native Carl Erskine starred in the Dodgers (both Brooklyn and Los Angeles) pitching line up for twelve seasons, from 1948 to 1959. His career highlights include two no-hitters, against the Cubs on June 19, 1952 and May 12, 1956 against the Giants. He pitched in the 1949, 1952, 1953, 1955, 1956 and 1959 World Series. His best year was 1953 with 20 wins and six losses. It was in that year that he achieved the World Series record with 14 strikeouts (in Game 3), a record that stood for 14 years.

Carl Erskine was elected into the Indiana Baseball Hall of Fame in 1979.

He features the World Series Buttermilk Cake in his book, *Tales From the Dodger Dugout*.

"During the 1955 season, the Dodgers were again the favorites to win the National League pennant. About mid-season, Frank Kellert, a rookie outfielder, received a package from his family in Oklahoma. It was a buttermilk cake. He shared it with the team before a game, and we won. The cake lasted long enough for us to win a couple more games. Sometime after that, the team went into a minor slump. Kellert was asked to contact his family for another buttermilk cake. The cakes kept coming, and we kept winning and clinched the pennant. During the World Series, we had a supply of buttermilk cakes. We beat the Yankees in seven games for the first and only world championship in the 75-year history of the Brooklyn Dodgers."

Carl Erskine's Series Winning Buttermilk Cake

That really is four **tablespoons** of vanilla. Use real vanilla for the best flavor. Butter can be used in place of shortening.

Preheat oven to 350 degrees.
1 cup shortening
2 cups sugar
4 whole eggs
Dash of salt
1 cup buttermilk
½ teaspoon baking soda, dissolved in buttermilk
4 tablespoons vanilla
3 cups all purpose flour
1 cup finely chopped pecans

Cream shortening and sugar together. Beat in eggs one at a time. Add flour and buttermilk, alternately. Add vanilla, stir well and fold in pecans.

Bake in a greased and floured tube pan for about 50 minutes, or until toothpick inserted in center comes out clean. Win World Series.

> *I've had a pretty good success facing Stan (Musial) by throwing him my best pitch and backing up third base.*
> —CARL ERSKINE

Gaylord Perry

A colorful and controversial pitcher, Gaylord Jackson Perry played for eight different teams from 1962-1983. When he makes personal appearances he wears a jersey that sports all eight team logos. However, when he was inducted into the National Baseball Hall of Fame in 1991, he wore the San Francisco Giants cap. The Giants retired his number, 36, in 2005.

Gaylord Perry was the first pitcher to win the Cy Young Award in both leagues, the first in 1972 while playing for the Cleveland Indians and again in 1978 for the San Diego Padres, at age 39. He had five seasons winning 20 or more games.

The controversy surrounding Gaylord Perry centered on throwing spitballs. Whether he did or he didn't, or how often, he entitled his biography, *Me and the Spitter*.

Like most pitchers, Gaylord Perry's strengths shone on the mound, not at the plate. In 1963, he was quoted as saying "They'll put a man on the moon before I hit a homerun." On July 20, 1969, just hours after Neil Armstrong stepped on the moon, Gaylord Perry hit his first homerun.

In his 22 year career, he never appeared in a World Series. Gaylord Perry is listed among The Sporting News 100 Greatest Baseball Players.

> *I reckon I tried everything on the old apple, but salt and pepper and chocolate sauce topping.*
> —GAYLORD PERRY

Debbie Catches Cy Young Pitcher with Chicken Parmesan

Gaylord Perry

~~~~~~~~~~~~

Serve with Bill Madden's Broccoli and Leek Sauté.

Preheat oven to 350 degrees.
2 eggs
¼ cup milk
2 cups Italian breadcrumbs
6 boneless chicken breasts
½ cup grated Parmesan cheese
½ cup chopped mushrooms
12 ounces shredded mozzarella
2 cups marinara sauce

Beat eggs with milk to make egg wash. Place bread crumbs in shallow dish.

Dip chicken breasts in egg mixture, then roll in breadcrumbs, coating well.

Place chicken breasts in baking pan and sprinkle with Parmesan cheese.

Cover with marinara sauce. Liberally scatter mozzarella over sauce. Add mushrooms evenly on top and around pan.

Bake about an hour.

Recipe courtesy of TJ's Place The Home Plate

The spitball was a legal pitch until 1920. After it was declared illegal, pitchers already playing in the major leagues were "grandfathered" and allowed to keep throwing "spitters."

Hall of Famer Burleigh Grimes threw the last legal spitball in the major leagues.

Ferguson Jenkins

Ferguson Jenkins, a nineteen-season right-handed hurler, moved the crowd and swelled North American pride at the 2004 Induction Ceremony with a heartfelt rendition of his country's national anthem, *O, Canada*. Inducted in 1991, "Fergie", an Ontario native, is the only Canadian member of the National Baseball Hall of Fame.

His stellar career began with the Philadelphia Phillies in 1963. After a single season, the Phils traded him to the Chicago Cubs where he became one of the best pitchers in the major leagues. Incredibly, the Phillies made the same trading error in 1982 when, after a single season, they also sent Ryne Sandberg to the Cubs. Ryne Sandberg joined Ferguson Jenkins in the Hall of Fame in 2005.

Ferguson Jenkins was a three-time All Star and, in 1971, a Cy Young Award winner. He had an incredible six consecutive seasons of 20+ wins and is one of only two pitchers to record more than 3000 strikeouts with fewer than 1000 walks (Greg Maddux is the other). Fergie also shone in basketball, playing with the Harlem Globetrotters.

Ferguson Jenkins retired with 267 complete games and 49 shutouts. He also holds the 9th-highest strikeout total in history with 3,192.

For more Ferguson Jenkins stats, rent the DVD *This is Spinal Tap*. Contained in the extra scenes is an amusing (and accurate) account of Ferguson Jenkins' shutout record as told by the unlikeliest fan.

Quail in Wine
Ferguson Jenkins

~~~~~~~~~~~~~~~~~~~~~~~~~~~~~~~~

This recipe is exceptional. If you don't happen to be a hunter, look for farm-raised quail at farmers' markets.

6 quail, cleaned and trussed
½ cup butter
2 onions, minced
2 whole cloves
1 teaspoon peppercorns
2 garlic cloves, minced
½ bay leaf
2 cups white wine
½ teaspoon salt
⅛ teaspoon pepper
1 teaspoon minced chives
2 cups cream or evaporated milk

In large pan, melt butter and add onions, cloves, peppercorns, garlic and bay leaf. Sauté several minutes over medium-low heat.

Add quail, browning on all sides. Add the wine, salt, pepper and chives. Cover and simmer until tender, about thirty minutes.

Remove quail and place in warmed serving dish. Strain cooking liquid and return to pan. Add cream and heat almost to boiling. Adjust seasonings to your taste. Pour sauce over quail.

> *During those 14 seasons, and for all my career really, I didn't consider pitching to be work— I was having fun getting most hitters out in the major leagues.*
> —FERGUSON JENKINS

Wade Boggs

Baseball and superstitions are inseparable. Babe Ruth always touched first base on his way in from right field. Jackie Robinson always walked in front of the catcher to reach the batter's box. With so much riding on a player's performance, who can blame them for using whatever works?

Wade Boggs took the practice to new heights. On game days he always awoke at the same time. Before night games, he took batting practice at exactly 5:17PM and ran sprints at exactly 7:17PM. He took precisely 150 ground balls. Before every at bat he drew the Hebrew sign of life, n-chai, in the batter's box. He famously ate chicken before every game, accumulating some great recipes.

A Nebraska native, third baseman Wade Boggs spent most of his career in Boston, playing also as a Yankee and finishing his career as a Tampa Bay Devil Ray, hitting the first home run in the expansion team's history. An amazing hitter, he is the only player to reach the 3000 hit mark with a homerun. He is the only 20th century player to have seven consecutive 200-hit seasons. In his 18-year career he reached base safely an astounding 80% of his games.

Wade Boggs is listed on The Sporting News' list of the 100 Greatest Players. The Tampa Bay Devil Rays retired his number 12 and he was inducted into the Boston Red Sox Hall of Fame in 2004.

Wade Boggs was inducted into the National Baseball Hall of Fame in 2005

Herb Chicken Casserole
Wade Boggs

~~~~~~

*W*ade Boggs is known for his pre-game traditions, including eating chicken before every game. He generously shares one of his favorite chicken recipes from his book, *Fowl Tips.*

Preheat oven to 350 degrees.
2-3 pounds chicken, cut up
3 slices bacon
¼ cup butter
5 tablespoons flour
1 teaspoon salt
⅛ teaspoon pepper
¼ teaspoon celery salt
¾ teaspoon sage
¾ teaspoon thyme
2 cubes chicken bouillon, dissolved in cup hot water
2 cups milk

Fry bacon and drain on paper towels. Crumble bacon and set aside. Brown the chicken pieces in bacon fat. As chicken browns, place in 2½ quart casserole dish, sprinkling crumbled bacon over each layer.

After chicken is browned, melt butter in same skillet. Remove from heat and stir in flour, salt, pepper and spices. Stir in chicken broth and milk, stirring over low heat until thickened and smooth. Pour over chicken.

Cover casserole and bake in 350 degree oven for 1 to 1½ hours, uncovering the last 15 minutes.

> *Boggs may have the best hand-eye coordination of anyone I've ever seen.*
> —TED WILLIAMS, 1985

Jim Konstanty

An Otsego County favorite son, ace Philadelphia Phillies reliever "Big Jim" Konstanty was first and foremost a coach and, like any good coach, he lead his team by example. He kept his arm strong; his head clear and took the 1950 "Whiz Kids" to the World Series.

In that magical 1950 season, pitcher Jim Konstanty was 33, well-educated, older than most of his teammates, and the adoring husband of his wife, Mary, and their two children, Jim and Helen.

In 1950 Jim Konstanty was also called the "Fireman" for his reliability on the relief mound, pulling the Phillies out of the flames and saving 22 games. He appeared in a then-record 74 games, putting 16 in the win column.

An unlikely hero, Jim Konstanty's palm ball, a confounding change-up pitch, was inspired by his friend Andy Skinner, a Worcester, NY, mortician who just happened to like to play pool and bowl. Andy and Jim worked together to translate the spin on billiard and bowling balls into a baseball pitch.

Their efforts were rewarded, with Jim heralding the emerging relief pitcher specialty. That year Jim was named the National League's Most Valuable Player, the first reliever to be so honored, the Associated Press' Athlete of the Year and The Sporting News' Pitcher of the Year.

> *He could hit you between the eyes with his best pitch and not give you a headache.*
> —LEO DUROCHER

After retiring from a major league career spanning 1944-1956, Jim Konstanty returned to Otsego County. He was instrumental in expanding the Athletic Department at Hartwick College, serving as its director from 1968 -1972. The Konstanty Sporting Goods store was a fixture on Oneonta's Main Street for nearly 40 years.

Jim Konstanty's Favorite Apple Pie
Jim Konstanty

~~~~~~

*T*his is a Konstanty family recipe that Jim's wife, Mary Burlingame Konstanty, perfected through the years. The layers of butter are key.

Preheat oven to 425 degrees.

Two 9" piecrusts
4-5 large tart apples (Northern Spy or Cortland are recommended)
¾ cup sugar
1 teaspoon cinnamon
⅓ cup butter

Pare and core apples and cut into slices. In a 9" piecrust, place random dabs of butter on bottom of crust. Arrange sliced apples in an even layer on top of butter. Mix sugar & cinnamon and sprinkle part of this mixture over the first layer of apples. Dot with butter. Add another layer of apples and sprinkle this layer with rest of sugar and cinnamon mixture. Dot randomly with rest of butter. Moisten edge of filled crust with cold water.

Make a design in the top crust, to allow steam to escape. Mary's favorite is a bicycle spoke pattern. Cover apple mixture with top crust. Crimp edges by squeezing together where the top and bottom crusts meet at the pan's edge.

Place in oven for 10 minutes. Turn oven down to 350 degrees and bake for 30 minutes more. Bake until crust turns brown. Caution: if apples are juicy, place a "collecting dish" or foil under the pie pan to keep juice from burning on oven.

> *Good apple pies are a considerable part of our domestic happiness.*
> —JANE AUSTEN

Marcelo Balboa

Known for his bicycle kicks, Chicago-born Marcelo Balboa was twice named U.S. Soccer Athlete of the Year, in 1992 and 1994. He is one of only three US players, (along with Tab Ramos and Eric Wynalda), to appear in three World Cups, anchoring the American defense in 1990, 1994 and 1998.

Playing the majority of his career with the Colorado Rapids, Balboa competed six seasons and ranked as the team's all time leader in numerous categories. During the two seasons he played in the Mexican League he became the first US player to break the 100-cap barrier, recognizing his international play. One of his spectacular bicycle kicks, a goal for the Rapids in 2000 was named Major League Soccer Goal of the Year. In 2005 he was named to the Major League Soccer All-Time Best XI.

Marcelo Balboa was elected to the National Soccer Hall of Fame in 2005, on the first ballot.

More information about Marcello Balboa and other soccer greats is available at the National Soccer Hall of Fame, Oneonta, NY, www.soccerhall.org

> *I was always taught as a kid if you do something, do it right. If not, go do something else. For me, soccer was life.*
> —MARCELO BALBOA

Meat Empanadas
Marcelo Balboa

~~~~~~

This Latin American favorite comes from the Spanish empanar, meaning "to coat with bread." It is similar to a calzone.

Dough (much like pie dough, but softer with less cutting in).

2 cups flour	2½ tablespoons unsalted butter
½ cup lard	½ cup (about) iced water

Cut fats into flour, preferably using your fingertips. Fat streaks should be visible. Stir in enough water to form a ball and knead lightly.

Refrigerate dough, at least an hour. Take from refrigerator and let dough return to room temperature (about an hour).

Working with half the dough at a time, roll on floured surface to ⅛" thick. Cut into 6" circles. Continue cutting and re-rolling until all dough is used. You should have about 24 empanada circles.

Meat Filling

1 ½ pounds ground beef	1 small onion, chopped
2 hard-boiled eggs, diced	7 or 8 green olives, chopped
Salt and pepper to taste	2 dozen empanada circles (tapas)
Vegetable oil for deep frying	

Brown ground beef and drain excess fat. Add eggs, onions and olives. Salt and pepper to taste. Heat mixture.

Wet the edges of tapas dough with a little water. Put about 3 tablespoons meat mixture in center of dough. Fold in half and seal edges, crimping with the tines of a fork.

Deep fry empanadas at 450 degrees until both sides are lightly browned. Let cool and drain on paper towels.

Shredded mozzarella and lean ham may be substituted for the beef mixture.

Paul Molitor

*H*all of Famer Paul Molitor is a great contributor to those statistics baseball fans find irresistible. He is surely a favorite of the Society of American Baseball Researchers (SABR).

Paul Molitor is the only member of the 3000 hit club to reach that magical number with a triple. In 1987, he tied the Major League record of three steals in one inning. He is third in stealing home, following Jackie Robinson and Rod Carew. Paul is one of only three players to hit over .300 after age 40 (Ty Cobb and Sam Rice are the others). He has the highest career batting average of any designated hitter.

In 1987 Paul Molitor excited the baseball world when he pursued the most elusive of records, Joe DiMaggio's 56 game hitting streak. Paul hit safely in 39 games, the seventh longest streak in major league history. His streak ended, as DiMaggio's did, against the Cleveland Indians.

Those figures, plus his impressive lifetime statistics, including a .306 batting average and 504 stolen bases, resulted in the baseball writers electing him to the Hall of Fame on the first ballot with 85.2 % of the vote in 2004.

Paul Molitor is the only designated hitter in the National Baseball Hall of Fame. He and team mate Robin Yount are the only inductees to wear a Milwaukee Brewers cap.

> *Baseball fans love numbers. They love to swirl them around their mouths like Bordeaux wine.*
>
> —PAT CONROY

Maple Glazed Asparagus
Paul Molitor

*T*his beautiful recipe is a hit in anyone's league. Bright green and delicious, it can be made ahead of time. Serve cold or at room temperature as an appetizer or side dish. The versatile Maple Glaze can also be used on other vegetables.

Maple Glaze:
2 tablespoons cider vinegar
1 tablespoon Dijon mustard
½ teaspoon salt
¼ cup olive oil
¼ vegetable oil
3 tablespoons maple syrup
1 tablespoon fresh tarragon, snipped (or 1 teaspoon dried)

Whisk together all ingredients. Cover and refrigerate.

2 bunches fresh asparagus (about three pounds)
2 hardboiled eggs, chopped
½ cup toasted nuts* (pine nuts, pecans or walnuts)

Steam asparagus until just tender and bright green. Plunge into or rinse in cold water to halt cooking. Refrigerate.

To serve, arrange on platter. Pour glaze over spears and sprinkle the eggs and nuts over all.

* To toast nuts, place in dry frying pan over low to medium heat. Heat and stir constantly, for a few minutes, until fragrant and lightly toasted.

Hal Bodley

USA Today

~~~~~~~~~~~~~~~~~~~~~~~

You could make the case that sportswriter Hal Bodley has seen it all. He has reported history as it happened at dozens of World Series and All-Star games, numerous Super Bowls, Olympiads, and Triple Crown races. With a roster of awards and a lifetime of experience, Hal Bodley is widely respected as a leading authority on baseball. It is likely more accurate to state that he, surely and modestly, simply knows everything about the game.

His journalism career began in 1958 and he has been the baseball editor-columnist of *USA Today* since its first edition in 1982. Hal Bodley's column is read by millions of subscribers. He is also the bestselling author of *The Team That Wouldn't Die,* about the 1980 Philadelphia Phillies, and *Countdown to Cobb,* about Pete Rose's pursuit of Ty Cobb's all-time career hits record.

Sporting events provide mileposts in our lives. We remember the World Series games heard on a transistor radio smuggled into school. We recall an Olympic moment that made us dewy-eyed with national pride, or the year an unbelievable steed, to the astonishment of all but the dark horse, won a jewel of the Triple Crown.

For nearly half a century, Hal Bodley has served as our national chronicler. Reporting baseball and sporting events from the small to the sweeping, his deft pen has illuminated our memories.

Ham Finale
Lima Bean Soup
Hal Bodley

*T*his "Sportswriter's Favorite" is Hal's mother's recipe. It came to *Home Plate,* via Hal's wife, Pat. *Home Plate* thanks all the Bodleys for their collective effort.

1 ham bone (leftovers from a half or whole boiled or baked ham)
2 cups diced cooked ham
1 6-ounce can tomato paste
1 teaspoon salt
½ teaspoon red pepper
⅛ teaspoon black pepper
2 pounds dried lima beans
1 cup raw macaroni
6 quarts water

Put ham bone, trimmings and seasonings into a large pot with the six quarts of water and bring to a rolling boil. Add tomato paste and washed lima beans. Reduce heat, cover and cook until beans are soft. Add macaroni and cook about ten minutes, until tender.

Makes 8 quarts, and can be frozen.

Some things in life you just can't buy- like great memories.
—DON DRYSDALE

Rollie Fingers

A 1992 National Baseball Hall of Fame Inductee and one of the best relievers to ever save a game, Rollie Fingers may be best known for his handlebar moustache. People on the periphery of baseball may not know he played for the Oakland Athletics, the San Diego Padres and the Milwaukee Brewers, they may not even know of his astounding pitching abilities, but they probably recognize those two perfect curls above his lip.

Growing the moustache was a Charlie Finlay marketing ploy, paying each of the Oakland A's $300 for the addition. Rollie Fingers accepted the bonus and, like his pitching, he did his a little better and more flawlessly than everyone else. His control, his durability and his moustache became his trademarks, on and off the field.

Baseball commentators are hard-pressed to identify any shortcomings in Finger's play. He retired as the greatest relief artist in baseball history after a 17 year career, highlighted with a host of honors, including both the American League Most Valuable Player and the Cy Young Awards while playing with the Brewers in 1981. When he hung up his cleats in 1985 he held the major league record for the most career saves (341) and World Series saves (7). He is among The Sporting News 100 Greatest Baseball Players.

Rollie Fingers is a familiar face, in Cooperstown and at many baseball venues. You can't miss the moustache.

> *A fellow has to have faith in God above and Rollie Fingers in the bullpen.*
> —ALVIN DARK

Apple of My Eye Salad
Rollie Fingers

*T*his salad features New York apples and is a wonderful mélange of contrasting flavors and textures. It is a perfect start to a dinner party or it can be expanded for a lunch or dinner salad by adding cooked poultry, ham or shrimp.

Salad

6 to 8 cups of mixed greens

2 sweet eating apples

Salt and pepper to taste

½ cup walnut or pecan halves

¼ cup chopped fresh Italian (flat leaf) parsley

8 ounces crumbled blue cheese

Rinse and spin greens and place in large salad bowl. Add nuts, parsley, and blue cheese. These steps may be done a few hours ahead of time. Refrigerate if not serving right away.

Immediately prior to serving, cut and core apples (no need to peel them; the color is too pretty to lose) and slice. Add to the salad greens and toss with Apple Cider Dressing.

Apple Cider Dressing

¼ cup apple cider vinegar

2 teaspoons Dijon-style mustard

Salt and pepper

¼ cup olive oil

Whisk ingredients in a bowl. This dressing seems a bit tangy at first, but it mellows beautifully when complementing the sweet apples and the blue cheese in the salad.

Brooks Robinson

*I*n the classic comedy *Sleepless in Seattle,* Annie Reed's (Meg Ryan) and Sam Baldwin's (Tom Hanks) romance would never have blossomed atop the Empire State Building had he disagreed with her introductory contention that Brooks Robinson "was the best third baseman ever."

The Annie Reed character is hardly alone in her opinion. Not only is Brooks Robinson generally acclaimed as the greatest defensive third-baseman of all time, the Arkansas native is also recognized as one of the most decent, generous players ever to don a uniform.

Brooks Robinson played his entire 23-season career (1955-1977), at third base, with the Baltimore Orioles. On a team known for their superior defensive play (including the graceful center fielding of team mate Paul Blair), Brooks Robinson's incomparable style earned him a slew of records and the moniker "the human vacuum cleaner."

Despite his opinion that he was "an average player," Brooks Robinson's consistent and frequently spectacular plays won him 16 consecutive Gold Gloves, a record only he and pitcher Jim Kaat hold. He was the starting third baseman on 15 consecutive All-Star teams and he holds the lifetime record for third baseman for most games (2,870), best fielding percentage (.971), most putouts (2,697), most assists (6,205), and most double plays (618). That's some definition of "average."

Brooks Calbert Robinson was inducted into the National Baseball Hall of Fame his first year of eligibility (1983) with a whopping 92% of the votes. He is on the Sporting News' list of the 100 Greatest Baseball Players, and was elected to the Major League Baseball All-Century Team. Fellow Hall of Famer George Brett chose his uniform number five in honor of Brooks Robinson.

> *Whether you want to or not, you do serve as a role model. People will always put more faith in baseball players than anyone else.*
> —BROOKS ROBINSON

Buffalo Chicken Dip

Brooks Robinson

~~~~~~

Buffalo Wings are an original creation of the Anchor Bar in Buffalo, New York. They are the unbreaded chicken wing parts (flats and drums), deep-fried and coated in a sauce of cayenne pepper sauce, white vinegar, butter, garlic and salt. The heat can vary with the addition of more cayenne pepper or other spices. Buffalo Wings are traditionally served with celery sticks and blue cheese dressing.

This easy dip uses the same flavorful ingredients as traditional Buffalo Wings, plus the smooth texture and pleasantly sharp bite of New York cheddar cheese. As Brooks says, "it's like eating wings without the bones".

Preheat oven to 350 degrees

6 chicken breasts
1 jar of Marie's Blue Cheese Dressing
1 (8 ounce) package of cream cheese, softened
2 cups of New York State shredded cheddar cheese
1 cup of Frank's Hot Sauce

Poach chicken breast until cooked, about 20-25 minutes. When cool enough to handle, shred the meat.

In a large bowl, combine the blue cheese dressing, cream cheese, shredded cheddar and hot sauce. Add the shredded chicken and mix together thoroughly. Transfer to an ovenproof casserole and bake until hot and bubbly, about 25 minutes

Serve with celery sticks, tortilla chips or crackers.

> *I will become a left-handed hitter to keep the ball away from that guy.*
> HALL OF FAMER JOHNNY BENCH
> ON BROOKS ROBINSON

VEGETABLES,
SIDES,
AND SAUCES

McCoy's Pure Raw Honey

I eat my peas with honey
I've done it all my life
It makes them taste quite funny
But it keeps them on my knife
—JOHN McCOY'S MOTHER

McCoy's Pure Raw Honey began in 1962 as a junior high school project. It has been humming ever since, with the current honey house opening in 1986.

McCoy's makes a wonderful stop on day trips in Otsego County. Watch the bees in John's observation hive and see the remarkable steps nature takes getting honey from blossom to jar. Field trips and groups are welcomed. Please call for an appointment.

Liquid, creamed, crystallized and comb honeys are available in the delightful bee-themed McCoy Bee House gift shop. Set halfway up Franklin Mountain, the views are as sweet as the honey. You'll also find honey candy, maple products, gifts and beekeeping supplies.

TO GET TO McCOY'S HONEY
From I-88 north, take Exit 14 at Oneonta. From I-88 south, take Exit 15. From either exit go south on State Highway 28, toward Delhi. You are ascending Franklin Mountain. Halfway up, where the passing lane begins, you'll find McCoy's Pure Raw Honey, the first drive on the right.

John McCoy
307 State Highway 28
Oneonta, NY 13820
607-432-0605

Open Year Round
Thursdays and Saturdays
Noon–5PM

Honey Cranberry Sauce
McCoy's Pure Raw Honey

*T*his beautiful red sauce makes a dazzling dip for egg rolls and Chinese dumplings. It is equally as good slathered on ribs and the honey-cranberry base makes it a natural accompaniment for turkey or chicken. If you're good at canning make extra to have on hand for hostess' gifts.

1 cup fresh or frozen cranberries
¾ cup honey
½ cup ketchup
½ cup red wine vinegar

1 tablespoon lemon juice
1 tablespoon Worcestershire sauce
¼ teaspoon black pepper

Optional: Add ¼ teaspoon red pepper flakes (more or less, according to taste,) if you like heat along with the sweet/tangy flavor combination.

Put all ingredients into a 2-quart saucepan and bring to a gentle boil.
Cover and cook 10-15 minutes, stirring frequently.

Uncover and continue to simmer another 10-15 minutes, stirring often, until desired thickness. The sauce will thicken slightly more when cool.

Correct the balance of flavors by adding more honey, vinegar and pepper to your liking.
Makes about 1½ cups. Store in the refrigerator in a covered jar. It should keep about a month.

Cooking with Honey Tips
To substitute honey for sugar use equal amounts but reduce other recipe liquids by one-quarter cup.
When baking with honey, reduce oven temperature by 25 degrees.
When measuring honey, coat spoon or cup with oil or butter to make clean up easier.
Cakes and cookies made with honey stay moist longer

Fly Creek General Store

*T*he Fly Creek General Store is local products central, and quite possibly the linchpin of life in Fly Creek. From local brews to bait, truly farm fresh eggs (the whites stand up like Jell-O) to Fly Creek fashions, syrup and honey to handmade brooms, no trip to Otsego County is complete without a stop at the Fly Creek General Store.

A brief historical aside: Fly Creek has no more of the pesky critters than anywhere else in Upstate New York. The "Fly" portion of their name comes from the area's many Dutch settlers and their word "vlie," which means "marsh." *Home Plate* thanks Fly Creek writer Jim Atwell for the clarification.

Most of life's crucial needs are met at the Fly Creek General Store. Morning java, auto fuel, the community news, bundles of firewood, handmade sandwiches to go with their homemade salads or a gallon of milk are all available at this friendly place.

Located at the slightly skewed Fly Creek four corners. The Fly Creek General Store welcomes customers Monday – Saturday from 6AM to 9PM, and on Sundays from 7AM to 6PM.

Tom Bouton
The Fly Creek General Store
State Route 28 (three miles north of Cooperstown)
Fly Creek, NY 13337
607-547-7274

Drawing by Anne Geddes-Atwell

Apple Slices in Cider Sauce

Fly Creek General Store

~~~~~~

*T*his is a lovely side dish, beautifully enhancing pork or poultry for dinner, or equally delicious at breakfast with sausage and pancakes.

4 to 6 New York State cooking apples
2 tablespoons butter
1 teaspoon cinnamon
2 tablespoons sugar
A handful of dried, sweetened cranberries for color, if desired

1 cup apple cider (leftover mulled cider is fine)
2 teaspoons cornstarch

Pare, core and peel apples. Cut into chunky slices. Melt butter in good-sized, heavy frying pan and add apple slices. Gently sauté for a few minutes, until apples begin to soften.

Gently stir in sugar and cinnamon. Add cranberries, if using, and continue to cook.

Place cornstarch in the bottom of a glass measuring cup. Add a splash of cold cider and stir to dissolve cornstarch. Add the remaining cider, stir thoroughly and add to apples.

Continue to cook over medium heat until cider sauce is thickened. If too thick, add more cider. If too thin, continue to cook apples until desired consistency is achieved.

This recipe lends itself to your own taste. Increase or reduce sugar and spices to suit yourself.

Essential Elements

*E*ssential Elements is a tranquil oasis in the heart of Cooperstown's activities. This full service day spa offers exactly what you need to relax, beautify and give yourself the attention you deserve. After a hectic day of work or travel, head to this pampering haven to calm jangled senses, quiet frazzled nerves, and refresh your spirit.

Owner Robin Gray has created the perfect retreat of rejuvenating body treatments amid the atmosphere of a sophisticated boutique. You'll find select clothing, accessories and marvelous jewelry, as well as one-of-a-kind gifts, local artwork and Bare Essentials cosmetics.

The professional Essential Elements staff offers an array of hand and foot treatments, massage, body scrubs and wraps, waxing, facials and make-up services. Gift Certificates Available. Reservations recommended.

Make sure to stroll through the soothing ambience of the Essential Elements "secret garden". This elm-shaded hideaway draws you in with its lush greenery, colorful flora and gurgling pool and fountain.

Shop online at www.essentialelementsdayspa.com

A shop for the spirit and an oasis for the soul.

Doubleday Parking Lot
137 Main Street
Cooperstown, NY 13326
607-547-9432
800-437-3265
FAX: 607-547-5791
www.essentialelementsdayspa.com

Be sure to enquire about the Apartment at Doubleday. This lovely two-bedroom apartment is available by the day or week.

Autumn Red Potato Casserole

Essential Elements Day Spa and Boutique

Like a good massage, this delicious casserole is warm and comforting.

8 medium red potatoes
3 cups New York State cheddar cheese (sharp or mild), grated
¼ cup butter
1 pint sour cream
⅓ cup green onions
¼ teaspoon salt
1 teaspoon pepper

Boil potatoes until tender, but still firm.
Let potatoes cool and then peel and dice.

In a heavy saucepan, combine cheese and butter over low heat. Stir until cheese melts. Remove from heat and stir in sour cream, onions, salt and pepper.

Pour sauce over potatoes and gently fold together. Transfer to casserole dish, dot with butter and bake for 30-40 minutes at 350 degrees. Excellent with pork, chicken or beef.

> *I have made a lot of mistakes falling in love, and regretted most of them, but never the potatoes that went with them.*
> —NORA EPHRON, *HEARTBURN*

Danny's Market

Danny's Market has been featured on The Food Network and in Country Living magazine for a throng of fresh, delicious reasons.

Established in Cooperstown for decades, mornings start with Danny's coffee and fresh baked goods as surely as the sun comes up over Otsego Lake. Tantalizing aromas meet you at the door and pleasant conversation greets you from the counter. Regulars and newcomers feel equally at home at Danny's. Linger over the lunch menu as you try to choose from Alice's multitude of fresh salads, soothing soups and appetizing sandwiches. Hint: Try Aged in Caves.

Sergio's fragrant artisan breads and the New York Times are reason enough to stop at Danny's, but imported cheese, local jams, specialty foods, microbrews and an appetizing deli case tempt you further.

Danny's fabulous food is also available at Glimmerglass State Park. Enjoy their fine fare at the waterside concession to make your perfect day on Lake Otsego completely satisfying.

Catering, gift baskets and gift certificates available.

Eat in or call for take out or delivery.

Alice and Sergio Gaviria
92 Main Street
Cooperstown, NY 13326
607-547-4053

Roasted Farmers' Market Vegetables
Danny's Market

Many Cooperstonians carry out a wonderful ritual every summer Saturday. Start with a morning trip to the Farmers' Market for the vendors' best goods and friendly conversation. Then cross Main Street to Danny's Market for great bread, cheese and specialty foods. Turn the corner at Pioneer for a fine bottle from Cooperstown Wine and Spirits. The weekend is set for good meals and good friends.

This recipe relies on your interpretation. Have fun!

Preheat oven to 350 degrees.

Ingredients:
A variety of farm fresh vegetables, based on color, quality and texture:
Orange, yellow and red peppers, green zucchini, broccoli, yellow squash and mushrooms are good choices.

An assortment of herbs: Dill, oregano, basil, chives, sage, parsley and thyme all work beautifully.

Olive Oil
Salt, pepper and garlic powder

Cut vegetables into chunks and finely chop herbs.
In a large bowl, mix vegetables and herbs together with olive oil, coating lightly, and generously sprinkle with salt, pepper and garlic powder.
Place on cookie sheet and bake about 20 minutes, until vegetables are desired softness. Arrange on a platter and serve at room temperature.
These prepared vegetables are great to have on hand to add to salads or soups or grilled sandwiches.

The TePee

At the northeastern gateway to Otsego County stands a four-story tepee. Try to travel the Scenic Route 20 Byway and not stop at this vestige of the ingenious businesses that dotted American roadways prior to the interstate system.

Built in 1950, The TePee is located on what was once known as the Cherry Valley Turnpike, the first divided roadway in the country. Across from the Tepee is one of the finest photo opportunities Upstate. This panoramic view of the Mohawk Valley extends 90 miles north to the Adirondack Mountains.

The TePee features great browsing. Select from Native made gifts, Minnetonka moccasins, sterling silver, drums, flutes, books and Native American music. Be sure to stop by TePee Pete's Chow Wagon.

The TePee is easy to find on Route 20 from Albany on your way to Cherry Valley, Cooperstown or Oneonta. Stop, take a photo and have a good time. Like Mount Everest, go just because it's there.

Hours:
July and August: Open seven days a week, 10AM-6PM, Sunday closing at 5PM
April – October: Same hours, closed Tuesdays
November and December:
Monday, Friday and Saturday 10AM-5PM, Sunday 11AM-4PM
January, February and March: Open by appointment, weather permitting

Dale and Donna Latella
7632 US Highway 20
Cherry Valley, NY 13320
607-264-3987
www.thetepee.net

Three Sisters Succotash
The TePee

~~~~~~

Corn, beans and squash (the three sisters) were the principal foods of the Haudenosaunee (Iroquois) people. They are called the three sisters because they grow in harmony with each other. The corn provides the stalk the beans need to climb. The beans fix the nitrogen in the soil that the corn depletes. The squash grows low to the ground with a broad leaf that helps keep moisture in the soil.

Preheat oven to 400 degrees

1 butternut squash
2 cups sweet corn kernels
2 cups cooked dried lima beans, or fresh or frozen beans
1½ cups vegetable broth or water
¼ cup bear or venison fat (butter is fine)
1 large onion, diced
2 bell peppers, diced (your choice of color)
Salt and pepper to taste

Split squash and remove seeds. Place cut side down in a baking dish and add a little water. Bake about 30 minutes, until squash is tender. Remove squash and let cool. When cool, peel and cut into 1" cubes.

In large saucepan, melt butter and sauté onions and peppers until onions begin to caramelize. Add corn, beans, squash and broth. Bring to a boil and cook until the liquid reduces by half. Salt and pepper to taste.

Anne Geddes–Atwell
Graphics and Book Design

*I*llustrator Anne Geddes-Atwell chooses an object, a significant person or animal from Jim Atwell's book *From Fly Creek: Celebrating Life in Leatherstocking Country* and her soft pencil makes them tangible and animate. Her uncluttered and captivating drawings portray the spirit and essence of the rich, daily life at Stone Mill Acres, the Fly Creek farm she and Jim nurture.

Anne's illustrations put an appealing, unpretentious face on her husband Jim's reflections, gracing many pages of his book. Through her perceptions you'll see important Fly Creek area landmarks, meet the Atwell's pig, Cholesterella, and view portraits of people who have influenced Jim's and Anne's journey.

The charm of Anne's pictures reach far beyond Fly Creek. Her Strawberry Picking Baskets, Doubleday Field, murderess Eva Coo's roadster, a variety of animal drawings and many others are available in digital print versions on archival paper to enhance your home. Purchase them on line and throughout the area.

Anne Geddes-Atwell
134 Allison Road
Fly Creek, NY 13337
(607) 547-5895
www.JimAtwell.com

Drawing by Anne Geddes-Atwell

Apple Lemon Coleslaw

Anne Geddes-Atwell
Graphics and Book Design

~~~~~~~~~~~~~~~~~~~~~~~~~~

*T*he Atwell's table is usually laden with vegetables from their garden. Both cabbages and carrots grow beautifully there, and apples are plentiful in Upstate New York. This refreshing lower calorie version of coleslaw is not lower in flavor.

1 small cabbage, finely sliced (8 cups)
2 apples, chopped
2 carrots, shredded

1/3 cup mayonnaise (light mayo is OK)
1 tablespoon sugar
2 tablespoons minced onion
1 teaspoon grated lemon rind
2 tablespoons fresh lemon juice
¼ teaspoon salt
¼ teaspoon pepper

Combine cabbage, apples, and carrots in a large bowl. Whisk together mayonnaise with the remaining ingredients. Toss with cabbage mixture. Cover and chill at least 1 hour. Makes four servings.

Recipe courtesy of Mary Margaret Kuhn

> *... there may be two or three*
> *Apples I didn't pick upon some bough.*
> *But I am done with apple-picking now.*
> *Essence of winter sleep is on the night,*
> *The scent of apples; I am drowsing off.*
> — ROBERT FROST

From Fly Creek: Celebrating Life in Leatherstocking Country
By Jim Atwell

W hat Jim Atwell sees, he perceives; when he listens, he hears; and the life he lives in Fly Creek, NY, he embraces.

In his book, *From Fly Creek: Celebrating Life in Leatherstocking Country,* Jim reflects on his Upstate transformation from a suit and tie college dean to a denim and sweatshirt farmer. He recalls his experiences (some humorous, some heartrending, all joyously human) that brought him and his artist wife, Anne, to the distinctive hamlet of Fly Creek, NY.

Jim's writing evokes the spirited and eloquent pens of E.B. White and Mark Twain. His reverent recollections of his first stumbling steps as a farmer and Arrie Hecox, the older mentor who took him under his wing, his empathy with life and death on the farm and on the most profoundly personal level, his respect for his neighbors and their (and now his) history are splendidly crafted in three dimensions. Jim's journey and passages are as touchingly relevant to city dwellers and suburbanites as they are to his fellow Upstaters.

Reading Jim Atwell is as warm and comfortable as wrapping yourself in a quilt in front of a generous fire.

Jim Atwell
134 Allison Road
Fly Creek, NY 13337
(607) 547-5895
www.JimAtwell.com

Drawing by Anne Geddes-Atwell

Broccoli Cranberry Slaw
Jim Atwell

~~~~~~

*T*his is a pretty version of what the original Dutch settlers called "koosla." Kool means "cabbage" and sla means "salad." The diverse textures, colors and complementary flavors make this slaw a year-round favorite.

4 cups finely sliced cabbage
2 cups broccoli florets, blanched
1¼ cups fresh or dried cranberries
1 small onion, minced
8 slices bacon, cooked and crumbled (optional)
1 cup raisins
1 cup coarsely chopped walnuts
⅓ cup sugar
2 tablespoons cider vinegar
1 cup mayonnaise (low fat is fine)

Toss broccoli, cranberries, cabbage, onion, raisins, bacon (if using) and nuts together in salad bowl.

Blend sugar, vinegar and mayonnaise in small bowl. Add to salad and toss gently. Cover and refrigerate 20 minutes to blend flavors.

Blanching means a quick plunge into boiling water for one to two minutes. Drain in a colander and rinse with cold water to arrest cooking.

Clark Sports Center

*T*he Clark Sports Center facility defines excellence in fitness. It continues Cooperstown's tradition of encouraging healthy activity, beginning when Alfred Clark opened the first gymnasium in 1891. The original facility was located on Main Street, where you'll now find the National Baseball Hall of Fame and Museum's administrative offices. Unusual for the times, women were encouraged to participate fully at the nineteenth century gymnasium. The present Clark Sports Center opened in 1986.

More than just a gym, the modern Clark Sports Center offers their patrons a broad selection of calorie burning, endorphin producing, and muscle-toning activities. Their complete exercise menu includes such diverse choices as racquetball, bowling, tennis, sand volleyball, rock wall climbing, aerobics and spinning classes. Also available: soccer fields, diving and swimming pools, saunas, basketball, yoga, personal trainers and much more. The Clark Sports Center offers something sure to appeal to everyone.

Men, children and women are (still) encouraged to participate fully.

Day passes are available.

For information about memberships and programs contact the Clark Sports Center.

124 County Highway 52
PO Box 80
Cooperstown, NY 13326
607-547-2800
www.clarksportscenter.com

Mediterranean Broccoli
Clark Sports Center

*T*his is an outstanding use of broccoli. The piquant ingredients make your taste buds stand up and salute. Better still, it is served at room temperature, allowing you to make it a couple of hours ahead. To enjoy the best color, serve the broccoli the same day it is prepared.

1 healthy bunch of broccoli (about a pound)
3 tablespoons olive oil
1 tablespoon red wine vinegar
2 tablespoons lemon juice (about a half lemon)
1 tablespoon capers, well drained
½ cup chopped Greek olives, or your favorite olives

Fill a two-quart saucepan about half full of water, enough to cover broccoli spears. Bring water to boil.

Cut broccoli stalks into spears. Discard any leaves and tough lower stems. Add broccoli spears to boiling water and cook, uncovered, 4 to 5 minutes. Spears should be tender, but firm, bright green and appealing.

Drain and put in serving dish. In small bowl, whisk together olive oil, red wine vinegar and lemon juice. Pour over broccoli and carefully toss. Season with salt and freshly ground pepper, as desired.

Add the olives and capers and gently turn the broccoli spears.

Be sure to cover the pot when bringing water to a boil;
it will boil much more quickly.

All and All Emporium

Take a stroll up Main Street in Cooperstown and turn left onto Railroad Avenue. Like Dorothy finding the Emerald City, here you'll find the All & All Emporium. This gem of a shop is a tribute to a timeless tradition of classic grace and whimsy, a marketplace where style and ideas meet at the crossroads of reasonable prices.

Owner Linda Parmalee's custom-made, one of a kind capes, scarves and dusters have to be seen. Take home something unique!

"Specialty" outfits and fashion accessories are the cornerstone for customer satisfaction. The clothing is unique, stylish and cosmopolitan. Linda's accessories, her hats, scarves and jewelry are incomparable.

If you are shopping for an ensemble for a special event, or just browsing for something new, at The All & All Emporium you are the event.

Linda will tend to your needs with the genuine hospitality and old-fashioned personal attention.

If you are of the mistaken impression that Cooperstown is all baseball shops, treat yourself to a visit to the All and All Emporium. It is a treasure trove of fashion and gifts for all seasons.

A Timeless Tradition of Classic Grace

Please call for seasonal hours or for a special appointment.
Linda Parmalee
21 Railroad Avenue
Cooperstown, NY 13326
607-437-1989
www.chamberofcommerce/allandall/

Confetti Orzo
All and All Emporium

Reminiscent of those boxed side dishes that end in "-roni," but so much better. This recipe is practically as quick, better tasting and healthier because it contains fresh vegetables and you control the salt content. The variations are limited only by your taste and imagination.

Orzo actually means "barley" in Italian, but in the United States this quick cooking and versatile pasta is known for its rice-like shape.

1 tablespoon butter
1 or 2 carrots, chopped
2 cloves garlic, chopped
4 cups chicken or vegetable broth
Salt and pepper to taste

2 cups uncooked orzo
3 cups fresh spinach, chopped
3 tablespoons Parmesan cheese
1 tablespoon fresh basil, chopped

Melt butter in 3-quart saucepan.

Sauté carrots and garlic in butter until carrots begin to soften. Add orzo and stir in broth. Bring to a boil, then reduce heat and simmer uncovered, until broth is absorbed.

Stir in spinach, cheese, salt, pepper and basil. The heat of the pasta will wilt the spinach, making it an appetizing bright green. The orange flecks of carrot, the spinach and the white orzo make the "confetti."

Variations: Keeping the other ingredients constant, change the broth flavor, vegetable and herbs for numerous versions of the same delectable theme. This is an excellent way to use leftover vegetables. Stir them in at the same time you would the spinach.

The National Baseball Hall of Fame and Museum

"Do you think the kid has a shot at Cooperstown?"

Any baseball announcer might ask that question as he watches a promising rookie steal second, pitch a deadly curve or hit a ball into the stratosphere. And when he asks the question, the world knows when he says, "Cooperstown" that he means The National Baseball Hall of Fame, so synonymous are the two.

The National Baseball Hall of Fame is the dignified steward of America's priceless game. Since 1939, historians and baseball fans have entrusted the Hall to preserve baseball's treasured artifacts and the American spirit they symbolize.

There is an almost palpable reverence as visitors gaze at an historic ball or a Hall of Famer's plaque. Recollections of games attended, astounding plays witnessed or heartbreaking losses endured, bubble to the surface. Unlike any other game or pastime, baseball spins threads that weave personal reminiscences and America's cultural tapestry.

The stately National Baseball Hall of Fame, with its noble respect for the game and all of those and all of us who have been a part of it, is a national treasure.

The National Baseball Hall of Fame and Museum is open seven days a week year-round, with the exception of Thanksgiving Day, Christmas Day and New Year's Day. Please call or visit their website for seasonal hours.

National Baseball Hall of Fame and Museum
25 Main Street
Cooperstown, NY 13326
607-547-7200
Toll Free: 888- HALL-OF-FAME or 888-425-5633
FAX: 607-547-2044
www.baseballhalloffame.org

Corn and Tomato Harvest Salad
The National Baseball Hall of Fame and Museum

~~~~~~~~~~~~~~~~~~~~~~~~~~~~~~~

*T*he sublime combination of these two all-American foods hits it out of the park. Like many recipes in *Home Plate,* this side dish is open to interpretation. You may vary the ratio of corn to tomatoes, add more cilantro if you like it, or omit it entirely if you don't. It is best served at room temperature, making it perfect for "bring a dish to share" gatherings.

P.S. It's a perfect accompaniment to hot dogs.

6 ears of fresh New York sweet corn, barely cooked (leftover is fine)
1 green pepper, diced
1 red bell pepper, diced
1 to 2 cups tomatoes, seeded and diced
1 cup minced onion, red or New York Empire Sweet
½ cup olive oil
2 teaspoons chili powder
1 teaspoon ground cumin
4 tablespoons fresh cilantro, chopped
3 tablespoons cider vinegar
Salt and pepper to taste

Cut corn kernels from cob. You should have about three cups.

Briefly sauté onions in ¼ cup of the olive oil. Add the chili powder and cumin and cook about minute longer. Cool.

Combine the corn, peppers, tomatoes and onion. Add the cilantro and vinegar, the other ¼ cup of olive oil and salt and pepper to taste. Serve in a beautiful bowl and enjoy the taste of summer.

> *It's difficult to think anything but pleasant thoughts while eating a homegrown tomato.*
> — LEWIS GRIZZARD

Brooks' House of Bar-B-Que

One of Otsego County's favorite homegrown success stories, Brooks' Bar-B-Que has been serving succulent chicken and ribs since 1951.

To find Brooks' just follow your nose. Entering Oneonta on Route 7, follow the smoky aroma wafting from Brook's 38 foot charcoal pit, the largest in the eastern United States. The Brooks' compound includes their 300-seat restaurant, the sauce production plant and the Brooks' Roost Banquet Room.

Now under the watchful tutelage of the third generation, Ryan and Beth Brooks and their faithful employees serve about 1100 people on any given weekend. And that hive of activity near their front door? It's just the usual crowd at the Brook's takeout window. Their catering operation takes the Brooks' Bar-B-Que show on the road to some 450 locations during the summer.

Take home the taste of Brooks with their own sauces and marinades. Brooks' famous barbeque sauce, speidie sauce, chicken marinade and seasoning can be ordered online, by mail or found at their restaurant and area retailers.

Brooks' House of Bar-B-Que
5560 State Highway 7, just off I-88 at exit 16
Oneonta, NY 13820
607-432-1782
800-498-2445
Fax: 607-432-2665

To order Brooks' sauce or for information:
www.brooksbbq.com
info@brooksbbq.com

Sauce Serving Ideas
Brooks' House of Bar-B-Que

Brooks' recipes are carefully guarded secrets, but they shared some best uses for their exceptional sauces and marinades.

Please do not to re-use sauces once they have been used as marinades and in contact with raw meats. Keep marinating meats refrigerated until cooked.

Barbeque Sauce—excellent added to ground meat when making hamburgers, meatloaf or meatballs. Brooks' Bar-B-Que sauce also adds a spicy kick to potato or macaroni salad and is an exceptional base for soups, stews and chili.

Speidie Marinade—a bottle of this classic Upstate New York sauce marinates two pounds of cubed chicken, beef or pork. Marinate for 24 hours, place on skewers and grill. Speidie sauce also marinates whole steaks.

Chicken Sauce—an excellent basting sauce for poultry and very good as a short time marinade for chicken or venison. Do not marinade meat in this sauce more than a few hours.

Meat Seasoning (Dry rub)—This is really an all-purpose seasoning, good rubbed on raw meat prior to grilling, but also a spicy addition to pasta sauces, vegetables and rice recipes.

Dipping—Brooks' Bar-B-Que and Chicken Sauces are wonderful for dipping. Simply warm and use for dipping sandwiches, French fries, seafood and meats.

SUNY College at Oneonta

SUNY-Oneonta is one of 64 campuses in the State University of New York system. Set in the scenic Oneonta hills, more than 5400 students are enrolled at this four-year university.

Established in 1889 as a state normal school to train teachers, the College at Oneonta became a founding member of the SUNY system in 1948. Among the 30 buildings on the 250-acre main campus is the James M. Milne Library. This expansive structure holds the second largest library collection among the SUNY Colleges of Arts and Sciences.

SUNY-Oneonta also maintains 2600 acres at the Biological Field Station and the Cooperstown Graduate Program in Museum Studies on Otsego Lake in Cooperstown. They also have the 284-acre College Camp, about two miles from the Oneonta campus.

SUNY-Oneonta offers undergraduate and master's degrees in liberal arts, teaching and sciences and is proud of their 18:1 student/ faculty ratio. SUNY-Oneonta is the home of the Red Dragons.

SUNY College at Oneonta
Ravine Parkway
Oneonta, NY 13820
607-436-3500
www.oneonta.edu

Salt Potato Salad

SUNY College at Oneonta

Salt potatoes originated in Syracuse, NY, which once a major salt production center. They are commonly sold throughout the Upstate area in five-pound bags; 4 ¼ pounds of new white potatoes with ¾ pound salt. Boiled in the briny water, the potatoes are wonderfully flavorful and versatile. They are also featured at New York fairs throughout the summer. Boil a bag of salt potatoes and keep them on hand in the refrigerator for potato salads, home fries or adding to soups.

This potato salad is served cold or at room temperature. It has no mayonnaise or eggs, making it preferable for picnics and summer dining.

About half a bag of boiled salt potatoes, cooked and cooled
1 large sweet New York onion, thinly sliced
¼ cup olive oil
3 tablespoons vinegar
1 clove garlic, finely minced
½ teaspoon salt
¼ teaspoon black pepper
1-2 tablespoons sugar
1 tablespoon finely chopped parsley

Slice potatoes in ¼" slices. Place in a large bowl with onion slices. In a small bowl, whisk remaining ingredients together. Pour over potatoes and onions and toss lightly. Season to taste with salt and pepper and refrigerate. For best flavor, refrigerate overnight. Add lightly cooked green beans or asparagus, or cooked, crumbled bacon for additional color and texture, if desired.

Triple Play Café

*J*ust a line drive's distance from the National Baseball Hall of Fame, the Triple Play Café's casual fare is a solid hit. You can slide into the comfort of their home style cooking for three square meals a day.

Owner Pat Governale's pride in his Main Street diner shows in his homemade rolls and baked goods and in his "in house" coleslaw and potato salads.

Traditional breakfasts, deli favorites for lunch and informal family dinners make Triple Play a great solution for the recurring question, "Where do we eat?"

Open for breakfast, lunch and dinner, Triple Play's daily specials are featured on the blackboard in the front window. Don't miss Pat's from scratch soups and cornbread.

TRIPLE PLAY DELIVERS!
Take out and catering also available

64 Main Street
Cooperstown, NY 13326
607-547-1395
Fax: 607-547-1355

Good **FOOD**

Stewed Zucchini
Triple Play Café

*W*hat to do with all the beautiful vegetables and herbs you just couldn't resist at the market? This simple, colorful recipe uses lots of them!

2 green zucchini, sliced in ¼ inch slices
1 yellow zucchini, sliced in ¼ inch slices
3 red, ripe garden tomatoes, diced
1 small onion, julienned (cut in matchstick pieces)
4 cloves garlic, chopped
1 tablespoon each: fresh oregano, basil, and parsley, coarsely chopped
1 bay leaf
1 tablespoon olive oil
1 tablespoon butter

Heat butter and olive oil in large skillet over medium heat. Sauté all ingredients, except tomatoes, 10-15 minutes. Gently stir in tomatoes, cover and cook on low to medium heat about 15 minutes more.

The Coca Cola Bottling Company of New York, Inc.

~~~~~~~~~~~~~~~~~~

*I*f there is one logo that defines the American icon it is surely Coca-Cola. The famous swirled "C" and red and white color combination is known in every pocket of the United States and every corner of the globe. Coca-Cola Enterprises, the world's largest bottler, makes sure the diverse selection of the Coca-Cola Company's beverages are available everywhere.

From the early days of Coke, the bottling, marketing and distribution has been a separate entity from the Coca-Cola Company. John Pemberton created his still secret Coca-Cola syrup in 1886. By 1901 the first bottling franchise was formed and this complementary association has been hugely successful for over a century.

The Coca Cola Bottling Company of New York, Inc. distributed 42 billion bottles and cans of Coca-Cola products in 2005, representing a fifth of the Coca-Cola's worldwide volume. As large as the company is, their philosophy of a "Close to Home" local focus and their longstanding commitment to being a good local citizen keeps The Coca Cola Bottling Company personal and accessible. They have an impeccable tradition of supporting community initiatives in education, youth sports, local charities, etc.

Coca-Cola Enterprises encourages positive choices about physical fitness, lifestyle and nutrition in their "Your Power to Choose... Fitness Health Fun" program. Making the choices easier is the broad array of Coca-Cola products, including still and sparkling waters, juices, sports drinks, coffee-based drinks, teas and, of course, Coca-Cola...the original and still the best.

Sweet and Sour Cabbage

The Coca-Cola Bottling Company of New York, Inc.

~~~~~~~~~~~~~~~~~~~~~~~~~~~~~

New York State is the nationwide leader in cabbage production. Paired with Coca-Cola, the nation's number one soft drink, this easy side dish is a flavorful way to enjoy cabbage's numerous benefits. The sweet Coke, the tangy vinegar and the smoky bacon work together beautifully. This cabbage is excellent with pork, beef or chicken.

Find more wonderful recipes using Coca-Cola products, many created at the Culinary Institute of America in Hyde Park, NY, at www2.coca-cola.com. Click on Heritage, and then Recipes.

About 1½ pounds red or green cabbage, finely cut
2 medium apples   ½ cup Coca-Cola®
2 tablespoons vinegar   2 tablespoons brown sugar
2 tablespoons bacon drippings   1 teaspoon salt
½ to 1 teaspoon caraway seeds (optional)

You should have about 3 cups cut cabbage. Core and dice unpeeled apples. In a large frying pan, heat bacon drippings. Add cabbage and sauté a few minutes. Add apples and remaining ingredients and toss together. Cover and simmer until cabbage is tender, about 25 minutes; stir occasionally. Balance flavors by adding more Coke or vinegar.

*To reduce foam for accurate measurement, use Coca-Cola at room temperature and stir rapidly

> *Life expectancy would grow by leaps and bounds if you could make your green vegetables smell like bacon.*
> —UNKNOWN

Cornell Cooperative Extension of Otsego County

"Times change, the need for knowledge never does" is one tenet of the Cooperative Extension system. "Wisdom is strength; knowledge is power' is another.

A unique achievement in American education, the Smith-Lever Act established the Cooperative Extension system in 1914. At that time President Woodrow Wilson called it " one of the most significant and far-reaching measures for the education of adults ever adopted by the government". For nearly a century, Cooperative Extension has provided the means to gain life skills and proficiency in what have been called "the mere mechanics of living" to every rural and urban community nationwide.

Information gleaned from the most trusted sources at Cornell University and their partners is available by phone, in the field, on the web, in workshops and in the classroom. Cooperative Extension educators and volunteers offer the benefits of higher education to all segments of the community.

Cornell Cooperative Extension of Otsego County provides programs in 4-H/Youth Development, life skills, nutrition and health, agriculture sustainability, environmental education, job skills, and community development. They are an invaluable resource and asset to Otsego County.

123 Lake Street
Cooperstown, NY 13326
607-547-2536
www.cce.cornell.edu/otsego
otsego@cornell.edu

Cornell Chicken Barbeque Sauce

Cornell Cooperative Extension of Otsego County

*T*his simple basting sauce makes an extraordinary difference in broiled chicken. As they say at Cornell, "Barbequed broilers without sauce are like bread without butter." Brush on broiler halves, a roasting chicken, or chicken breasts every few minutes during cooking.

1 cup cooking oil
1 pint (16 ounces) New York State apple cider vinegar
3 tablespoons salt*
1 tablespoon poultry seasoning
½ teaspoon black pepper
1 egg

In a large bowl, beat or whisk the egg. Add the oil and beat again. Add remaining ingredients and stir together.

Leftover sauce can be stored in a glass jar in the refrigerator for several weeks.

* Adjust the quantity or eliminate salt to meet individual health needs and taste. Frequently basted chicken will be saltier than lightly basted.

For more information request the Cornell Cooperative Extension publication Barbequed Chicken and Other Meats.

The Otsego County Empire Zone Program

*T*our our Otsego County roads and you'll see the signs of a flourishing agricultural economy. There are seemingly endless acres of well-tended fields and forests. The Holstein dairy cattle dotting the hillsides produce milk for New York cheddar, European-style yogurt, and sweet butter. Herds of goats provide milk and fine cheese, and beef cattle supply flavorful meats to New York City's markets and finer restaurants.

In March, look for maple trees trimmed with bright blue tubing. These tubes carry the sap that feeds the nation's appetite for Grade "A" 100% pure maple syrup. During summer, a sharp eye can spot wild hops growing along the roadsides, a vestige of the hops industry that quenched America's thirst for beer in the nineteenth and early twentieth centuries. Today, Otsego County is home to several successful microbreweries.

The Otsego County Economic Development Department helps entrepreneurs tap the county's natural assets, create jobs, and preserve its scenic beauty. It supports the community with a variety of loan programs, technical assistance, Empire Zone tax benefits, and other business re-location and expansion services. Their staff is dedicated to helping make your business plans a reality in Otsego County.

"A Key Ingredient to Economic Success"

Otsego County Economic Development
242 Main Street
Oneonta, NY 13326
607-432-8871
www.otsegoeconomicdevelopment.com

Business à la King
The Otsego County Empire Zone Program

~~~~~~~~~~~~~~~~~~~~~~~~~~~~~~~~~~~

*I*f you are planning to start or expand a business in Otsego County, contact the professional staff at the Otsego County Empire Zone Program for a wealth of information and guidance. Let them help you make the most of your Otsego County opportunities.

Ingredients:
(There are no substitutions for the following)

1 great idea for a product line
1 determined entrepreneur
1 solid business plan
1 Otsego County loan program
1 production plant, located in a tax-advantaged Empire Zone
5 motivated, affordable, loyal employees

Add:

A dash of passion

A pinch of perseverance

A sprinkle of publicity

Cook over a hot fire until hungry customers are standing in line for your product. Set out on porch to cool. Count your profits.

DESSERTS

Nicoletta's Italian Café

How do you say "luscious" in Italian? It may well be "Nicoletta's."

This comfortable upscale eatery with its authentic Italian cuisine and hand-selected wines is the frequent answer to the oft-asked Cooperstown question, "Can you recommend a good restaurant?"

From their signature Lobster Ravioli Pomodoro to their smartly attired and professional wait staff to a tiramisu that rivals the last best one you ever tasted, are a just few reasons patrons return to Nicoletta's time and again.

Nicoletta's interior is tastefully decorated with an understated blend of great American icons- baseball and Frank Sinatra. If you're dining in fine weather, ask for seating in the back al fresco area.

Nicoletta's is located in the heart of Cooperstown's Main Street. It is open seven days a week from 4PM on. Reservations are recommended.

96 Main Street
Cooperstown, NY 13326
607-547-7499
www.nicolettasitaliancafe.com

P.S. "Luscious" in Italian is *succulento*.

Honey Apricot Ricotta Cheesecake
Nicoletta's Italian Café

~~~~~~~~~~~~~~~~~~~~~~~~~~~~~~~~~~~~~

A food processor is helpful when making this lovely cheesecake. It is very rich, so you can get a lot of servings from one cake.

Ingredients

8 ounces biscotti
6 tablespoons unsalted butter, melted
12 ounces whole milk ricotta cheese, drained
16 ounces cream cheese, at room temperature
¾ cup sugar

¼ cup New York honey
¼ cup finely diced dried apricots
1 tablespoon orange zest
4 large eggs

- Preheat oven to 300 degrees.
- Wrap the outside of a 9" spring-form pan with two layers of heavy-duty foil.
- Finely grind the biscotti in a food processor. Add melted butter and process until crumbs are moistened.
- Press crumbs on the bottom of the prepared pan. Bake about 15 minutes, until golden. Cool completely.
- Blend the ricotta in processor until smooth. Add cream cheese and sugar and blend. Add honey, apricots and orange zest. Add eggs and pulse until just blended.
- Pour cheese mixture over crust. Place spring-form pan in large roasting pan. Add enough water to come halfway up the sides of the spring-form pan. Bake about 1 hour, until cheesecake is golden. Center will be jiggly.
- Transfer cake to rack and let cool 1 hour. Refrigerate cake at least 8 hours. Cut in wedges and serve garnished with fresh fruit (sliced peaches, apricots, blueberries, strawberries, etc.) and sprigs of mint.

The Rose and Kettle Restaurant

O ne of the finest restaurants in Otsego County, The Rose & Kettle offers gourmet dining in a two-hundred-year-old house in historic Cherry Valley, New York. It is well worth the scenic 12-mile drive from Cooperstown or the beautiful ten miles from the Glimmerglass Opera.

From their signature cocktails to their signature desserts, the Rose and Kettle is a treasure in this unique country town, and a culinary gift to Otsego County.

Chef-owned and operated, The Rose and Kettle features a seasonal menu with an emphasis on fresh, local ingredients. The food is American, but with the southern European influences of French and Italian cuisines. Clem and Dana's wine cellar features many unusual wines from small, excellent producers.

Reservations are recommended for this exceptional restaurant, especially in July and August.

July and August: Open everyday except Wednesday. Dinner served from 5PM.
September–June: Open Thursday–Sunday nights at 5PM
Open year round for Sunday Brunch 10AM to 2PM

Please call ahead if you will be visiting during winter months.

Clem Coleman and Dana Spiotta
4 Lancaster Street
Cherry Valley, NY 13320
607-264-3078
dana@roseandkettle.com
www.roseandkettle.com

Goat Cheese Panna Cotta with Berries
The Rose and Kettle Restaurant

*P*anna Cotta is chilled Italian custard with an infinite number of variations. It is a stunning and easy dessert. The Rose and Kettle makes Goat Cheese Panna Cotta with local chevre (goat cheese) and the best berries they can find. Strawberries, raspberries, blackberries and currants are all delicious. Preparation time is minimal, but allow a couple of hours for the dessert set in the refrigerator. Serves 4

1 pint (16 ounces) heavy cream
1 teaspoon powdered unflavored gelatin
4 tablespoons white sugar
¼ cup chevre (goat cheese)
1 teaspoon vanilla extract
1 pint fresh berries
Whipped cream and fresh mint or basil for garnish

Dissolve gelatin in 3 teaspoons warm tap water.

Warm the heavy cream in a saucepan until it is hot but not boiling. Whisk in the sugar and vanilla. Turn off the heat and mix in the chevre, letting the cheese melt away and fuse with the cream. Taste for a desirable balance of sweetness, tanginess and touch of vanilla. Adjust flavor by adding sugar, vanilla or a bit more cheese.

Add the gelatin, whisking and looking for clumpy bits.

Pour mixture through a fine strainer to catch strays. Discard these and divide the mixture evenly among pretty serving dishes- martini glasses, sundae dishes or something festive.

Refrigerate servings about two hours. Serve with whipped cream and fresh berries and garnish with mint or basil.

Daylily Dreams
Bed and Breakfast

"*D*aylily Dreams" is more than just a pretty name. Beautiful, fragrant lilies grace the grounds of this welcoming bed and breakfast, delighting guests and hummingbirds alike.

Continuing with this pretty theme, each of Bob and Rae's inviting guest rooms are named for a type of lily. You'll sleep sweetly in the Meadowsweet, Velvet Rose, Paper Butterfly or Moondazzle rooms.

The Consigli's are members of the American Hemerocallis Society and theirs has been designated as an official display garden for the AHS. Some of their lily varieties are for sale, so you may take home a lasting reminder of your stay in Cooperstown.

Daylily Dreams and their lily fields are just outside of Cooperstown, five minutes from Main Street.

Rae and Bob Consigli
1599 County Route 33
Cooperstown, New York 13326

Toll free 866-547-1888
www.daylilydreams.com
info@daylilydreams.com

If you have two loaves of bread, sell one and buy a lily.
—CHINESE PROVERB

Pumpkin Chocolate Chip Mini Muffins
Daylily Dreams Bed and Breakfast

*Y*ummy enough for dessert, these are also wonderful for brunch.

Preheat oven to 350 degrees

1 ⅔ cup flour	1 ⅓ cup sugar
1 teaspoon baking powder	½ teaspoon baking soda
½ teaspoon salt	½ teaspoon nutmeg

½ cup chocolate or cinnamon chips	¼ cup toffee flavored bits (optional)
½ cup diced walnuts or pecans	1 teaspoon vanilla extract
⅓ cup melted butter or vegetable oil	2 large eggs
1 cup (half of a 15-ounce can) packed pumpkin	
⅓ cup water	

Glaze

1 cup confectioner's sugar, sifted	2 tablespoons melted butter
1 tablespoon milk	¼ teaspoon cinnamon

Beat together; add milk to achieve desired consistency.

Stir flour, sugar, baking powder, baking soda, salt and nutmeg together in large bowl. In separate bowl whisk together vanilla, melted butter, eggs, pumpkin and water. Stir wet and dry ingredients together until just combined. Fold in chocolate chips and toffee bits. Spoon into 24 lined mini muffin cups, or 12 regular sized muffin cups. Bake for 25-30 minutes.

Glaze when muffins are completely cool.

Glimmerglass Opera

~~~~~~~~~~~~~~~~~~~~~~~~

Simultaneously intimate and pastoral, Glimmerglass Opera offers opera experiences beyond the expected. Beginning with their magnificent productions, set on the breathtaking shores of Otsego Lake, to their Young American Artists Program to their after-show Cabaret performances, a Glimmerglass outing can entail far more than a single performance.

You can be a part of opening night receptions, opera previews, Seminar and Gala Weekends, backstage tours or production changeovers. The Glimmerglass grounds make a picture-perfect picnic setting. Their concession offers wine and casual gourmet fare, or order picnics delivered to the theater. You are welcomed to bring your own feast and enjoy the rural grandeur of the Glimmerglass campus before the performance. New to the 2006 season is Family Weekend, a perfect opportunity to share your love of opera with family members of all ages.

Call or visit the Glimmerglass Opera website to take advantage of all Glimmerglass offers to create a complete and unforgettable opera experience.

PO Box 191
Cooperstown, NY 13326
607-547-2255
www.glimmerglass.org

Ticket Office:
18 Chestnut Street
Cooperstown, NY 13326

> *I have always believed that opera is a planet where the muses work together, join hands and celebrate all the arts.*
> —FRANCO ZEFFIRELLI

Strawberry Rhubarb Crunch
Glimmerglass Opera

*T*hese two spring crops marry well for wonderful strawberry-rhubarb crisps, pies, salsas, jams etc. Rhubarb is one two perennial vegetables (asparagus is the other). Once established, it produces a great crop that freezes beautifully for winter enjoyment. This recipe is a perfect use for a big rhubarb plant in the garden.

Preheat oven to 375 degrees.
1 cup white sugar
3 tablespoons all-purpose flour
3 cups sliced fresh strawberries
3 cups diced rhubarb
1 1/2 cups all-purpose flour
1 cup packed brown sugar
1 cup butter
1 cup rolled oats

In a large bowl, mix white sugar, 3 tablespoons flour, strawberries, and rhubarb. Place the mixture in a 9"x13" inch baking dish. Mix 1½ cups flour, brown sugar, butter, and oats until crumbly. You may want to use a pastry blender for this. Crumble on top of the rhubarb and strawberry mixture. Bake 45 minutes in the preheated oven, or until crisp and lightly browned.

BlueStone Farm

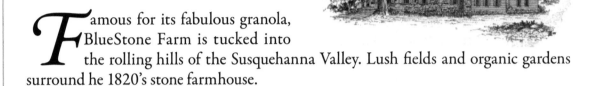

Famous for its fabulous granola, BlueStone Farm is tucked into the rolling hills of the Susquehanna Valley. Lush fields and organic gardens surround he 1820's stone farmhouse.

In Otsego County, and well beyond our borders, BlueStone Farm means granola. It's a family recipe and the delectable result of countless combinations tried in the BlueStone Kitchens. Their granola is hand made in small batches using twenty ingredients. And, unlike commercial granola that might sit on a shelf for months, BlueStone Farm Granola is always fresh.

BlueStone Farm puts in everything you could want in granola, using fresh, natural ingredients. Find wholesome oats, crunchy walnuts, chewy apricots and cranberries, sunflower seeds, plus the sweetness of local clover honey, just to name a few. Fresh, natural ingredients, brimming with health and flavor, all make the beginning of a perfect morning and a great snack anytime.

Marty Bernardo
Bissell Road
Cooperstown, NY 13326
www.bluestonefarm.org
bluestone@capital.net
607-547-8227

Charlie's Granola Cookies
BlueStone Farm

~~~~~~

*T*hese satisfying cookies are great for hikes and lunch boxes.

Preheat oven to 350 degrees.

6 tablespoons butter, softened
1 cup brown sugar
½ cup granulated sugar
2 eggs
1 teaspoon vanilla
1 ½ cups all purpose flour
1 teaspoon baking powder
1 teaspoon ground cinnamon
3 cups BlueStone Farm Granola

Cream butter and sugar until together. Add eggs and vanilla, beating well.
Stir together flour, baking powder and cinnamon in separate bowl. Add to butter mixture and mix well. Stir in BlueStone Farm Granola.
Drop by rounded tablespoons onto ungreased cookie sheet. Bake 10-12 minutes or until cookie bottoms are golden brown.
Cool 1 minute on cookie sheet. Remove to wire cooling rack.

> *A balanced diet is a cookie in each hand.*
> —UNKNOWN

The Susquehanna SPCA

*F*ounded in 1916, the Susquehanna SPCA is committed to a time when there are no more homeless animals and every animal will be guaranteed a loving home.

To reach their goal, they sponsor educational and spay and neuter programs and, of course, adoptions. Thorough in their background checks and high in their standards, the Susquehanna SPCA strives to make every placement of every homeless animal successful.

Adoption fees vary, with special rates for senior adoptions. Your potential new best friend is spayed or neutered, wormed, tattooed and vaccinated. Canine pals are bathed and given obedience training. Cats are tested for feline leukemia.

Memberships to the Susquehanna SPCA are available from $15 to $1000. The Susquehanna SPCA is open Tuesday-Saturday, 11AM-4PM.

Be sure to stop at the Better Exchange Thrift Shop, a great place for bargains and a fundraising enterprise for the Susquehanna SPCA, located right next door.

4841 State Highway 28
Cooperstown, NY 13326
607-547-8111
sspca@stny.rr.com
www.sspca.petfinder.org

Walt Disney film's Benji, The Shaggy Dog and Old Yeller were all rescued from animal shelters. So was the first, second, third and fourth ginger tabby to play Morris the Cat, of Nine Lives cat food fame.

Fresh Apple Cake
Susquehanna SPCA

〜〜〜〜〜〜〜〜〜〜〜〜〜〜〜〜〜〜〜〜

Preheat oven to 325 degrees

Fresh Apple Cake

2⅓ cups flour

2 cups granulated sugar

2 teaspoon baking soda

¾ teaspoon table salt

1 teaspoon cinnamon

½ teaspoon ground ginger

¼ teaspoon each ground cloves and freshly ground nutmeg

4 cups NYS cooking apples, peeled, cored and chopped

½ cup unsalted butter, softened

½ finely chopped walnuts

2 eggs, gently beaten

In large bowl, stir together flour, sugar, soda, salt and spices, mixing well.

Add apples, butter, nuts and eggs. Using an electric mixer on low speed, or by hand, beat until well blended. Be careful not to puree apples.

Pour batter into a greased and floured 9"x13" pan. Bake for 45 minutes, or until cake springs back when touched in the middle.

Let cool in pan on wire rack. Frost when completely cooled.

Caramel Frosting

⅓ cup salted butter

½ cup firmly packed dark brown sugar

Dash of salt

3 tablespoons whole milk

1½ cups sifted confectioners sugar

¼ teaspoon real vanilla

Melt butter in small saucepan. Add brown sugar and salt. Stir over medium heat until sugar melts.

Stir in milk; bring to a boil, stirring constantly. As soon as mixture boils, pour into mixing bowl and let cool for 10 minutes.

Add confectioners' sugar and vanilla; beat to spreading consistency, adding more sugar if necessary. Spread on Fresh Apple Cake.

Recipe courtesy of Jane Duel

Pumpkin Fest

New York grows more pumpkins than any other state. We bake them into pies, carve them into jack 'o lanterns, sail them on Otsego Lake and puree them into soup. What? Back up one. What was that thing before the soup?

The Pumpkin Regatta is one of the high points of Pumpkin Fest, the Cooperstown Chamber of Commerce's celebration of this glorious gourd. Mammoth pumpkins, weighing between 700-800 pounds, are skillfully carved into seaworthy craft. Seating a lone oarsman, they make an exuberant orange flotilla on an autumn afternoon.

A mere 800-pound pumpkin is a runt among the really big ones vying for the biggest pumpkin championship. Pumpkins from around the state, tipping the scales at upwards of 1500 pounds, weigh-in at Doubleday Court. There really is a Great Pumpkin, Charlie Brown, and he visits Cooperstown the first days of October.

Pumpkin Fest is splendid family fun, featuring a craft fair, professional and amateur pumpkin carving, games for the kids, food, music and lots of pumpkin edibles.

Make plans to join the Pumpkin Fest party. Contact the Chamber for more information and to make reservations.

Cooperstown Chamber of Commerce
31 Chestnut Street
Cooperstown, NY 13326
607-547-9983
www.cooperstownchamber.org
info1@cooperstownchamber.org

Apple Muffins
Cooperstown Chamber of Commerce

~~~~~~

*F*eatured in Bon Appetit, these incredible "muffins" are a cross between a muffin and a cookie. They are a wonderful use of New York autumn apples.

The key to these great muffins is to treat the dough gently at all times, so that the apples don't break down too much.

Preheat oven to 350 degrees
3 cups coarsely chopped apples (Granny Smith, Braeburn or Rome)

3½ cups all-purpose flour	1 teaspoon cinnamon
2 cups sugar	1 teaspoon baking soda
1 teaspoon salt	12 ounces vegetable oil
1 teaspoon vanilla	½ cup chopped nuts (optional)

In large bowl, combine apples, flour, sugar, cinnamon, salt and baking soda. Mix together gently. Add vegetable oil, vanilla and nuts and mix just until blended. You may want to use your clean hands to get the mixture to hold together. Dough will be stiff.

Spoon mixture into sprayed and floured muffin tins, or use paper liners. Bake for 20-25 minutes until tops are golden and firm. Makes 60 small muffins or 24 large. These muffins freeze well.

An original recipe courtesy
Polly and Jim Renckins

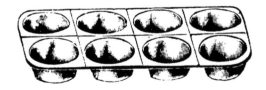

Greater Cherry Valley Chamber of Commerce

A Short History of Cherry Valley Commerce

The Greater Cherry Valley Chamber of Commerce represents many enterprises in this charming community and it can recount the comings and goings of businesses since the town of Cherry Valley was formed in 1791.

Cherry Valley has a long history of renaissance, beginning when settlers returned to the area after the 1778 Cherry Valley Massacre. Fortunes have ebbed and flowed but, people have always been drawn to Cherry Valley.

Cherry Valley thrived at the beginning of the nineteenth century when the Great Western Turnpike was built, growing to be the largest settlement west of Albany. Business declined in 1825 when the Erie Canal drew interests elsewhere. However, Cherry Valley professionals and politicians brought rail service to the area, once again boosting commerce. The early twentieth century saw Cherry Valley's economic heyday when it boasted multiple retailers, restaurants, a movie theater, five car dealerships, a bowling alley and, for almost 80 years, the Armstrong & Son Chair Factory.

In 1954 the Cherry Valley bypass left Cherry Valley out of the traffic loop and rail service stopped. The population and business community dwindled and "progress" passed by Cherry Valley. However, with the new millennium, many businesses have rediscovered Cherry Valley. Once again it is growing, boasting new businesses, fine restaurants, bed and breakfasts and a renewed population.

Maggie Gage, Secretary
PO Box 37
Cherry Valley, NY 13320
607-264-3755
www.cherryvalleyny.com
maggieg.cv@gates-cole.com

Cherry Nut Cake

Greater Cherry Valley Chamber of Commerce

*U*nlike muffins, which require only minimal mixing by hand, most cakes benefit from thorough beating. A good electric mixer is a boon to making light cakes with a tender crumb. This luscious and pretty pink cake makes a lovely dessert or addition to teatime.

Preheat oven to 350 degrees
Sift together in large mixing bowl:
2 ¼ cups flour
1 1/3 cups sugar

1 tablespoon baking powder

Optional ingredients
½ cup chopped pecans

In separate bowl combine:
½ cup butter, melted
¼ cup cherry syrup (from a jar of
  maraschino cherries)
16 maraschino cherries,
  finely chopped
½ cup milk

1 can "extra fruit" cherry pie filling

Combine flour and butter mixtures. Beat 2 minutes with an electric mixer.

Add 4 egg whites and beat an additional 2 minutes. Do not substitute two whole eggs for the whites; the yellow yolks interfere with the delicate pink color. Fold in ½ cup chopped pecans.

Pour batter into greased and floured cake pans and bake for 25-30 minutes, or until a toothpick inserted in center comes out clean. Makes two 9" round layers or one 9"x13" sheet cake. Fill between layers with a few spoons of cherry pie filling and frost with a vanilla or cherry icing.

Or, put half of batter into a prepared bundt or tube pan. Spoon a half to a whole can of cherry pie filling over batter, pressing down slightly. Cover with remaining batter, spreading evenly. Bake about 30 minutes. After cake is cool, cover with glaze made of powdered sugar, enough milk for dripping consistency and a little cherry syrup for color and flavor, if desired.

For the Love of Cake by Kelly

Restrain yourself just a moment before slicing into one of Kelly Calhoun's beautiful creations and take a snapshot. Her hands-down luscious cakes are as pleasing to the eye as to the taste buds and should be preserved for memories. Got the picture? Now, dive in with abandon and let all sensations but taste fade for the moment.

Kelly Calhoun makes an artful cake, tailoring her flair to reflect your special taste and style. Her birthday, wedding, anniversary and other special occasion cakes feature only the best ingredients, skillfully crafted for your celebration.

Butter cakes, spice cakes, cheesecakes and pound cakes use fresh butter, fragrant spices, whole eggs or fine chocolate. Fillings feature fresh fruit purees, liqueurs or lemon curd. Choose icings of mousseline buttercream, dark chocolate ganache or fondant. Cakes may also be adorned with fresh flowers.

Guarantee that your special occasion will be truly memorable. Let Kelly bake the cake.

Kelly Calhoun
156 Perkins Road
Cooperstown, NY 13326
607-293-8465

Maple Pumpkin Cheesecake

For the Love of Cake

〜〜〜〜〜〜〜〜〜〜〜〜〜〜〜

*P*reheat oven to 375 degrees

Graham Cracker Crust:
½ pound graham crackers, finely crumbed
½ cup butter, melted
Mix crumbs and butter and press into bottom and partway up the sides of a
10" spring form pan. Bake 5 minutes.

Fabulous Pumpkin Filling:
1¼ pounds cream cheese, beaten smooth
Add and whip together until creamy:
1¾ cups pumpkin puree
1½ cups maple syrup
1 egg
½ cup whipping cream
1 teaspoon blackstrap molasses
2 tablespoons cornstarch or arrowroot
1 tablespoon vanilla extract
½ teaspoon cinnamon
½ teaspoon powdered ginger
A pinch each of ground cloves, allspice and nutmeg

Pour filling evenly over crust and bake for about an hour. Cake will be done even if center is not completely set. Allow cheesecake to cool completely and cover. Refrigerate overnight before unmolding and serving.

Bear Pond Winery

*W*inemaking is equal parts art, science, intuition and attention to detail. Every careful process and each temperamental ingredient affects the vintage. Soil, climate, rainfall, cuttings, sugar, type of yeast, exposure to heat and oxygen, even the color of the bottle can alter the quality of the wine.

Bear Pond Winery successfully meets these challenges as it celebrates New York State's winemaking renaissance. Their wines are made from carefully selected New York grapes grown on their property or from other small New York vineyards. Bear Pond's top quality vintages are competitive in national and international markets.

Tour their facilities and try the Bear Pond varieties. You can taste the care, the years of experience, the attentiveness and the sun, rich soil and sweet rain that produce a fine vintage.

Plan a stop at the Bear Pond Winery, located between Cooperstown and Oneonta, near Goodyear Lake. Browse their giftware while tasting and selecting your favorites. Custom labels are available in house, making a very special gift.

Enjoy the good wine and good times with good friends, here in the country.

Mark Lebo
Brenda Lebo
Michael Bordinger

2515 State Highway 28
Oneonta, NY 13820
www.bearpondwines.com
taste@bearpondwines.com
607-643-0294
Fax: 607-643-0219

Creamy Blueberry Sorbet with Blueberry Compote
Bear Pond Winery

*T*his glorious dessert sings New York. Absolutely beautiful and equally as luscious, pick extra blueberries in August and freeze to enjoy this summery jubilation when winter grows long. You'll need an ice cream freezer.

Sorbet
2 cups granulated sugar
4 cups water
1 cup Bear Pond Blueberry Wine
Juice of one lemon
Juice of one orange
2 cups pureed blueberries
2 cups vanilla yogurt

In a saucepan combine sugar, wine, blueberries and water. Bring to a boil and cook and stir for five minutes. Stir in lemon and orange juice and refrigerate overnight.
Combine yogurt with berry-wine mixture. Process according to ice cream freezer directions.

Blueberry Compote
8 cups fresh or frozen blueberries
2 cups granulated sugar
½ cup Bear Pond Blueberry Wine, plus 2 tablespoons
Juice of half of an orange
1 teaspoon orange zest

Combine berries, sugar, ½ cup wine, juice and zest in saucepan and bring to a boil. Turn heat to simmer and cook until liquid reduces by half. Remove from heat and stir in reserved 2 tablespoons of wine. Serve over sorbet. Also great warm or cold on pancakes, waffles or desserts.

Davidson's Jewelry and Augur's Books

*T*his alluring combination of jewelry, books, giftware and treasures is located in an attractive historic building at the corner of Main and Pioneer Streets, in the heart of Cooperstown.

Davidson's Jewelry specializes in custom designs in gold and sterling silver. Among the cases of beautiful adornments you'll find many unique pieces in their broad line of baseball jewelry, the largest selection in Cooperstown. You'll find just the right gift in their selection of beautiful gemstones and watches. Davidson's also offers engraving and repairs.

For over a century, Augur's Books had been known for their quality lines of stationery, fine gifts, pens, Swiss Army knives and more, as well as bestsellers. Don't miss their complete selection of Cooperstown related books and baseball themes. Special book orders are cheerfully filled.

Open Monday to Saturday, 9AM-5:30PM.

73 Main Street (by the flagpole)
Cooperstown, NY 13326
607-547-2422
607-547-5099
www.cooperstownjewelry.com
augurs@capital.net

Spicy Pumpkin Oat Squares

Davidson's Jewelry and Augur's Books

~~~~~~~~~~~~~~~~~~~~~~~~~~~~~~~

*T*hese are so good, they never made it out of the test kitchen. The spicy pumpkin custard and the oatmeal crisp make a dynamite combination. These squares are delicious warm out of the oven or as an out of hand snack when cool. They are delectable with whipped cream or ice cream. Then again, isn't everything?

Preheat oven to 375 degrees
1½ cups old fashioned or quick oats (not instant)

1¼ cups all purpose flour	¾ cup brown sugar, firmly packed
½ cup chopped nuts (pecans or walnuts)	½ teaspoon salt
½ teaspoon baking soda	¾ cup soft butter

Mix all ingredients and beat or cut in the butter until crumbly. Reserve 1½ cups of this mixture and press the rest into the bottom of a lightly buttered 9"x13" baking pan. Bake for 10 minutes.

Filling

One 16-ounce can of pumpkin puree	⅔ cup milk
⅓ cup brown sugar, packed	1 egg
1 tablespoon pumpkin pie spice	

While bottom crust bakes, combine all filling ingredients. Spread pumpkin mixture on top of baked crust and then sprinkle with reserved crumb mixture. Bake about 25 minutes longer, until lightly browned.

> *Vegetables are a must on a diet. I suggest carrot cake, zucchini bread, and pumpkin pie.*
>
> —JIM DAVIS,
> CREATOR OF GARFIELD

Cooperstown Cookie Company

The Cooperstown Cookie Company makes the sweetest baseball souvenirs. Their buttery traditional shortbread is baked in the shape and size of a regulation baseball. These delightful cookies break along the "stitching," making them easy to share.

Cooperstown Cookies are baked by hand, in small batches at Pathfinder Village, a residential community for children and adults who have Down's syndrome. Cooperstown Cookie Company shares a portion of its profits with Pathfinder Village. Cooperstown Cookies are made using all natural ingredients, with no additives or preservatives.

These shortbread cookies have been a favorite with locals, visitors, Major League Baseball, and sweet tooths everywhere since their debut at the National Baseball Hall of Fame in 2004. Each tin of Classic Baseball Shortbread includes a tricky baseball trivia question.

Cooperstown Cookies make a perfect gift. Packed in decorated tins, they travel and ship well. The Cooperstown Cookie Company happily fills your custom order.

Classic Baseball Shortbread is available on line and at many vendors in the Cooperstown area.

To order or for more information contact:

Cooperstown Cookie Company
PO Box 64
Cooperstown, NY 13326
607-547-9146 or 607-435-5789
goodies@cooperstowncookiecompany.com
www.cooperstowncookiecompany.com

Classic Baseball Shortbread

The Cooperstown Cookie Company

*T*his really is Pati Drumm Grady's family recipe, the same one she uses for Classic Baseball Shortbread.

Preheat oven to 325 degrees

2 cups flour
½ pound (2 sticks) unsalted butter at room temperature
½ cup granulated sugar
½ teaspoon salt
½ teaspoon pure vanilla extract

Sift flour and salt into a small bowl and set aside. Place butter in bowl and beat with an electric mixer, using the paddle attachment, if available. Cream butter until fluffy. Add sugar and vanilla and continue beating, about 2 minutes.

Gradually add flour mixture; combine on low, scraping sides of bowl with spatula until flour is incorporated and dough sticks together.

Roll dough on parchment paper to ¼" thickness.

Using a 2½" round cookie cutter, cut circles in dough. With a pastry crimper, or ravioli cutter, lightly make two inverted "C" shapes to simulate baseball stitching on each circle. Transfer to baking sheets. Gather scraps together, re-roll and cut shapes.

Bake until firm and light in color, 15-20 minutes. Cool on wire rack; store in airtight container.

Cooperstown Natural Foods

Cooperstown Natural Foods is a family-owned complete grocery, fully stocked with natural and organic products. They showcase many locally made products in this clean and bright store, and serve as a year-round forum for local producers, such as *Home Plate* contributors Chutney Unlimited, Bluestone Farms Granola, Stannard's Maple Products and Cooperstown Cookies.

Their excellent 100% certified organic produce department is a key feature of this attractive shop. From apples to zucchini, the Poulette's offer the widest selection of fresh organic produce for many miles.

Cooperstown Natural Foods carries many gluten-free and casein-free items, as well as vegetarian and vegan items. They also have a most satisfying array of organic chocolates.

The Cooperstown Natural Foods Store's dead-end street location at the end of Linden Avenue assures a parking spot, even during Cooperstown's busiest months of July and August,

The Poulette family looks forward to meeting you.

Ellen Poulette
607-547-8613
61 Linden Avenue
Cooperstown, NY 13326
Cooperstownnaturalfoods@verizon.net

Applesauce Cake
Cooperstown Natural Foods

～～～～～～～～～～～～～～～

*T*his spicy, moist cake stores well and successfully ships to friends and family at a distance.

12 New York State cooking apples (organic Cortlands preferred)
peeled, cored and sliced
2 tablespoons water
1 cup sugar

½ cup butter, melted
2 cups unbleached flour
2 teaspoons baking soda
½ teaspoon salt
1 teaspoon each cinnamon and nutmeg
½ teaspoon ground cloves
1 cup raisins

Place apples in saucepan with water and sugar. Heat, covered, over low heat, stirring occasionally. When reduced to applesauce, remove from heat and let cool a bit.

Preheat oven to 350 degrees.

Mix flour, soda, salt and spices in small bowl and set aside.

Add sugar and butter to cooled applesauce, stirring well. Add flour mixture and stir just until combined. Fold in raisins. Pour into greased 8"x8" cake pan. Bake 45-55 minutes.

Citigroup Smith Barney

The Morgan McReynolds Group offers professional guidance for wealth management for the residents of and newcomers to Otsego County. Careful financial planning can be a daunting challenge, with many options and much potential. A local, experienced professional and a known guiding hand is an invaluable asset when investing.

The Morgan McReynolds expertise covers stocks and bonds, mutual funds, government securities, annuities, commodities and options. Financial and retirement planning is a specialty. They can help you understand the best uses for your money.

They invite you to call for a complimentary personal review of your investments.

493 Chestnut Street
Oneonta, NY 13820
607-432-5000 or 800-962-2357

Success depends in a very large measure upon individual initiative and exertion, and cannot be achieved except by a dint of hard work.
—ANNA PAVLOVA

Strawberry Pavlova

Citigroup Smith Barney

~~~~~~~~~~~~~~~~~~~~~~~~~~~~~~~~~~~~

Named for the ballerina Anna Pavlova, this dramatic meringue dessert is the national favorite in New Zealand where it is made with kiwi. A meringue shell filled with fruit and whipped cream, it makes an unforgettable impression that belies how easy it is to make. Though suitable with most fruits, to make it a star, use New York strawberries or blueberries.

Shell
1 cup sugar
6 egg whites

1 teaspoon white vinegar
1 tablespoon cornstarch

Filling
1-2 quarts strawberries, halved (leave a few whole for decoration)
3-4 tablespoons sugar
1 cup heavy cream, whipped
Parchment Paper

Preheat oven to 275 degrees
Line a baking sheet with parchment or grease and sprinkle generously with sugar.
Beat egg whites until stiff peaks form. Slowly add sugar and continue beating. Meringue will be stiff and glossy. Sprinkle cornstarch over meringue, add vinegar and fold in gently. Pile onto prepared baking sheet and spread into a large round, forming a slight hollow in the center. It will look like a billowy pizza crust. Bake for 1½ hours until the pavlova is lightly browned and like marshmallow in the center.

Let cool to room temperature and peel off paper. At this point the shell may be stored for up to a week in an airtight container. When ready to serve, pile half of whipped cream in shell, add fruit and finish with remaining whipped cream. Garnish with whole berries.

The Perennial Field

Ruby Mitchell's Perennial Field is, literally, a breath of spring. She's filled the big field by her farmhouse with lovely, fragrant plants including perennial flowers, biennials, herbs, hostas and ornamental grasses. All plants are grown in-ground and accustomed to the Otsego County climate, your assurance that Ruby's lush plants are hardy and cold tolerant. Large clump sizes, ranging from one to five-gallon pots, bloom the first season.

The Perennial Field is floriculture at its most direct. Choose any of Ruby's gorgeous flowers and ornamental grasses and she digs them for you on the spot. You can stroll the garden and select from over 300 varieties,

Lilies, hosta, irises, bleeding hearts, bee balm, and lots more thrive in Ruby's care. You'll surely find something special for your garden at the Perennial Field, located in the beautiful Susquehanna Valley in Otego, New York, just ten minutes from Oneonta and 35 minutes from Cooperstown.

The Perennial Field is easy to find from I-88. Take exit 12 to Otego and go west on Route 7. The Perennial Field is one-half mile, on the right.

Hours: May and June 10AM to 6PM, seven days a week
        July, August and September 10AM to 6PM Tuesday
        Saturday

Ruby Mitchell
25 Main Street
Otego, NY 13825
607-988-9009
www.perennialfield.com

Lavender Cookies
for Teatime
The Perennial Field

~~~~~~

*F*ragrant and different, try teaming these butter cookies with the Rose Petal Drink from *Home Plate* contributor, The Cherry Valley Historical Society, as well as your favorite tea.

Preheat oven to 350 degrees
⅔ cup butter, softened
⅓ cup sugar
1 egg
1 tablespoon dried lavender flowers
1½ cups flour
½ teaspoon baking soda
½ teaspoon cream of tartar
¼ teaspoon salt

Sift together flour, baking soda, cream of tartar and salt. Stir lavender into dry ingredients. Set aside.

Cream butter and sugar together in large mixing bowl. Add egg and beat well. Gradually add dry ingredients to butter mixture and blend well.

Drop by teaspoonful onto greased or parchment lined cookie sheet.
Bake 12-14 minutes.

Willys Farm and Cider Mill

*T*his old-fashioned cider mill is another great reason to visit Otsego County in the autumn. Willys Farm presents an enchanting and satisfying glimpse into Otsego County agriculture. This family-run operation offers apples, mazes, local artwork and delicious food and cider. Willys is one of the few cider mills that will custom press apples for you.

Willys' is FUN. Enjoy beautiful views, wonderful autumn activities and open fields suitable for active children. There are free corn mazes for the kids and grass mazes for the tots. Meet the Pumpkin People, Louie the Donkey and Pia the Goat. Visit the corn teepee and weaving wall. Ride in the wagon and take in the breathtaking autumn colors. Finish your day back at the barn with hot cider and a sing-along.

Set on a hill in Schenevus, NY, Willys grows and sells pumpkins and other autumn favorites. Their delicious apple pies and cider doughnuts are made from scratch. Find homemade jams and jellies and locally produced farm products including syrup, honey, cheese, soaps and more! Local artists and family members create the photography, paintings, jewelry, tin ware, woodcrafts and fiber arts in the retail area.

Open weekends only during autumn, Willys offers an unforgettable visit to a real New York cider mill.

Willys Farm and Cider Mill is located about four miles from Schenevus on Badeau Hill Road. Take exit 18 off I-88 and follow the red and white signs.

Open Labor Day Weekend through the first weekend of November, including Labor Day Monday and Columbus Weekend Monday.
Hours: Friday 9AM-5PM   Saturday 9AM-5PM   Sunday 11AM-5PM

Weekdays by appointment for school and tour groups.
(Call early; they fill quickly!)

Custom pressing by appointment. Call 607-638-9449 or 607-547-2186

Apple Pie

Willys Farm and Cider Mill

*P*reheat oven to 425 degrees

Crust for a double crust 8" pie
2 cups flour   1 teaspoon salt
2/3 cup, plus 2 tablespoons shortening   4 to 5 tablespoons cold water

Mix flour and salt in large mixing bowl. Cut in shortening thoroughly. Sprinkle in water, one tablespoon at a time, until flour is moistened and a ball forms "cleaning" the sides of the bowl. You may need another spoon or two of water.

Divide dough in half. On a floured board, roll each half into a circle two inches larger than pie pan. Line pie pan with bottom crust and fill.

Apple Filling
½ cup sugar
3 tablespoons flour (a bit more if you use a juicier apple, such as an Empire)
¼ teaspoon cinnamon
A dash of salt
5 cups thinly sliced apples (Paula Reds preferred, but use your own favorite)
1 tablespoon butter

Mix sugar, flour, cinnamon and salt with apple slices. Pour into pastry line pie pan. Dot with butter. Cover with top crust. Cut slits to allow steam to escape. Seal and flute.

Bake for 15 minutes at 425 degrees. Reduce oven temperature to 350 degrees and bake another 40 to 50 minutes until crust is golden brown, the pie bubbles and the apples feel tender when poked with a fork. You may need to bake a bit longer if using a firmer apple.

The Rose and Thistle Bed and Breakfast

You'll find wisps of enchantment at The Rose and Thistle bed and breakfast. This lovingly maintained turn-of-the-century Queen Anne Victorian combines old world charm with new world luxury, accented with a beautiful rose theme.

Relax in the Rose and Thistle's warm and welcoming atmosphere. Take full advantage of the wraparound porch, or enjoy a book or a game in the front parlor. For the energetic, climb the backyard stairs to wander among the tall pines and tranquil brook.

Congenial hosts Steve and Patti D'Esposito will make your stay in Cooperstown memorable with great food, comfortable accommodations and friendly ambience.

The Rose and Thistle Bed and Breakfast
132 Chestnut Street
607-547-5345
Cooperstown, NY 1332

www.roseandthistlebb.com
stay@roseandthistlebb.com

Bread Pudding

The Rose and Thistle Bed and Breakfast

~~~~~~

*I*n France, what we call French toast is *pain perdu,* literally "lost bread". It puts stale bread to a thrifty and delicious purpose. Steve expands that same idea in his Bread Pudding, using a variety of leftover bread products. Since the components vary, the scrumptious result is always a bit different. This is one of Steve's signature dishes.

Preheat oven to 350 degrees
13 ounces cubed French bread; leftover pancakes, waffles, danish or muffins may be used in addition to or in place of the bread.
4 cups milk
2 cups sugar
½ cup melted butter
4 eggs
2 tablespoons vanilla
1 tablespoon cinnamon
1 tablespoon nutmeg
1 cup raisins, optional
1 cup pecans, optional
New York State maple syrup

Spray or grease a 13"x9" baking pan. Place bread in pan, evenly. In a bowl, mix milk, sugar, butter, eggs, vanilla, cinnamon and nutmeg. Combine well and pour over bread. The bread should be moist, but not soupy. If too liquid, add more bread.

Bake for about one hour and 15 minutes. Oven temperatures vary so check after an hour. Pudding is done when the top is golden brown. Serve with maple syrup, whipped cream, etc. It is outstanding with *Home Plate* contributor Assemblyman Bill Magee's New York Maple Dried Cherry Syrup.

The Plaide Palette

Harboring the soul of Ireland in Cherry Valley, NY, the Plaide Palette is an unforgettable stop. Owner Sue Miller offers an impressive array of all things Celtic, including food, jewelry, music and those fabulous knits.

If your world is a little off-kilter without your "cuppa tea," browse Sue's extensive line of teas and tea accessories, including *Tiny Teapot* necklaces. Her front porch pantry is filled with biscuits (Americans, read "cookies") to go with your tea and other fine fare from the British Isles. Heinz baked beans, McVitie's chocolate digestives, Malteasers and Rose's lime marmalade are sure to ring a bell and warm the heart of any Anglophile or wandering Brit.

Once inside the shop, choose from sweaters, scarves, tapestries, soaps and candles. Sue carries figurines, hats, kilts, children's clothing, drums, bagpipes and Irish music accessories. From Celtic crosses to garden statuary to custom- made wedding cake toppers, be sure to stop at the Plaide Palette; there is no place like it in Otsego County.

The Plaide Palette is located in the historic Oliver Judd Homestead, circa 1804. Sue invites you for tea, for conversation while browsing, and a stroll in the garden.

45 Main Street
PO Box 464
Cherry Valley, NY 13320
Phone: 607-264-3769
Fax: 607-264-9320
www.plaidepalette.com

Old Fashioned Fruit Cake

The Plaide Palette

Fruitcake has been much maligned and the butt of too many jokes. This delicious recipe will convert even the most skeptical to a fruitcake fan. The bourbon helps keep this delicious cake for months.

2 cups chopped dried peaches
1 cup chopped dried cherries
1 large apple, coarsely chopped
1¾ cups bourbon or dark rum
2½ cups unbleached all-purpose flour
½ teaspoon salt
¾ teaspoon grated nutmeg
1 cup crushed walnuts
½ cup molasses
2/3 cup heavy cream or buttermilk
¼ cup honey

2 cups golden raisins
1 cup chopped dried pineapple
¾ cup fresh orange juice

¾ teaspoon ground cloves
½ teaspoon baking soda

1½ sticks unsalted butter, softened
½ cup sugar
4 large eggs

In a large mixing bowl, combine the dried fruits, chopped apple, 1¼ cups bourbon and the orange juice. Cover and refrigerate overnight.

Preheat the oven to 325 degrees. Grease and flour a 10-cup Bundt pan.

Sift 1 cup of the flour with the cloves, nutmeg, salt and baking soda into a small bowl and set aside.

Add the remaining 1½ cups flour, molasses, cream and walnuts to the fruit and bourbon mixture. Mix thoroughly and set aside. Beat butter and sugar in a large mixing bowl until light and fluffy, using an electric mixer at medium speed. Add the eggs, one at a time, beating well after each addition. Fold the batter into the fruit mixture and stir well.Scrape the mixture into the prepared pan. Smooth the top. Bake about1 hour and 20 minutes, or until a toothpick inserted in the center comes out clean. Cool the cake in the pan for 10 minutes, and then turn it out onto a rack. Combine honey and the remaining ½ cup bourbon in a small saucepan. Cook over low heat, stirring until combined. Brush half of the hot glaze over the top and sides of the cake. Gently turn the cake over, and brush on the remaining glaze. Let the cake cool thoroughly.

Wrap the cake tightly in plastic wrap or wax paper, then in heavy-duty aluminum foil. Let the cake mellow a couple of days at room temperature before serving.

Walker Planning and Design

~~~~~~~~~~~~~~~~~~~

*A*ppealing and efficiently usable community areas, recreational centers, and welcoming public places are no accident. They are the satisfying results of astute planning and gifted design.

Walker Planning and Design meets the demands of site planning and development issues with forethought, vision, and over 30 years experience in landscape architecture, master planning, project management, regulatory review and grants administration. Walker projects, including parks, baseball stadiums and sports facilities, business zones and roadways are seen throughout Upstate New York. In the near future, look for the Walker designed community heritage park in Worcester, NY.

Walker Planning and Design works with your ideas, applies their extensive expertise in multiple specialties and creates bricks and mortar reality.

Edward B. Walker, RLA, AICP
20 Chestnut Street
Cooperstown, NY 13326
607-547-5745

By far the greatest and most admirable form of wisdom is that needed to plan and beautify cities and human communities.

—SOCRATES

Pumpkin Carrot Bars

Walker Planning and Design

~~~~~~~~~~~~~~~~~~~~~~~~~

*T*hese are an easy favorite. Very flavorful and moist, they travel well, freeze well* and are a hit for coffees and lunch boxes.

Preheat oven to 350 degrees

Stir together in mixing bowl:

2 cups all-purpose flour
2 teaspoons baking powder
1 teaspoon orange zest
½ teaspoon baking soda
¼ teaspoon salt
1 cup finely grated carrots

Combine in separate bowl:

3 eggs, beaten
1 ½ cups brown sugar, packed
1 cup canned pumpkin
2/3 cup cooking oil
1 teaspoon vanilla

Orange Icing

1 cup chopped walnuts
1-2 tablespoons orange juice or liqueur

1½ cups powdered sugar

Combine wet and dry ingredients, stirring until just combined.

Pour batter into a prepared baking pan. Use a 15"x10" jelly roll pan for bars or a 13"x9" pan for a sheet cake. Bake bars 15-20 minutes; bake cake 25-30 minutes, or until toothpick inserted comes out clean.

When cake or bars are cool, frost with orange icing. Mix powdered sugar with orange liqueur or orange juice to make a glaze of desired consistency. Drizzle over bars or spread over cake. Decorate with chopped nuts or walnut halves, if desired.

*Freeze unfrosted. Ice after cake or bars have thawed.

Smokey Hollow Maple Products

For over seventeen years, family-run Smokey Hollow Maple Products have "tapped the mountain" on their 330 acre farm. A cat's cradle of bright blue sap tubing connects over 1700 sugar maple trees. Every March the trees convey their precious liquid by gravity and vacuum to George Loft's pump house on Sparrow Hawk Creek.

The sap is transported to the Smokey Hollow Sap House where it is transformed into premium quality syrup, maple cream, maple sugar and sprinkles. Their maple products are available for shipping and they count loyal customers nationwide and overseas.

You'll enjoy Smokey Hollow Maple Products at Sugaring Off Sundays at The Farmers' Museum, numerous area pancake breakfasts and at the Otsego County Fair, every August in Morris. Please call before stopping by the Smokey Hollow Sap House.

Smokey Hollow Maple Products is easy to find. From Interstate 88, take exit 18 to Route 7, Schenevus. Turn left onto Route 7 and right onto Smokey Avenue, just before Schenevus High School. Smokey Hollow is about two miles on the right.

George and Inga Loft
436 Smokey Avenue
Schenevus, NY 12155
607-638-9393

Why is sap tubing blue? It limits the ultraviolet light to the sap, keeping it cooler as late winter days start warming. Sap must be kept under 40 degrees to keep from fermenting.

Maple Syrup Cherry Bars

Smokey Hollow Maple Products

~~~~~~~~~~~~~~~~~~~~~~~~~~

D elicious and easy, this recipe makes big pan of bars, perfect to take to class, the office, or a picnic or potluck.

Preheat oven to 375 degrees

1 cup butter, softened

2 cups maple syrup

2 eggs

3 cups flour

1 cup chopped nuts

3 cups uncooked oatmeal

1 cup chopped maraschino cherries

Maple Frosting

1 teaspoon salt

4 teaspoons baking powder

½ cup milk

Maple Sprinkles or maple sugar

2 cups powdered sugar, sifted

1 tablespoon soft butter

3 to 4 tablespoons maple syrup

Beat together butter, syrup and eggs. Sift together flour, salt and baking powder; add to syrup mixture and then stir in milk. Add nuts, oats and cherries and thoroughly combine. Grease a 15"x10"x1" jelly roll pan, or line the pan with aluminum foil and mist with cooking spray. Spread mixture evenly in pan. Bake 10-15 minutes. When completely cool, ice with maple frosting and generously scatter Maple Sprinkles from Smokey Hollow Maple Products.

Maple Frosting: Beat together butter and ½ cup of the powdered sugar. Beat in maple syrup and remaining sugar. Add more maple syrup to achieve desired consistency.

These bars are a great way to use the cherries leftover from baking the Cherry Nut Cake from *Home Plate* contributor, the Greater Cherry Valley Chamber of Commerce

Dancing Veggie Farm

Garlic and brooms are two components essential to daily life. Fortunately, both are beautifully produced on Dancing Veggie Farm. Warren Ainslie's handcrafted brooms are made on the farm using 19th century tools and techniques. They are featured in the 2006 issue of *Early American Life* magazine. He and his wife Rachel also grow about a ton of Elmer's Topset Garlic annually on their family farm, set in the quiet, scenic hills between Otsego and Canadarago Lakes.

The Ainslie's Garlic Harvest Celebration is the last weekend of August. They fill their 1840s post and beam barn with cookbooks, garlic keepers, garlic related wares and garlic hanging from the rafters. Garlic and garlic accoutrements, Warren's wonderful brooms and one of the prettiest drives in Otsego County, make a wonderful August afternoon.

Dancing Veggie Farm takes their show on the road in September at garlic fests throughout the region, including The Susquehanna Garlic Festival in Milford right here in Otsego County. They also visit The Southern Vermont Garlic and Herb Festival on Labor Day Weekend and the Hudson Valley Garlic Festival in Saugerties. In October, they plant next year's garlic crop.

The Ainslie's use traditional biodynamic farming methods, maximizing the vitality of their crops. Using crop rotation and natural fertilizers in a contained environment, the result is high fertility, healthier soils and better crops.

Warren and Rachel Ainslie-Hamblin
246 Ainslie Road
Richfield Springs, NY 13439
315-858-0506

Garlic Peach Upside Down Cake
Dancing Veggie Farm

*T*his is not just a novelty dessert. The complex flavors of garlic add a pleasant background for the peaches. With most varieties of garlic, the "heat" will cook out.

Preheat oven to 350 degrees.

½ cup butter, melted
1 cup brown sugar
1-2 cans sliced peaches*
½ cup dried tart cherries (optional)
1-2 bulbs (whole heads, not cloves) New York State garlic, peeled and diced
1 box yellow cake mix, or your favorite yellow cake recipe

Pour melted butter in bottom of a greased 9"x13" pan. Sprinkle brown sugar over butter. Place peaches or pineapple in single layer over sugar and scatter cherries and diced garlic evenly over all.

Prepare cake batter and pour evenly over fruit. Bake for 25-30 minutes, or until cake springs bake when touched. Cool slightly before turning upside down to serve.

*8 slices of canned pineapple may be substituted.

Tomatoes and oregano make it Italian; wine and tarragon make it French.
Sour cream makes it Russian; lemon and cinnamon make it Greek.
Soy sauce makes it Chinese; Garlic makes it Good.
—ALICE MAY BROCK

42 Montgomery Bed and Breakfast

*T*his strikingly renovated Victorian bed and breakfast falls right in step with the serene, artistic charm of the Historic Village of Cherry Valley.

Warmth, welcome and tranquility are the hallmarks of this beautiful property, gracefully positioned on a knoll within earshot of church bells.

Guests are treated to oversized soft robes, book-laden shelves, inviting common areas and a lovely garden, as well as the comfortable beds, delicious breakfasts and other amenities expected at a well-appointed B&B.

Mornings greet you with repasts from whole-grain porridge with embellishments to an indulgent apple-cinnamon bread pudding with Bavarian cream sauce. Espresso, cappuccino and lattes are specialties of the house.

All are invited to sit on Melanie's wide front porch and let daily stress drift away as you listen to the opera voices practice in the summer, or as the pastoral peacefulness of this beautiful valley envelops you.

Melanie Crawford
42 Montgomery Street
PO Box 521
Cherry Valley, NY 13320
607-264-9974
www.42montgomery.com
Melanie@42montgomery.com

> *To sit in the shade on a fine day, and look upon verdure is the most perfect refreshment.*
> —JANE AUSTEN

Melanie's Apple Cake
42 Montgomery Bed and Breakfast

*T*his dessert recalls traditional farm cakes, complete with boiled frosting.

Preheat oven to 350 degrees

4 cups New York apples, pared, cored and chopped
1 cup walnut or pecan pieces
1 cup maple sugar
1 cup white sugar
Mix together and let sit for 40 minutes

1 cup vegetable oil
2 eggs
1 teaspoon vanilla
Whisk together and then stir into apple mixture.

3 cups whole wheat or all-purpose flour (or a blend of the two)
1 teaspoon salt
1 teaspoon baking soda
2 teaspoons cinnamon
Stir together, and then add to apple mixture. If batter seems too thick, add ¼ cup apple or orange juice.

Pour batter into well greased 9"x13" baking pan or a Bundt pan.
Bake 35-55 minutes, or until toothpick inserted in center comes out clean.

Maple Glaze

1 cup maple sugar	½ cup buttermilk
1 teaspoon baking soda	1 tablespoon corn syrup

Put all ingredients in saucepan and bring to a boil. Boil over medium heat for 7 minutes. Stir in ½ teaspoon vanilla and pour over warm cake.

NEW YORK FOOD AND FARMING

Amazing New York

*I*f you think New York means mostly skyscrapers and traffic, then you are in for a surprise. This remarkably bountiful state, with its curvy topography and beautiful valleys, rocky soils and challenging winters ranks in the top ten nationwide in the production of a bounty of farm goods and is second nationally in agricultural diversity. *Home Plate* salutes the New York agriculturalists that have earned these impressive statistics. We respect your incomparable work ethic. Thank you for keeping us well fed and preserving a beautiful New York.

APPLES—New York ranks second nationally in apple production. McIntosh, Empire, Rome, Idared, and Red Delicious are our leading varieties.

CABBAGE—We are Number One! We are Number One!

DAIRY PRODUCTS—New York is the third largest producer of milk in the nation. Nothing compares to New York cheddar.

GRAPES—New York is third nationwide in wine and juice grape production. Wine is one of our fastest growing agricultural industries.

MAPLE SYRUP—Number three in sap volume, and number two in syrup value.

ONIONS—Those muck farms have made us number eight in onion production.

PEARS—New York shines when com-"pear"ed to other states. We rank fourth in nationwide pear production.

PUMPKINS—New York is first in pumpkin production.

SNAP BEANS—New York is number two in fresh snap beans and number three in processed beans.

STRAWBERRIES—Strawberries are our third most valuable fruit, following apples and grapes. These are real strawberries, not the "plastic" kind that ship better than they taste. We place seventh in nationwide production.

SWEET CORN—New York is number three nationally in fresh corn, and number six in processed corn. Always stop at a New York fresh sweet corn farm stand!

TART CHERRIES—New York production ranks third in the nation. Can we bake a cherry pie, Billy Boy? Yes!

VEGETABLES—New York ranks sixth in fresh market vegetables, making New York great for farmers' markets and community-supported agriculture. We are ninth in processing vegetables. When you grab a can of green beans, think New York! Leading crops in New York are cabbage, sweet corn and onions.

AND JUST FOR GOOD MEASURE...

Wait, there's more! New York also holds these rankings for the following crops:

CAULIFLOWER—According to Mark Twain, cauliflower is nothing but cabbage with a college education. New York is number three in cauliflower production, number one in cabbage.

CUCUMBERS and GREEN PEAS—New York ranks fourth in both crops.

FLORICULTURE—our bedding plants are beautiful! We rank number 5.

OATS—Number nine in oat production. Good morning! Have your breakfast and a New York oatmeal cookie.

SQUASH—New York is fifth in nationwide production, from acorn to zucchini.

TOMATOES—New York is number eight. That's a lot of salads and sauce!

Savor New York

How Do You Say That?

The Otsego County area place names boast a rich Native American history and the influence of Dutch and other European settlers. Below is a phonetic guide to pronouncing a few of the sometimes-puzzling names bestowed on our geography and entities.

Canadarago Lake – CANADA-RA-GO   Canajoharie – CAN-A-JO-HAIR-EE
Chenango-SHE-NANG-O   Delhi- DELL- HIGH
NYSHA- KNEE-SHA   Oneida- OH-NY-DA
Oneonta – OWN-KNEE-ON-TA   Otego – O-TEE-GO
Otsego- OTT-SEE-GO   Schenevus- SKIN-KNEE-VUS
Schoharie- SKO-HAIR-EE   Schuyler Lake: SKY-LER Lake
Susquehanna- SUSS-KWE-HAN-NA   Unadilla- YOON-A-DILL-A
Worcester- WUSS-TER

Otsego County Farmers' Markets

COOPERSTOWN FARMERS' MARKET
Pioneer Alley
Cooperstown, NY 13326
607-547-6195
www.cooperstownfarmersmarket.org
Open Saturdays; May to August 8AM-2PM;September to mid-November 9AM-2PM; Mid-November to mid-December 10AM-2PM; Look for special holiday markets!

RICHFIELD SPRINGS FARMERS' MARKET
Spring Park, corner of Main (Route 20) and Church Streets
Richfield Springs, NY
315-858-3520
Early June through October; Thursdays 4PM-8PM; Saturdays 8AM-2PM

ONEONTA FARMERS' MARKET
Main Street Plaza
Oneonta, NY 13820
607-431-6034
Open Saturdays; Mid-May through October 9AM-2PM; Open Tuesdays; Mid-June through September 2PM-6PM

GILBERTSVILLE FARMERS' MARKET
The Gilbertsville Farmers' Market is open in conjunction with Music at the Major's, weekly evening concerts held at the Major's Inn.

Post Office Park
Gilbertsville, NY
607-783-2112
Wednesdays in July, August 4:30PM – closing; Wednesdays in September by demand

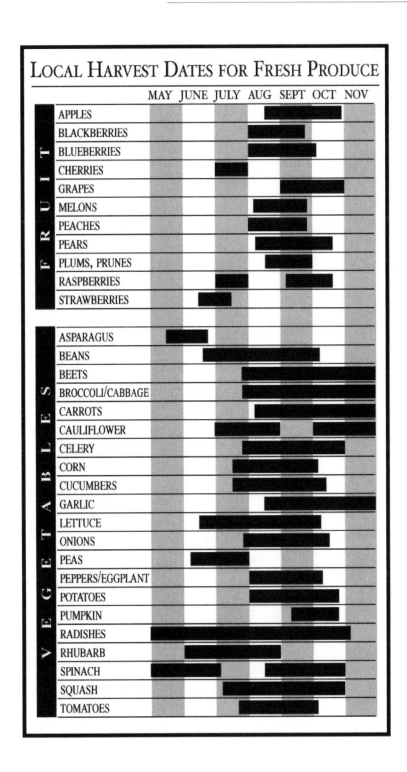

LOCAL HARVEST DATES FOR FRESH PRODUCE

Otsego County Agri-Tourism Events and Festivals

"*A*gri-tourism" events and celebrations are frequent attractions in Otsego County. Food and farm related themes provide the backdrop for many events; look for bake sales and barbecues at various celebrations, and homemade food and non-edible agricultural goods at craft fairs. Here we've listed some of our favorite happenings. This list is by no means all-inclusive; celebrations go on in Otsego County year round. Check local newspapers or chambers of commerce to see what's happening during any given week. Please reference the phone numbers or websites listed to learn specific dates and locations.

FEBRUARY
February is National Cherry Month

COOPERSTOWN WINTER CARNIVAL
Cooperstown, NY
1-800-843-3394
www.cooperstowncarnival.org

ANNUAL CHILI BOWL AND COOK-OFF
Oneonta, NY
Super Bowl Sunday
Upper Catskill Community
      Council of the Arts (UCCCA)
607-432-2070
www.uccca.com

ANNUAL LENTEN PANCAKE BREAKFASTS
Featuring genuine
      New York State maple syrup
Most Lenten Saturday mornings
United Methodist Church
Morris, NY
      607-263-5162

Snow Fest
Cooperstown
Cooperstown Chamber of Commerce
607-547-9983
www.cooperstownchamber.org

Winterfest
Milford, NY
Milford Central School
607-286-7721

<u>March</u>
National Nutrition Month
*Look for Pancake Breakfasts held throughout
Otsego County at schools, churches, firehouses, and meeting halls.*

Sugaring Off Sundays Pancake Breakfasts,
featuring Otsego County Maple Syrup
The Farmers' Museum
Cooperstown, NY
607-547-1450
www.farmersmuseum.org

Historical Dining at Bump Tavern Series
Featuring evenings of local food and local lore.
The Farmers' Museum
Cooperstown, NY
607-547-1450
www.farmersmuseum.org

<u>April</u>
April is National Food Month

The Farmers' Museum opens
Cooperstown, NY
607-547-1450
www.farmersmuseum.org

EPICUREAN FESTIVAL, FOOD TASTING AND BENEFIT
 AUCTION
Cooperstown, NY
607-432-6773
www.cahpc.org

FOOD FOR THOUGHT LUNCHEONS BEGIN
The Farmers' Museum/Fenimore Art Museum
Cooperstown, NY
607-547-1450
www.farmersmuseum.org

MAY
May is National Strawberry Month

THE COOPERSTOWN FARMERS' MARKET OPENS
Pioneer Alley
Cooperstown, NY
607-547-6195
www.cooperstownfarmersmarket.org

ONEONTA FARMERS' MARKET OPENS
Main Street Plaza
Oneonta, NY
607-431-6034
www.cadefarms.org/markets

SPRING FESTIVAL AT THE FARMERS' MUSEUM
Cooperstown, NY
607-547-1450
www.farmersmuseum.org

HERITAGE PLANT SALE
The Farmers' Museum
Cooperstown, NY
607-547-1450
www.farmersmuseum.org

ANNUAL MASTER GARDENER PLANT SALE
Cornell Cooperative Extension
Cooperstown
607-547-2536
www.cce.cornell.edu/otsego

CHERRY VALLEY MEMORIAL WEEKEND
Featuring the Cherry Bake-off
Cherry Valley, NY
607-264-3755
www.cherryvalleyny.com

JUNE
June is Dairy Month

RICHFIELD SPRINGS FARMERS' MARKET OPENS
Spring Park
Richfield Springs, NY
315-858-3520

ANNUAL FRIENDSHIP CRAFT FESTIVAL AND BBQ
Spring Park
Richfield Springs, NY
315-858-2182
www.rscocu.com

THE FARMERS' MUSEUM ANNUAL BENEFIT HORSE
SHOW
Iroquois Farm
Cooperstown, NY
607-547-1450
www.farmersmuseum.org

JULY
July is National Ice Cream Month

GILBERTSVILLE FARMERS' MARKET OPENS
Post Office Park
Gilbertsville, NY
607-783-2112

GRAND OLD 4TH OF JULY CELEBRATION
        at The Farmers' Museum
Cooperstown, NY
607-547-1450
www.farmersmuseum.org

FOURTH OF JULY PARADE, BARBEQUE AND PIE SALE
Springfield Center, NY
315-858-5802

INDEPENDENCE DAY ICE CREAM SOCIAL
First Presbyterian Church
Cooperstown
607-547-8496

OTSEGO LAKE FESTIVAL
Lake Front Park
Cooperstown, NY
607-547-4488
www.otsegolakefestival.com

JUNIOR LIVESTOCK SHOW
Iroquois Farm
Cooperstown
607-547-1450
www.farmersmuseum.org

BROOKWOOD GARDEN FUNDRAISER AUCTION
        AND PLANT SALE
Cooperstown, NY
607-547-2170
www.brookwoodgarden.com

UNADILLA CARNIVAL OF SALES
Community Grounds
Unadilla, NY
607-530-9737 or 888-530-7937

MIDDLEFIELD COMMUNITY DAY
*Featuring Brook's BBQ, New York State ice cream and
        baked goods*
Middlefield, NY
607-547-9515

AUGUST
August is Harvest Month

DANCING VEGGIE FARM GARLIC FEST
Richfield Springs, NY
246 Ainslie Road
315-858-0506

HOP PICKERS' PICNIC AND BALL
The Farmers' Museum
Cooperstown, NY
607-547-1450
www.farmersmuseum.org

LEATHERSTOCKING SHEEP DOG TRIALS
Beaver Meadow Road
Cooperstown, NY
607-293-8385

OTSEGO COUNTY FAIR
Morris, NY
607-263-5289
www.otsegocountyfair.org

SEPTEMBER
September is National Honey Month

SUSQUEHANNA GARLIC FESTIVAL
Milford, NY
607-638-9016

THE FARMERS' MUSEUM AUTUMN HARVEST
FESTIVAL
The Farmers' Museum
Cooperstown, NY
607-547-1450
www.farmersmuseum.org

LABOR DAY ARTS AND CRAFTS SHOW
Clark Sports Center Grounds
Cooperstown, NY
607-847-6641

OCTOBER
October is National Apple Month

PUMPKIN FEST
Cooperstown, NY
Cooperstown Chamber of Commerce
607-547-9983
www.cooperstownchamber.org

NOVEMBER
November is National Pepper Month

Cooperstown Holiday Farmers' Markets Begin
607-547-6195
www.cooperstownfarmersmarket.org

CORNELL COOPERATIVE EXTENSION
Benefit Auction and Celebrity Chefs
Hunt Union, SUNY Oneonta
607-547-2536
www.cce.cornell.edu/otsego

DECEMBER
December 25 is National Pumpkin Pie Day

CANDLELIGHT EVENING
The Farmers' Museum
Cooperstown, NY
607-547-1450
www.farmersmuseum.org

OTSEGO COUNTY BUYING GUIDE

Home Plate Buying Guide

Otsego County Specialty Foods and Agricultural Products

A Rose is a Rose Flowers
Jackie Hull
17 Main Street
Cherry Valley, NY 13320
607-264-3100
800-243-9501
aroseisarose17@hotmail.com

The Taste of Britain Bakery
Perry Owen
Norwich, NY 13815
607-336-3333
pvowen@cnyconnect.net

Bates Hop House Lilacs
George Alverson
54 Lancaster Street
Cherry Valley, NY 13320
607-264-3450

Bear Pond Winery
Mark and Brenda Lebo
2515 State Highway 28
Oneonta, NY 13820
607-643-0294
Fax: 607-643-0219
www.bearpondwines.com
taste@bearpondwines.com

BlueStone Farm Granola
Marty Bernardo
Bissell Road
Cooperstown, NY 13326
www.bluestonefarm.org
bluestone@capital.net
607-547-8227

Breezie Maples Products
Rick Newman and Larry Roseboom
2269 County Highway 34
Westford, NY 13488
607-638-9317
800-950-9676
www.breeziemaples.com

Chutney Unlimited
Tanna Roten
52 Pioneer Street
Cooperstown, NY 13326
607-547-7272
www.chutneyunlimited.com
tanna@chutneyunlimited.com

Cooperstown Brewing Company
Stan Hall
110 River Street
PO Box 276
Milford, NY 13807
607-286-9330 or 1-877-FINE ALE
www.cooperstownbrewing.com
taproom@cooperstownbrewing.com

COOPERSTOWN COOKIES
Pati Drumm Grady
PO Box 64
Cooperstown, NY 13326
607-547-9146 or 607-435-5789
goodies@cooperstowncookiecompany.com
www.cooperstowncookiecompany.com

CREEK'S EDGE ELK FARM
Stacy Handy or Susan Keith
894 State Highway 80
Fort Plain, NY 13339
518-568-5476
518-993-4014 (Sue at the Farm)

DANCING VEGGIE FARM
Warren and Rachel Ainslie-Hamblin
246 Ainslie Road
Richfield Springs, NY 13439
315-858-0506

DISMAL INN SUGAR COMPANY
Bruce and Lucia Phillips
Hartwick, NY 13348
607-293-6488
607-293-6164

DOWN IN THE COUNTRY
Jackie Jones
2388 County Highway 11
Mount Vision, NY 13810
607-293-8333
www.downinthecountry.com
Jackie@downinthecountry.com

FOR THE LOVE OF CAKE
Kelly Calhoun
156 Perkins Road
Cooperstown, NY 13326
607-293-8465

FOX HOLLOW NURSERY
Neil and Bonnie Monzeglio
2751 State Highway 23
West Oneonta, NY
607-263-5764
bmonzeglio@stny.rr.com

LIBERTY MARKET BAKERY
Bonnie Fayssoux
187 Joe Chamberlain Road
Cherry Valley, NY 13320
518-234-9642 or
607-264-8327
www.libertymarket.net

MCCOY'S PURE RAW HONEY
John McCoy
307 State Highway 28
Oneonta, NY 13820
607-432-0605

PERENNIAL FIELD
Ruby Mitchell
25 Main Street
Otego, NY 13825
607-988-9009
www.perennialfield.com

SMOKEY HOLLOW MAPLE PRODUCTS
George and Inga Loft
436 Smokey Avenue
Schenevus, NY 12155
607-638-9393

STANNARD'S MAPLE AND ELK
Warren, Mary and Julie Stannard
166 Stannard Hill Road
Cherry Valley, NY 13320
stannardsmaple@msn.com
607-264-3090

WILLYS FARM AND CIDER MILL
The Gartung Family
Badeau Hill Road
Schenevus, NY 12155
607-638-9449

Restaurants

BROOK'S BAR-B-QUE
Ryan and Beth Brooks
5560 State Highway 7
Oneonta, NY 13820
607-432-1782
800-498-2445
Fax: 607-432-2665
Website: www.brooksbbq.com
E-Mail: info@brooksbbq.com

COOLEY'S STONE HOUSE TAVERN
Tim Gould
49 Pioneer Street
Cooperstown, NY 13326
607-544-1311
www.cooleystavern.com

DANNY'S MARKET
Alice and Sergio Gaviria
92 Main Street
Cooperstown, NY 13326
607-547-4053

FENIMORE CAFÉ
Fenimore Art Museum
5775 State Highway 80 - Lake Road
Cooperstown, NY 13326
607-547-1450
www.fenimoreartmuseum.org

FRENCH CORNER
Mark McCoy
161 Main Street
Cooperstown, NY 13326
607-547-6106

HARMONY HOUSE CAFÉ AND ANTIQUES
Richard and Mary Lou Votypka
6208 State Highway 28
Fly Creek, NY 13337
Harmony House Café: 607-547-5077
Fax: 607-547-6011
Harmony House Antiques: 607-547-4071

HERDER'S COTTAGE
The Farmers' Museum
5775 State Highway 80 - Lake Road
Cooperstown, NY 13326
607-547-1450
www.farmersmuseum.org

HOFFMAN LANE BISTRO
Mark Loewenguth
2 Hoffman Lane
Cooperstown, NY 13326
607-547-7055
www.hoffmanlanebistro.com
mark@hoffmanlanebistro.com

NICOLETTA'S
96 Main Street
Cooperstown, NY 13326
607-547-7499
www.nicolettasitaliancafe.com

ROSE AND KETTLE RESTAURANT
Clem Coleman and Dana Spiotta
4 Lancaster Street
Cherry Valley, NY 13320
607-264-3078
dana@roseandkettle.com
www.roseandkettle.com

STELLA LUNA RISTORANTE
Antonio and Vincente Avanzato
58-60 Market Street
Oneonta, NY 13820
Phone: 607-433-7646
Fax: 607-433- 9623
www.stellalunas.com

SWEETTOOTH SCHOOLHOUSE
Harriet and Richard Sessler
540 State Highway 165
Pleasant Brook, NY
607-264-3233
www.sweettoothschoolhouse.com

TJ'S PLACE THE HOME PLATE
Ted Hargrove and Diane Howard
124 Main Street
Cooperstown, NY 13326
607-547-4040
800-860-5670
Fax: 607-547-4042
www.tjs-place.com

TEPEE PETE'S CHOW WAGON
Pete Latella
7632 US Highway 20
Cherry Valley, NY 13320
607-264-3987
www.thetepee.net
thetepee@capital.net

TRIPLE PLAY CAFÉ
Pat Governale
64 Main Street
Cooperstown, NY 13326
607-547-1395
Fax: 607-547-1355

Retail

ALL AND ALL EMPORIUM
Linda Parmalee
21 Railroad Avenue
Cooperstown, NY 13326
607-437-1989
www.chamberofcommerce/allandall/

ARTISANS' GUILD
Deborah Blake
148 Main Street
Oneonta, NY 13820
607-432-1080

ATWELL, JIM AUTHOR
From Fly Creek: Life in Leatherstocking Country
Fly Creek, NY 13337
(607) 547-5895
www.JimAtwell.com

COOPERSTOWN BASEBALL BRACELET
Anne Hall and Jennifer Stewart
607-437-1492
www.cooperstownbaseballbracelet.com
cooperstownbaseballbracelet@yahoo.com

COOPERSTOWN BOOK NOOK
Karen Johansen
61 Main Street
Cooperstown, NY 13326
607-547-2578
bnook@aol.com

COOPERSTOWN NATURAL FOODS
Ellen Poulette
607-547-8613
61 Linden Avenue
Cooperstown, NY 13326
Cooperstownnaturalfoods@verizon.net

COOPERSTOWN WINE AND SPIRITS
Ed Landers
45 Pioneer Street
607-547-8100
Cooperstown, NY 13326

DAVIDSON'S JEWELRY AND AUGUR'S BOOKS
73 Main Street
Cooperstown, NY 13326
607-547-2422
607-547-5099
www.cooperstownjewelry.com
augurs@capital.net

ESSENTIAL ELEMENTS
Robin Gray
Doubleday Parking Lot
137 Main Street
Cooperstown, NY 13326
607-547-9432
800-437-3265
Fax: 607-547-5791
www.essentialelementsdayspa.com

FLY CREEK GENERAL STORE
Tom Bouton
State Route 28
Fly Creek, NY 13337
607-547-7274

GEDDES-ATWELL, ANNE, ILLUSTRATOR
From Fly Creek: Life in Leatherstocking Country
134 Allison Road
Fly Creek, NY 13337
(607) 547-5895
www.JimAtwell.com

GILBERT BLOCK QUILT SHOP
Nona Slaughter
9 Commercial Street
PO Box 351
Gilbertsville, NY 13776
607-783-2872

HAGGERTY ACE HARDWARE
5390 State Highway 28
Cooperstown, NY 13326
607-547-2166
haggertyhardware@stny.rr.com

HILTON BLOOM ART STUDIO
Jane Evelynne Higgins
24 Bloom Street
PO Box 12
Gilbertsville, NY 13776-0012
607-783-2779
www.gilbertsville.com
jane.al@frontiernet.net

LADYBUG
Doris Mark
108 Main Street
Cooperstown, NY 13326
607-547-1940

LAKE CLEAR WABBLER
Tom Delaney
PO Box 301
10 Spring Street
Gilbertsville, NY 13776
Phone: 607-783-2587
Fax: 607-783-2538
www.lakeclearwabbler.com
lcwabbler@stny.rr.com

MICKEY'S PLACE
Vin Russo
74 Main Street
Cooperstown, NY 13326
607-547-5775
800-528-5775
Fax: 607-547-6212
www.mickeysplace.com
info@mickeysplace.com

NATURA PRODUCTS
Scottie Baker
PO Box 77
Fly Creek, NY 13337
607-547-5356
www.naturaproductions.com
scottieb@naturaproductions.com

PLAIDE PALETTE
45 Main Street
PO Box 464
Cherry Valley, NY 13320
Phone: 607-264-3769
Fax: 607-264-9320
www.plaidepalette.com

PRICE CHOPPER
Route 7
Oneonta , NY 13820
(607) 432-8905
1 Main Street
Richfield Springs 13439
(315) 858-1171
www.pricechopper.com

RIVERWOOD GIFTS
Rick Gibbons
88 Main Street
Cooperstown, NY 13326
607-547-4403
www.riverwoodgifts.com
riverwood@verizon.net

SIEGFRIED STONEWARE
Alice Siegfried, Potter
Oneonta, NY 13326
607-432-8673

THE TEPEE
Dale and Donna Latella
7632 US Highway 20
Cherry Valley, NY 13320
607-264-3987
www.thetepee.net
thetepee@capital.net

Accommodations

42 MONTGOMERY BED AND BREAKFAST
Melanie Crawford
42 Montgomery Street
PO Box 521
Cherry Valley, NY 13320
607-264-9974
Website: www.42montgomery.com
E-mail: Melanie@42montgomery.com

BARNWELL INN
Mark and Tara Barnwell
48 Susquehanna Avenue
Cooperstown, NY 13326
1-607-547-1850
E-mail: Barnwellinn@aol.com
Website: www.Barnwellinn.com

BRYN BROOKE MANOR
John, Brenda and Elizabeth Brooke Berstler
6 Westridge Road
Cooperstown, NY 13326
607-544-1885
607-287-0162
www.brynbrookemanor.com
brookebb@stny.rr.com

DAYLILY DREAMS BED AND BREAKFAST
Rae and Bob Consigli, Innkeepers
1599 County Rte. 33
Cooperstown, New York 13326
Toll free 866-547-1888
www.daylilydreams.com
info@daylilydreams.com

INN AT COOPERSTOWN
Marc and Sherrie Kingsley
16 Chestnut Street
Cooperstown, NY 13326
607-547-5756
www.innatcooperstown.com
info@innatcooperstown.com

ROSE AND THISTLE BED AND BREAKFAST
Steve and Patti D'Esposito
132 Chestnut Street
607-547-5345
Cooperstown, NY 1332
www.roseandthistlebb.com
stay@roseandthistlebb.com

SUNNY SLOPE FARM BED AND BREAKFAST
Cliff and Patti Brunner
211 Brunner Road
Cooperstown, NY 13326
607-547-8686
sunnyslope@mymailstation.com

WHITE HOUSE INN
Ed and Margie Landers
46 Chestnut Street
Cooperstown, NY 13326
607-547-5054
607-547-1100 fax
www.thewhitehouseinn.com
stay@thewhitehouseinn.com

Attractions and Services

BROOKWOOD GARDEN
Pat Thorpe
6000 West Lake Road (Route 80)
Cooperstown, NY 13326
607-547-2170
www.brookwoodgarden.com
info@brookwoodgarden.com

CHERRY VALLEY HISTORICAL SOCIETY
49 Main Street
Cherry Valley, NY 13320
607 264-3303
607 264-3098
museum@HistoricCherryValley.com
www.cherryvalleymuseum.org

COOPERSTOWN CHAMBER OF COMMERCE
31 Chestnut Street
Cooperstown, NY 13326
607-547-9983
www.cooperstownchamber.org
info1@cooperstownchamber.org

COOPERSTOWN/OTSEGO TOURISM
Deb Taylor
242 Main Street
Oneonta, NY 13820
Phone: 800-843-3394
Fax: 607-432-5117
www.VisitCooperstown.com
info@visitcooperstown.com

COOPERSTOWN WINTER CARNIVAL
1-800-843-3394
www.cooperstowncarnival.org
Cooperstown, NY 13326

GLIMMERGLASS OPERA
PO Box 191
Cooperstown, NY 13326
607-547-2255
www.glimmerglass.org
Ticket Office:
18 Chestnut Street
Cooperstown, NY 13326

GREATER CHERRY VALLEY CHAMBER OF COMMERCE
Maggie Gage, Secretary
PO Box 37
Cherry Valley, NY 13320
607-264-3755
www.cherryvalleyny.com
maggieg.cv@gates-cole.com

NATIONAL BASEBALL HALL OF FAME AND MUSEUM
25 Main Street
Cooperstown, NY 13326
607-547-7200
888-HALL-OF-FAME (888-425-5633)
Fax: 607-547-2044
www.baseballhalloffame.org

NATIONAL SOCCER HALL OF FAME AND MUSEUM
18 Stadium Circle
Oneonta, New York 13820
(607) 432-335
www.soccerhall.org
nshof@soccerhall.org

NYSHA
THE FARMERS' MUSEUM AND FENIMORE ART MUSEUM
5775 State Highway 80 - Lake Road
Cooperstown, NY 13326
607-547-1450
www.farmersmuseum.org
www.fenimoreartmuseum.org

OTSEGO CHAMBER
Rob Robinson
12 Carbon Street
Oneonta, NY 13820
877-5-OTSEGO
www.otsegocountychamber.com

OTSEGO COUNTY FAIR
Morris, NY
607-263-5289
www.otsegocountyfair.org

WIETING MEMORIAL
168 Main Street
PO Box 472
Worcester, NY 12197
607-397-7309

WORCESTER HISTORICAL SOCIETY
144 Main Street
Worcester, NY 12197
607-397-1700
www.worcesterhistoricalsociety.org

Professional Resources and Services

BASSETT HEALTHCARE
One Atwell Road
Cooperstown, NY 13326
1-800-BASSETT (1-800-227-7388)
1-607-547-3456
www.bassett.org
Public.Relations@bassett.org

CITICORP SMITH BARNEY
493 Chestnut Street
Oneonta, NY 13820
607-432-5000 or 800-962-2357

CLARK SPORTS CENTER
124 County Highway 52
Cooperstown, NY 13326
607-547-2800
www.clarksportscenter.com

CORNELL COOPERATIVE EXTENSION
123 Lake Street
Cooperstown, NY 13326
607-547-2536
cce.cornell.edu/otsego
Otsego@cornell.edu

GLIMMERGLASS LEARNING CENTER
PO Box 1105
Cooperstown, NY 13326
607-547-9988
www.gclcenter.org
607-547-8434 (kitchen)
www.gourmetroadshow.com
jillians@localnet.com

KONSTANTY LAW OFFICE
James Konstanty
252 Main Street
Oneonta, NY 13820
607-432-2245
866-432-2245
www.konstantylaw.com
law_info@konstantylaw.com

LEATHERSTOCKING MASSAGE
Robert Fiorentino
PO Box 213
180 Smith Road
Springfield Center, NY 13468
315-858-9486
315-868-2119
rfmassage@usadatanet.net

LETTIS AUCTION SERVICE
Kevin Herrick
23 Reynolds Street
Oneonta, NY 13820
607-432-3935

NBT BANK
One Wall Street
Oneonta, NY 13820
(607) 432-5800
www.nbt.com

ONEONTA ELKS CLUB
Bryan Bennett
Oneonta Elks Lodge
82-86 Chestnut Street
Oneonta, NY 13820
607-432-1312

OTSEGO COUNTY ECONOMIC DEVELOPMENT
Carolyn Lewis
242 Main Street
Oneonta, NY 13326
607-432-8871
www.otsegoeconomicdevelopment.com

SIDNEY FEDERAL CREDIT UNION
53 Market Street
Oneonta, NY 13820
1-877-642-7328

SUNY-ONEONTA
SUNY COLLEGE AT ONEONTA
Ravine Parkway
Oneonta, NY 13820
607-436-3500
www.oneonta.edu

SUSQUEHANNA SPCA
4841 State Highway 28
Cooperstown, NY 13326
607-547-8111
sspca@stny.rr.com
www.sspca.petfinder.org

SYLLABLES PRESS
SYLLABLES WEB SERVICES
Curt Akin
2388 County Highway 11
Mount Vision, NY 13810
607-293-8202
www.syllables.com
Curt@Syllables.com

WALKER PLANNING AND DESIGN
Edward B. Walker, RLA, AICP
20 Chestnut Street
Cooperstown, NY 13326
607-547-5745

WILBER BANK
Main Office(24 Hour ATM)
245 Main Street
Oneonta, NY 13820
607-432-1700 or
1-800-374-7980
www.wilberbank.com

Touring Otsego County

~~~~~~~~~~~~~~~~~~~~~~~~~~~~~~~~

*W*elcome to the adventure of discovering Otsego County. If you're new to the area, visiting for a while, or even if you have lived here for years, we'd like you to get to know the County a little better. We've put together a few suggestions, by area, to help you make the most of your time and mileage.

If you are unaccustomed to country roads and small towns, relax. Otsego Countians are friendly and helpful. Refer to our maps, enjoy the views and respect the speed limit; avoid hitting any of our abundant animal life or getting a ticket! Keep a lookout for signs and shingles along the way; you'll probably find farmers or artists selling their wares en route.

Visit some of our *Home Plate* contributors and let them know you found them here. If you don't see familiar fast food signs, don't panic. Almost any local general/grocery store has a deli counter with great sandwiches and sides.

Refer to our contributor's pages for more specific information. Have fun!

COOPERSTOWN

For a village of 2,000 residents (more or less), there is a lot to see and do in Cooperstown. The Village is a little over a mile square and almost everything is within easy walking distance. As a point of reference, Otsego Lake lies north of Cooperstown.

Many Otsego County villages have "four corners", the intersection of two main thoroughfares forming the north-south and east-west arteries. Main and Chestnut Streets form Cooperstown's "four corners." It is the location of the Village's only traffic light.

At Main and Chestnut, find fine dining at *The French Corner*. A block south on Chestnut Street (Route 28) is the *Cooperstown Chamber of Commerce*, a fountain of information and visitor advice. Make sure to travel west on Upper Main to Railroad Avenue for a variety of shops, including the *All and All Emporium* for fine women's clothing and gifts.

Heading east on Main Street toward the *National Baseball Hall of Fame and Museum* takes you into a hub of activity and dining. Feed the team and find great memorabilia at *TJ's The Home Plate*. A broad selection of unique items awaits at *Ladybug*, and you can indulge in terrific Italian dinner fare at *Nicoletta's*. *Danny's Market* is next door with great eats and specialty foods. Visit *Riverwood* for fascinating shopping.

Across Main Street and down Pioneer Alley, the *Cooperstown Farmers' Market* is open on Saturday mornings, in season. Just a few steps away in Doubleday Court, enjoy well-deserved pampering at *Essential Elements*.

Look for the flagpole in the center of the next intersection, Main and Pioneer. On one corner, it's *Mickey's Place* for the baseball collector and on the other it's jewelry, books and gifts at *Davidson's Jewelry and Augur's Books*. Turn up Pioneer for fine potables at *Cooperstown Wine and Spirits*. Just a couple of steps away is *Cooley's Stone House Tavern*. *NBT Bank* (ATM) is located diagonally across Pioneer Street.

Back on Main Street, just a few doors down from Mickey's Place is *Wilber National Bank* (ATM) and the *Triple Play Café* for breakfast, lunch or dinner. Just off Main Street, peek down Hoffman Lane (next to the Post Office) and find the *Hoffman Lane Bistro*. Across Main Street, explore the shelves of the *Cooperstown Book Nook*.

Across Main Street from the Post Office and just a base hit from the headwaters of the Susquehanna River is the *National Baseball Hall of Fame and Museum*.

Outside the center of the Village are two mainstays of good health. Traveling south on Chestnut, turn onto Susquehanna Avenue to find the *Clark Sports Center*. Farther down Chestnut, just across the railroad tracks, turn onto Walnut and then immediately onto Linden Avenue. Follow it nearly to the end and find *Cooperstown Natural Foods*.

Returning to Chestnut and leaving Cooperstown, you are now on the Route 28 Corridor between Cooperstown and Oneonta on to the south.

ROUTE 28 CORRIDOR: COOPERSTOWN SOUTHERLY TO ONEONTA

Make some stops along Route 28 between the Village of Cooperstown and the City of Oneonta. There are several opportunities to replenish your wallet. Look for *Wilber National Bank* (ATM) just outside of Cooperstown. *NBT Bank* (ATM) is located three miles southerly at the Cooperstown Commons.

Just prior to the Wilber National Bank as you leave Cooperstown, stop at *Haggerty Ace Hardware*, and find just what you need, from batteries and duct tape to jeans and maple syrup. Two miles farther, beyond the sign for the hamlet of "Index," *The*

Susquehanna SPCA's Better Exchange Thrift Shop is next door to the *SPCA* building and is a wellspring of great bargains.

When you go six miles farther south to the Milford stoplight, look for the signs and turn left onto Route 166 to visit the *Cooperstown Brewing Company* for great beer and great gifts. Either stay on Route 166 and go to Roseboom and Cherry Valley, or return to Route 28. As you head towards Oneonta on Route 28, after about five miles look for *Bear Pond Winery* in Milford Center, across from Goodyear Lake, for wonderful vintages from New York grapes.

WORCESTER/SCHENEVUS

Where Route 28 meets Interstate 88, turn west to Oneonta or east to Worcester. On I-88 take exit 18 to Route 7 and the Schenevus/ Worcester area. A left turn on Route 7 takes you to *Smokey Hollow Maple Products*; follow the signs and turn right onto Smokey Avenue, at the Schenevus High School; they're about two miles up the hill. During the glorious autumn months, follow the signs to *Willys Cider Mill* for great fun and fall food.

At I-88 exit 18, turn right onto Route 7 and head 5 miles east to the pleasant village of Worcester and summer weekend movies at the Wieting Memorial. Spend some time in the *Worcester Historical Society Museum* and learn how this small Upstate town connects to many facets of American history. Check the hours first.

ONEONTA/OTEGO

From Route 28, turn west on Interstate 88 and discover the Oneonta/Otego area. Oneonta is the only city in Otsego County (pop. 13,000).

Several exits from I-88 lead into Oneonta. Take Exit 16 to Route 7 and turn left toward town. One of Otsego County's two *Price Chopper Supermarkets* is on your left. Just a stone's throw (and a deep breath, if they are cooking) away is *Brooks' Bar-B-Que*. A mile or two farther on Route 7, turn on Reynolds Street (across from a cemetery) to the *Lettis Auction Room*. If you're in Oneonta on a Thursday evening, that's the place to be.

Stay westerly on Route 7 and head into downtown Oneonta (from I-88 take exit 15 to downtown). Across Main Street from the stately *Wilber National Bank* (ATM) building is the *Regional Visitors Center,* the retail venue of *Cooperstown/Otsego County Tourism* and a great source of local information and gifts. Next door is the *Konstanty Law Office.* The Main Street Plaza is home to the *Oneonta Farmers' Market,* a great stop on Tuesdays and Saturdays, in season. Another block down on Main Street is the *Artisans' Guild,* an emporium of exceptional local art and one of the homes of *Siegfried Stoneware.*

A block over from Main Street is Market Street. Across from the **Sidney Federal Credit Union** (ATM) is the fabulous **Stella Luna Restaurant.**

The beautiful **SUNY-Oneonta** campus and the **Oneonta County Chamber** offices are also in central Oneonta.

While you are in the Oneonta area, discover **McCoy's Pure Raw Honey** and visit the bees on Thursdays and Saturdays. The **National Soccer Hall of Fame** is easy to find— just take Exit 13 from I-88. Take Exit 12 from I-88 (or just continue west on Route 7), and go to Otego and Ruby Mitchell's **Perennial Field** for simply gorgeous plants.

West Oneonta/Morris/Gilbertsville

Exit 13 from I-88 puts you on Route 205. Follow Route 205 to Route 23 and go west through West Oneonta. Stop at the **Fox Hollow Nursery** farm stand for garden produce, pumpkins or holiday greenery. Enjoy the ride to Morris, ten miles westerly on Route 23 and, in August, spend a day at the **Otsego County Fair.** From Morris, go south seven miles on Route 51 through the beautiful Butternut Valley to the lovely village of Gilbertsville. Visit the many artists represented at the **Hilton Bloom Art Studio.** Stop at the **Gilbert Block Quilt Shop** for wonderful finds in gifts, fabrics, and more art. If you are a fisherman, call the Delaney's ahead of time and arrange a time to visit **Lake Clear Wabblers.** The **Gilbertsville Farmers' Market** on summer Wednesday evenings is another must!

Cooperstown to Springfield
Route 80 Corridor

If you leave Cooperstown via Route 80, north along the west side of Otsego Lake, you'll be treated to a beautiful ten-mile drive along Otsego Lake and the location of some of our most treasured places.

Just outside the Village of Cooperstown limits, on Route 80 you'll find **The Farmers' Museum** and **Fenimore Art Museum.** Neither should be missed by anyone visiting the area. The tranquil and enchanting **Brookwood Garden** graces Otsego Lake, just two miles beyond the Museums, Look for a small sign on the Lake side of the road. If you get to Three Mile Point Park, you've gone too far! Another six miles along the lake James Fenimore Cooper called "Glimmerglass", brings you to the phenomenal *Glimmerglass Opera*. Not an opera fan? Go anyway, just to experience it. You might just become one.

Drive another two miles into Springfield Center and find the professional and rejuvenating care of *Leatherstocking Massage*. Make the sharp left turn on Smith Road.

Route 80 intersects with Route 20 at Springfield Center. Heading east on Route 20 will lead to the Route 166 South turn to Cherry Valley. If you overshoot the turn-off about two miles, you will find *The Tepee* and *TePee Pete's Chow Wagon* for casual food, fun shopping and a fantastic view. This is an easy stop when traveling to and from Albany.

Or, turn west on Route 20 and it will take you to Richfield Springs. From Richfield, Route 28 south 11 miles leads to Fly Creek and then three miles to Cooperstown.

CHERRY VALLEY/ROSEBOOM

Cherry Valley is a charming village in the northeast part of the County, just two miles off of the Route 20 Scenic Byway and 12 miles from Cooperstown. From Route 20, take the Route 166 turn to Cherry Valley. Roseboom is six miles south of Cherry Valley, on Route 166.

Wander through Cherry Valley and stop at the *Plaide Palette* for Celtic charm and gifts. Next door, you can stroll the *Cherry Valley Museum* and learn of colonial life and the Cherry Valley Massacre. *A Rose is a Rose* is a wonderful stop for floral gifts and fresh flowers. *NBT Bank* (ATM) is in the neat stone building on the corner. That same building has housed a bank since 1818.

If you are in Cherry Valley at dinnertime, do not miss the sublime food at *The Rose and Kettle*. Up the Lancaster Street hill from the Rose and Kettle is the *Bates Hop House*. George's 150 varieties of stunning lilacs are available May, June and the first half of July. The *Greater Cherry Valley Chamber of Commerce* can advise you about events and other places of interest in Cherry Valley.

Leaving Cherry Valley south on County Route 166 to Route 165 takes you to Roseboom and Pleasant Brook. Be sure to stop at *Stannard's Maple and Elk* for syrup and other maple products, elk and great recipes. Plan to be at *The SweetTooth SchoolHouse* in Pleasant Brook in time for lunch or tea. Harriet and Dick's food is reason enough to go to the Roseboom area. After experiencing the SweetTooth, drive up LaFleure Road (by the Pleasant Brook Hotel) and visit *Breezie Maples Farm*, especially if you're here in March. Give them a call ahead of time. A bit of advice: LaFleure Road ascends a hill and parts are unpaved, so keep adverse weather conditions in mind.

When leaving Roseboom, go back to Route 166 and continue south, toward Milford. After about five miles, you can turn onto Route 52 to go to Cooperstown. The sign says "Cooperstown 3 ½ Miles." About a mile onto Route 52, at the multiple sharp curve arrows, is one of the most magnificent views in the County. Stay on Route 52 to Route 33. Stay left on Route 33 to Main Street, Cooperstown.

Or, if you pass the Route 52 turn to Cooperstown and continue south on Route 166 you will find the *Cooperstown Brewing Company* in Milford. Route 166 connects with the Route 28 corridor at Milford, which runs between Cooperstown and Oneonta.

FLY CREEK/RICHFIELD SPRINGS AREA

About three miles from Cooperstown, north on combined Routes 28 and 80, is an Otsego County treasure in the hamlet of Fly Creek. Look for Fly Creek author *Jim Atwell's* book *From Fly Creek: Celebrating Life in Leatherstocking Country* and his wife, *Anne Geddes-Atwell's* black and white illustrations. You'll find both at the *Fly Creek General Store* along with a host of other local products including coffee, gas, sandwiches, brews, bait and Warren Ainslie's (*Dancing Veggie Farms*) handmade brooms. *Harmony House Café and Antiques* offers sumptuous breakfasts and lunches, Internet access and wonderful browsing. Just beyond the Fly Creek blinking light, turn left on Bissell Road and look for the bounty of fresh produce and homemade granola at Marty Bernardo's *BlueStone Farm,* about a mile and a half down the road.

A few miles north of Fly Creek, on the way to State Route 20 or Interstate 90, is Richfield Springs. Visit *Price Chopper* for great produce, meats, flowers, etc. An *NBT Bank* (ATM) is available on Main Street and the *Richfield Springs Farmers' Market* is open Thursdays and Saturdays in summer.

Head east on Route 20 from Richfield Springs to Springfield Center. At the intersection of Route 20 and Route 80, travel 11 miles south on Route 80 to go to Cooperstown.

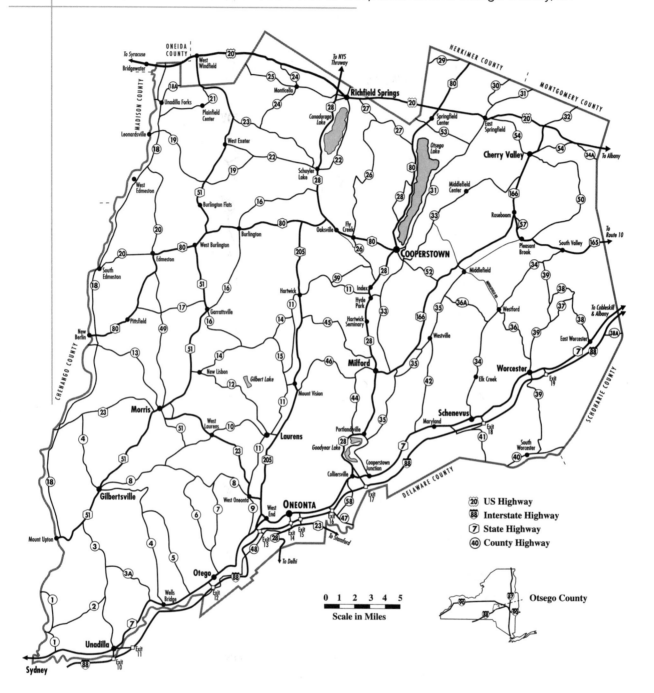

Otsego County, in its entirety. The following pages each contain an enlarged area from the above map.

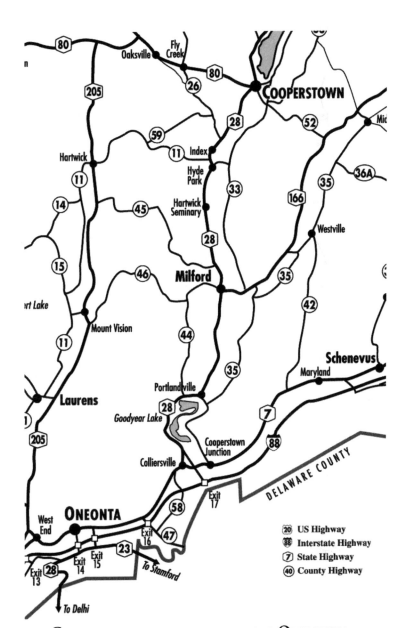

COOPERSTOWN SOUTHERLY TO ONEONTA:
ROUTE 28 CORRIDOR

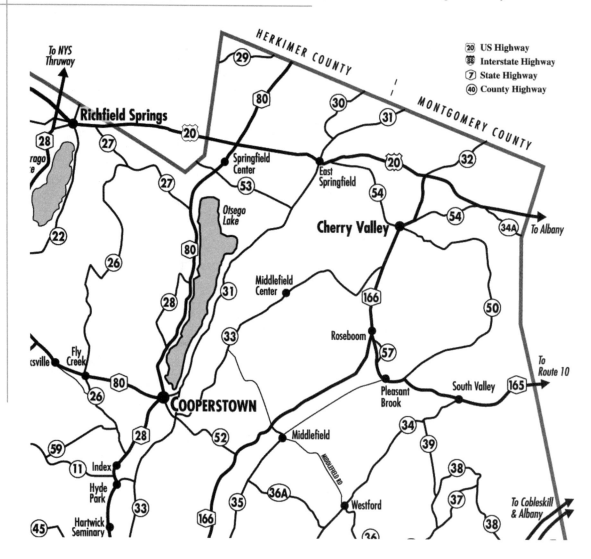

CHERRY VALLEY/ROSEBOOM; COOPERSTOWN TO SPRINGFIELD: ROUTE 80 CORRIDOR; FLY CREEK/RICHFIELD SPRINGS AREA; COOPERSTOWN

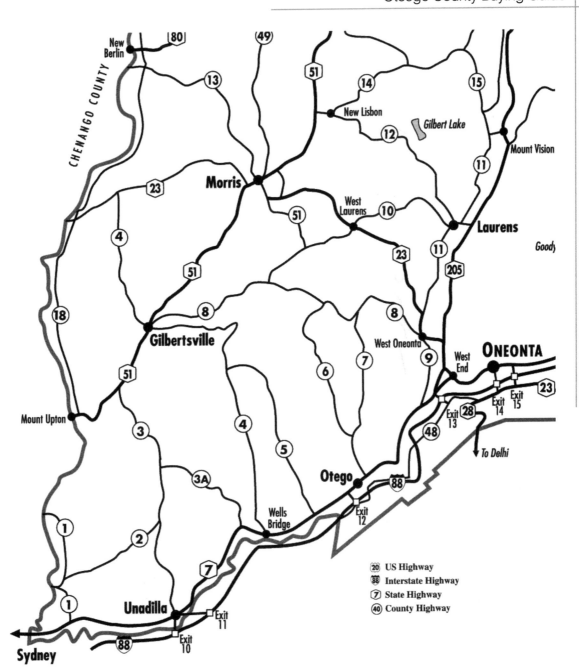

WEST ONEONTA/MORRIS/GILBERTSVILLE; ONEONTA/OTEGO

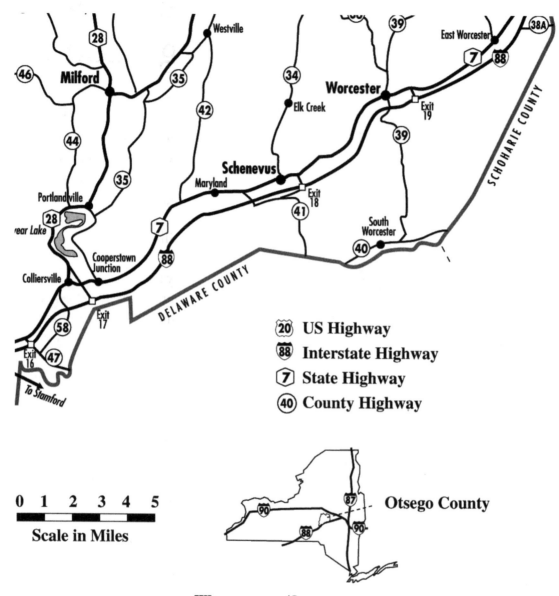

Westville

28

46 **Milford** 35

42

34 **Worcester** East Worcester 7 88 38A

Elk Creek Exit 19

44

35 39

Schenevus

Maryland Exit 18

Portlandville 41

28

ear Lake 7 South Worcester

Cooperstown Junction 88 40

Colliersville

Exit 17

58 DELAWARE COUNTY

Exit 16 47

To Stamford

SCHOHARIE COUNTY

39

Legend

20 US Highway
88 Interstate Highway
7 State Highway
40 County Highway

0 1 2 3 4 5
Scale in Miles

87 **Otsego County**
90
88 90

WORCESTER/SCHENEVUS

Reflections on Otsego County

*D*uring the Colonial era, the area that would become Otsego County was considered the "western wilderness." The reputation was not without credence; the Cherry Valley Massacre of 1778 duly frightened Easterners, already wary of the roaming wildlife, Native Americans and French and English conflicts of the 18th century unstructured west.

Immigrants came anyway (as is evident by the number of hills named for the settlers' birth countries—Dutch Hill, Scotch Hill, Irish Hill, etc.) and, in 1791, New York State recognized Otsego County, the same year the State helped ratify the United States Bill of Rights, and just two years after the U.S Constitution was adopted. Many villages were established well before New York made the area an official county. Most have remained contentedly small, though some have known heady periods of increased wealth and population based either on a quickly growing plant indispensable to brewing, or slightly smelly natural springs that promise rejuvenation, or the arrival of railroads, assuring easier transportation and financial boons, or the discovery of a well-worn baseball.

Throughout Otsego County's economic swells and ebbs, agriculture has remained constant, experiencing its own vicissitudes. Vestiges of the creameries once common in every County nook are found in antique shop milk bottle collections. County road names indicate industries that once flourished, such as Rendering Works, Chicken Farm Hill, Stone Quarry or Potato Farm Roads. Others denote farming families such as Kukenberger or Fassett, whose generations lived on them long enough that the road became known as theirs.

Otsego County's 62,000+ residents represent less than 1½ percent of the population of New York State. In a state with a population density of 402 persons per square mile, Otsego County is just shy of 62. We treasure all that open space and draw our sustenance from it. We work both to preserve Otsego County's finest asset and be smart about how we use it. Though we are no longer considered "western" we still have a considerable amount of "wilderness" and a treasury of characters, past and present, giving it vibrant color.

Every year Otsego County welcomes hundreds of thousands of visitors, over ten times its population. They come pursuing their passions in sport, music, history, theater or outdoor recreations of golf, fishing, hunting, hiking and camping. Our pristine state parks are reason enough to visit.

There is a significant contingent of visitors who come to Otsego County and stay. Bewitched by the lush rolling hills; the dramatic, changing seasons; the breathtaking views; and the potential of genuine human experiences; they make Otsego County home. They come in spite of the sometime grueling winters and the dearth of large town "services" of multiplexes, franchises and food courts, preferring the hand-made to the mass-produced and choosing the challenges of weather to those of congested traffic.

Regardless of vocation, in Otsego County people remain connected to nature and to farming. The tractor or hay truck in front of the line of cars dictates the pace in this wonderfully rural county. It is a most effective traffic-calming device, Or, when temperatures dip well below zero, the compelling focus, regardless of other projects and deadlines, is keeping everyone and everything warm and functioning.

Farming constants set the tone. Vegetables ripen at their pace, dependent as they have always been on rain, sun and temperature. Cows still have to be milked twice a day, apples rely on bees to transform from blossom to fruit, and maple sap becomes syrup with the freeze-thaw wizardry that occurs only in this small corner of the planet. Instant gratification is for the suburbs; nature decrees that we work and wait for those rewards.

Comfortable with the agrarian tempo and embracing the substance it conveys, newcomers and natives alike deplore any sprawling sameness that might despoil this Brigadoon-like place. They thrive in the fulfillment and assuring familiarity that comes from the oft-decried small town trait of "everybody knows everybody else."

Industries fall and rise, tourists pass through, and Otsego County changes, but agriculture remains our touchstone. It teaches us patience, a fundamental reverence for our environment and, on any given day, it instills in us a sense of wonder.

In Otsego County, as abundant in life's precious intangibles as it is in agriculture, it is our measure of respect for farming and our natural surroundings that reflects and defines who we are and where we are—safe at home.

Brenda Berstler
Summer, 2006

Author Bio

A Missouri native, Brenda Berstler has lived in the Susquehanna Valley since 1999, choosing to settle in Otsego County after years of hopscotching around the United States and Europe. She and her husband, John, and daughter, Elizabeth, own Bryn Brooke Manor Bed and Breakfast in the Village of Cooperstown.

With broad-based area support, Brenda founded the Walking Example Group Organization (WE GO) in 2002. WE GO's mission is to establish destination trails and pathways allowing walking and cycling accessibility to all of Otsego County. WE GO's goal is to help create a healthy infrastructure that encourages a healthier population. WE GO supports smart growth that preserves our heritage and open spaces and strives to create a premium quality of life in Otsego County.

Combining her fascination with food and her respect of farming, with her desire for a healthier environment, Brenda worked with Rich McCaffery of Cornell Cooperative Extension of Otsego County and Curt Akin of Syllables Press to create *Home Plate: The Traveler's Food Guide to Cooperstown and Otsego County*. All proceeds from the sale of the book and associated items benefit community programs of WE GO and CCE-Otsego County.

> *Restore human legs as a means of travel. Pedestrians rely on food for fuel and need no special parking facilities.*
>
> —Lewis Mumford

Contributors
Index

42 MONTGOMERY BED AND BREAKFAST
Melanie Crawford
42 Montgomery Street
PO Box 521
Cherry Valley, NY 13320
607-264-9974
www.42montgomery.com
Melanie@42montgomery.com

A ROSE IS A ROSE FLOWERS
Jackie Hull
17 Main Street
Cherry Valley, NY 13320
607-264-3100
800-243-9501
aroseisarose17@hotmail.com

ALL AND ALL EMPORIUM
Linda Parmalee
21 Railroad Avenue
Cooperstown, NY 13326
607-437-1989
www.chamberofcommerce/allandall/

ARTISANS' GUILD
Deborah Blake
148 Main Street
Oneonta, NY 13820
607-432-1080

ATWELL, JIM
134 Allison Road
Fly Creek, NY 13337
(607) 547-5895
www.JimAtwell.com

BARNWELL INN
Mark and Tara Barnwell
48 Susquehanna Avenue
Cooperstown, NY 13326
1-607-547-1850
www.Barnwellinn.com
Barnwellinn@aol.com

BASSETT HEALTHCARE
One Atwell Road
Cooperstown, NY 13326
1-800-BASSETT (1-800-227-7388)
1-607-547-3456
www.bassett.org
Public.Relations@bassett.org

BATES HOP HOUSE
George Alverson
54 Lancaster Street
Cherry Valley, NY 13320
607-264-3450

BEAR POND WINERY
Mark and Brenda Lebo
2515 State Highway 28
Oneonta, NY 13820
607-643-0294
Fax: 607-643-0219
www.bearpondwines.com
taste@bearpondwines.com

BLUESTONE FARM, LLC
Marty Bernardo
Bissell Road
Cooperstown, NY 13326
607-547-8227
www.bluestonefarm.org
bluestone@capital.net

BREEZIE MAPLES FARM
Rick Newman and Larry Roseboom
2269 County Highway 34
Westford, NY 13488
607-638-9317
800-950-9676
www.breeziemaples.com

BROOKS BAR-B-QUE
Ryan and Beth Brooks
5560 State Highway 7
Oneonta, NY 13820
607-432-1782
800-498-2445
Fax: 607-432-2665
Website: www.brooksbbq.com
E-Mail: info@brooksbbq.com

BROOKWOOD GARDEN
Pat Thorpe
6000 West Lake Road (Route 80)
Cooperstown, NY 13326
607-547-2170
www.brookwoodgarden.com
info@brookwoodgarden.com

BRYN BROOKE MANOR
John, Brenda and Elizabeth Brooke Berstler
6 Westridge Road
Cooperstown, NY 13326
607-544-1885
607-287-0162
www.brynbrookemanor.com
brookebb@stny.rr.com

CHERRY VALLEY HISTORICAL SOCIETY
49 Main Street
Cherry Valley, NY 13320
607 264-3303
607 264-3098
museum@HistoricCherryValley.com
www.cherryvalleymuseum.org

CHUTNEY UNLIMITED
Tanna Roten
52 Pioneer Street
Cooperstown, NY 13326
607-547-7272
www.chutneyunlimited.com
E-mail: tanna@chutneyunlimited.com

CITICORP SMITH BARNEY
493 Chestnut Street
Oneonta, NY 13820
607-432-5000 or 800-962-2357

CLARK SPORTS CENTER
124 County Highway 52
PO Box 850
Cooperstown, NY 13326
607-547-2800
www.clarksportscenter.com

COOLEY'S STONE HOUSE TAVERN
Tim Gould
49 Pioneer Street
Cooperstown, NY 13326
607-544-1311
www.cooleystavern.com

COOPERSTOWN BASEBALL BRACELET
Anne Hall and Jennifer Stewart
607-437-1492
www.cooperstownbaseballbracelet.com
cooperstownbaseballbracelet@yahoo.com

COOPERSTOWN BOOK NOOK
Karen Johansen
61 Main Street
Cooperstown, NY 13326
607-547-2578
bnook@aol.com

COOPERSTOWN BREWING COMPANY
Stan Hall
110 River Street
PO Box 276
Milford, NY 13807
taproom@cooperstownbrewing.com
www.cooperstownbrewing.com
607-286-9330 or 1-877-FINE ALE

COOPERSTOWN CHAMBER OF COMMERCE
31 Chestnut Street
Cooperstown, NY 13326
607-547-9983
www.cooperstownchamber.org
info1@cooperstownchamber.org

COOPERSTOWN COOKIE COMPANY
Pati Drumm Grady
PO Box 64
Cooperstown, NY 13326
607-547-9146 or 607-435-5789
www.cooperstowncookiecompany.com
goodies@cooperstowncookiecompany.com

COOPERSTOWN NATURAL FOODS
Ellen Poulette
607-547-8613
61 Linden Avenue
Cooperstown, NY 13326
cooperstownnaturalfoods@verizon.net

COOPERSTOWN/OTSEGO TOURISM
Deb Taylor
242 Main Street
Oneonta, NY 13820
Phone: 800-843-3394
Fax: 607-432-5117
www.VisitCooperstown.com
info@visitcooperstown.com

COOPERSTOWN WINE AND SPIRITS
Ed Landers
45 Pioneer Street
607-547-8100
Cooperstown, NY 13326

COOPERSTOWN WINTER CARNIVAL
1-800-843-3394
www.cooperstowncarnival.org
Cooperstown, NY 13326

CORNELL COOPERATIVE EXTENSION
123 Lake Street
Cooperstown, NY 13326
607-547-2536
cce.cornell.edu/otsego
Otsego@cornell.edu

CREEK'S EDGE ELK FARM
Stacy Handy or Susan Keith
894 State Highway 80
Fort Plain, NY 13339
518-568-5476
518-993-4014 (Sue at the Farm)

DANCING VEGGIE FARM
Warren and Rachel Ainslie-Hamblin
246 Ainslie Road
Richfield Springs, NY 13439
315-858-0506

DANNY'S MARKET
Alice and Sergio Gaviria
92 Main Street
Cooperstown, NY 13326
607-547-4053

DAVIDSON'S JEWELRY AND AUGUR'S BOOKS
73 Main Street
Cooperstown, NY 13326
607-547-2422
607-547-5099
www.cooperstownjewelry.com
augurs@capital.net

DAYLILY DREAMS BED AND BREAKFAST
Rae and Bob Consigli, Innkeepers
1599 County Route 33
Cooperstown, New York 13326
Toll free 866-547-1888
www.daylilydreams.com
info@daylilydreams.com

DISMAL INN SUGAR COMPANY
Bruce and Lucia Phillips
Hartwick, NY 13348
607-293-6488
607-293-6164

DOWN IN THE COUNTRY
Jackie Jones
2388 County Highway 11
Mount Vision, NY 13810
607-293-8333
www.downinthecountry.com
Jackie@downinthecountry.com

ESSENTIAL ELEMENTS
Robin Gray
Doubleday Parking Lot
137 Main Street
Cooperstown, NY 13326
607-547-9432
800-437-3265
FAX: 607-547-5791
www.essentialelementsdayspa.com

FLY CREEK GENERAL STORE
Tom Bouton
The Fly Creek General Store
State Route 28
Fly Creek, NY 13337
607-547-7274

FOR THE LOVE OF CAKE
Kelly Calhoun
156 Perkins Road
Cooperstown, NY 13326
607-293-8465

FOX HOLLOW NURSERY
Neil and Bonnie Monzeglio
2751 State Highway 23
West Oneonta, NY
607-263-5764
bmonzeglio@stny.rr.com

FRENCH CORNER
Mark McCoy
161 Main Street
Cooperstown, NY 13326
607-547-6106

GEDDES-ATWELL, ANNE
134 Allison Road
Fly Creek, NY 13337
(607) 547-5895
www.JimAtwell.com

GILBERT BLOCK QUILT SHOP
Nona Slaughter
9 Commercial Street
PO Box 351
Gilbertsville, NY 13776
607-783-2872

GLIMMERGLASS LEARNING CENTER
PO Box 1105
Cooperstown, NY 13326
607-547-9988
www.gclcenter.org
607-547-8434 (kitchen)
www.gourmetroadshow.com
jillians@localnet.com

GLIMMERGLASS OPERA
PO Box 191
Cooperstown, NY 13326
607-547-2255
www.glimmerglass.org
Ticket Office:
18 Chestnut Street
Cooperstown, NY 13326

GREATER CHERRY VALLEY CHAMBER OF COMMERCE
Maggie Gage, Secretary
PO Box 37
Cherry Valley, NY 13320
607-264-3755
www.cherryvalleyny.com
maggieg.cv@gates-cole.com

HAGGERTY ACE HARDWARE
5390 State Highway 28
Cooperstown, NY 13326
607-547-2166
haggertyhardware@stny.rr.com

HARMONY HOUSE CAFÉ AND ANTIQUES
Richard and Mary Lou Votypka
6208 State Highway 28
Fly Creek, NY 13337
Harmony House Café: 607-547-5077
Fax: 607-547-6011
Harmony House Antiques: 607-547-4071

HILTON BLOOM ART STUDIO
Jane Evelynne Higgins
24 Bloom Street
PO Box 12
Gilbertsville, NY 13776-0012
607-783-2779
www.gilbertsville.com
jane.al@frontiernet.net

HOFFMAN LANE BISTRO
Mark Loewenguth
2 Hoffman Lane
Cooperstown, NY 13326
607-547-7055
www.hoffmanlanebistro.com
mark@hoffmanlanebistro.com

INN AT COOPERSTOWN
Marc and Sherrie Kingsley
16 Chestnut Street
Cooperstown, NY 13326
607-547-5756
www.innatcooperstown.com
info@innatcooperstown.com

KONSTANTY LAW OFFICE
James Konstanty
252 Main Street
Oneonta, NY 13820
607-432-2245
866-432-2245
www.konstantylaw.com
law_info@konstantylaw.com

LADYBUG
Doris Mark
108 Main Street
Cooperstown, NY 13326
607-547-1940

LAKE CLEAR WABBLER
Tom Delaney
PO Box 301
10 Spring Street
Gilbertsville, NY 13776
Phone: 607-783-2587
Fax: 607-783-2538
www.lakeclearwabbler.com
lcwabbler@stny.rr.com

LEATHERSTOCKING MASSAGE
Robert Fiorentino
PO Box 213
180 Smith Road
Springfield Center, NY 13468
315-858-9486
315-868-2119
rfmassage@usadatanet.net

LETTIS AUCTION
Kevin Herrick
23 Reynolds Street
Oneonta, NY 13820
607-432-3935

LIBERTY MARKET BAKING
Bonnie Fayssoux
187 Joe Chamberlain Road
Cherry Valley, NY 13320
518-234-9642 or
607-264-8327
www.libertymarket.net

MCCOY'S PURE RAW HONEY
John McCoy
307 State Highway 28
Oneonta, NY 13820
607-432-0605

MICKEY'S PLACE
Vin Russo
74 Main Street
Cooperstown, NY 13326
607-547-5775
800-528-5775
Fax: 607-547-6212
www.mickeysplace.com
info@mickeysplace.com

NATIONAL BASEBALL HALL OF FAME AND MUSEUM
25 Main Street
Cooperstown, NY 13326
607-547-7200
888-HALL-OF-FAME (888-425-5633)
FAX: 607-547-2044
www.baseballhalloffame.org

NATIONAL SOCCER HALL OF FAME AND MUSEUM
18 Stadium Circle
Oneonta, New York 13820
(607) 432-335
www.soccerhall.org
nshof@soccerhall.org

NATURA PRODUCTS
Scottie Baker
PO Box 77
Fly Creek, NY 13337
607-547-5356
www.naturaproductions.com
scottieb@naturaproductions.com

NBT BANK
One Wall Street
Oneonta, NY 13820
607 432-5800
www.nbt.com

NICOLETTA'S
96 Main Street
Cooperstown, NY 13326
607-547-7499
www.nicolettasitaliancafe.com

NYSHA
THE FARMERS' MUSEUM AND FENIMORE ART MUSEUM
5775 State Highway 80 - Lake Road
Cooperstown, NY 13326
607-547-1450
www.farmersmuseum.org
www.fenimoreartmuseum.org

ONEONTA ELKS CLUB
Bryan Bennett
Oneonta Elks Lodge
82-86 Chestnut Street
Oneonta, NY 13820
607-432-1312

OTSEGO COUNTY CHAMBER
Rob Robinson
12 Carbon Street
Oneonta, NY 13820
877-5-OTSEGO
www.otsegocountychamber.com

OTSEGO COUNTY ECONOMIC DEVELOPMENT
Carolyn Lewis
242 Main Street
Oneonta, NY 13326
607-432-8871
www.otsegoeconomicdevelopment.com

OTSEGO COUNTY FAIR
Morris, NY
607-263-5289
www.otsegocountyfair.org

PERENNIAL FIELD
Ruby Mitchell
25 Main Street
Otego, NY 13825
607-988-9009
www.perennialfield.com

PLAIDE PALETTE
45 Main Street
PO Box 464
Cherry Valley, NY 13320
Phone: 607-264-3769
Fax: 607-264-9320
www.plaidepalette.com

PRICE CHOPPER
Route 7
Oneonta , NY 13820
(607) 432-8905
1 Main Street
Richfield Springs 13439
(315) 858-1171
www.pricechopper.com

RIVERWOOD GIFTS
Rick Gibbons
88 Main Street
Cooperstown, NY 13326
607-547-4403
www.riverwoodgifts.com
riverwood@verizon.net

ROSE AND KETTLE RESTAURANT
Clem Coleman and Dana Spiotta
4 Lancaster Street
Cherry Valley, NY 13320
607-264-3078
dana@roseandkettle.com
www.roseandkettle.com

ROSE AND THISTLE BED AND BREAKFAST
Steve and Patti D'Esposito
132 Chestnut Street
607-547-5345
Cooperstown, NY 1332
www.roseandthistlebb.com
stay@roseandthistlebb.com

SIDNEY FEDERAL CREDIT UNION
53 Market Street
Oneonta, NY 13820
1-877-642-7328
www.sfcuonline.com

SIEGFRIED STONEWARE
Alice Siegfried, Potter
Oneonta, NY 13326
607-432-8673

SMOKEY HOLLOW MAPLE PRODUCTS
George and Inga Loft
436 Smokey Avenue
Schenevus, NY 12155
607-638-9393

SUSQUEHANNA SPCA
4841 State Highway 28
Cooperstown, NY 13326
607-547-8111
www.sspca.petfinder.org
sspca@stny.rr.com

STANNARD'S MAPLE AND ELK
Warren, Mary and Julie Stannard
166 Stannard Hill Road
Cherry Valley, NY 13320
E-Mail: stannardsmaple@msn.com
607-264-3090

STELLA LUNA RISTORANTE
Antonio and Vincente Avanzato
58-60 Market Street
Oneonta, NY 13820
Phone: 607-433-7646
Fax: 607-433- 9623
www.stellalunas.com

SUNNY SLOPE FARM AND B&B
Cliff and Patti Brunner
211 Brunner Road
Cooperstown, NY 13326
607-547-8686
sunnyslope@mymailstation.com

SUNY-ONEONTA
SUNY COLLEGE AT ONEONTA
Ravine Parkway
Oneonta, NY 13820
607-436-3500
www.oneonta.edu

SWEETTOOTH SCHOOLHOUSE
Harriet and Richard Sessler
540 State Highway 165
Pleasant Brook, NY
607-264-3233
www.sweettoothschoolhouse.com

SYLLABLES PRESS
SYLLABLES WEB SERVICES
Curt Akin
2388 County Highway 11
Mount Vision, NY 13810
607-293-8202
www.syllables.com
Curt@Syllables.com

THE TASTE OF BRITAIN
Perry Owen
Norwich, NY 13815
607-336-3333
pvowen@cnyconnect.net

THE TEPEE
Dale and Donna Latella
7632 US Highway 20
Cherry Valley, NY 13320
607-264-3987
www.thetepee.net
thetepee@capital.net

TePee Pete's Chow Wagon
Pete Latella
7632 US Highway 20
Cherry Valley, NY 13320
607-264-3987
www.thetepee.net
thetepee@capital.net

TJ's Place The Home Plate
Ted Hargrove and Diane Howard
124 Main Street
Cooperstown, NY 13326
607-547-4040
800-860-5670
Fax: 607-547-4042
www.tjs-place.com

Triple Play Café
Pat Governale
64 Main Street
Cooperstown, NY 13326
607-547-1395
Fax: 607-547-1355

Walker Planning and Design
Edward B. Walker, RLA, AICP
20 Chestnut Street
Cooperstown, NY 13326
607-547-5745

White House Inn
Ed and Margie Landers
46 Chestnut Street
Cooperstown, NY 13326
607-547-5054
607-547-1100 fax
www.thewhitehouseinn.com
stay@thewhitehouseinn.com

Wieting Memorial
168 Main Street
PO Box 472
Worcester, NY 12197
607-397-7309

Wilber Bank
Main Office
(24 Hour ATM)
245 Main Street
Oneonta, NY 13820
607-432-1700
800-374-7980
www.wilberbank.com

Willys Farm and Cider Mill
The Gartung Family
Badeau Hill Road
Schenevus, NY 12155
607-638-9449

Worcester Historical Society
144 Main Street
Worcester, NY 12197
607-397-1700
www.worcesterhistoricalsociety.org

COLOPHON

Without the proper tools, both cooking and setting type would be tedious indeed. *Home Plate* was set using Adobe's InDesign, a program which has matured into a tool allowing attention to the page and not the process; Adobe is to be revered. The body text is Garamond, a face originally designed by 16th-century type designer Claude Garamond. Headings are set in Christiana, a face designed by Gudrun Zapf-von Hesse in 1991 for the H. Berthold AG Typefoundry, Berlin. The distinctive type used for "Home Plate" on the cover and in the running heads is Algerian, designed by Philip Kelly in 1968. Running heads are Swiss 721

To many of us brought up in the tradition of fine typesetting, the advent of the OpenType format was a long-awaited gift that allows painless access to ligatures, fractions, and other devices once so prevalent in well designed and set books, but absent from computer-set type for years.